RESPECT FOR NATURE

STUDIES IN MORAL, POLITICAL,
AND LEGAL PHILOSOPHY

General Editor: Marshall Cohen

RESPECT FOR NATURE

A Theory of Environmental Ethics

Paul W. Taylor

PRINCETON UNIVERSITY PRESS
PRINCETON, NEW JERSEY

Copyright © 1986 by Princeton University Press
Published by Princeton University Press
41 William Street
Princeton, New Jersey 08540
In the United Kingdom:
Princeton University Press, Guildford, Surrey

Library of Congress Cataloging in Publication Data
will be found on the last printed page of this book
ISBN 0-691-07709-6
ISBN 0-691-02250-X (pbk.)

This book has been composed in Linotron Palatino

Clothbound editions of Princeton University Press books
are printed on acid-free paper, and binding materials
are chosen for strength and durability. Paperbacks,
although satisfactory for personal collections,
are not usually suitable for library rebinding

Printed in the United States of America
by Princeton University Press
Princeton, New Jersey

To the Earth's Wild Living Things

CONTENTS

ACKNOWLEDGMENTS

I wish to thank the faculty and administration of Brooklyn College and the City University of New York for permitting me to take a sabbatical leave of absence during the spring semester of 1982. This gave me the opportunity to bring to completion a first version of the book, which I had been working on since 1977.

To Tom Regan my thanks are also due. When he was Visiting Distinguished Professor at Brooklyn College in the Fall of 1982, he kindly read the last chapter of the book and made extensive comments on it. I benefited greatly from this, as well as from discussions with him concerning various matters related to other parts of the book.

The entire manuscript has been read and critically evaluated by Professors Michael Ruse, Mary Anne Warren, and C. G. Beer. Their detailed criticisms and suggestions were very helpful to me, and the book was much improved as a result. I am of course fully responsible for whatever errors and confusions remain.

I am grateful to Professor Eugene C. Hargrove, Editor-in-Chief of *Environmental Ethics*, for permission to use material from two of my articles: "The Ethics of Respect for Nature," vol. 3, no. 3, Fall 1981, pp. 197-218; and "Are Humans Superior to Animals and Plants?" vol. 6, no. 2, Summer 1984, pp. 149-160.

Finally, I would especially like to thank the Editor-in-Chief of Princeton University Press, Sanford G. Thatcher, for his careful, patient, and expert guidance in directing the manuscript through all its successive stages of development and revision.

Brooklyn College,
City University of New York
September 1985

RESPECT FOR NATURE

ENVIRONMENTAL ETHICS AND HUMAN ETHICS

1. Introduction

Environmental ethics is concerned with the moral relations that hold between humans and the natural world. The ethical principles governing those relations determine our duties, obligations, and responsibilities with regard to the Earth's natural environment and all the animals and plants that inhabit it. I shall use the term "the natural world" to refer to the entire set of natural ecosystems on our planet, along with the populations of animals and plants that make up the biotic communities of those ecosystems.

The idea of a natural ecosystem as it is to be understood in this book means any collection of ecologically interrelated living things that, without human intrusion or control, maintain their existence as species-populations over time, each population occupying its own environmental niche and each shaped by the evolutionary processes of genetic variation and natural selection. Two types of natural ecosystems may be distinguished. First, there are those that have never been exploited by humans and have not undergone any major changes as the effect of human culture and technology. Examples are remote expanses of northern tundra, mountain forests, savannah grasslands, cactus deserts, and the marshlands of river estuaries. Insofar as such ecosystems are left undisturbed by humans, they remain in pristine condition and their biotic communities exist in a genuinely wild state. Some of them are preserved in their natural condition because they have been intentionally set aside as wilderness areas by humans.

The second type of natural ecosystem, like the first, includes a biotic community of wild animals and plants that now maintains its existence without being interfered with by human activities. But unlike ecosystems of the first type, these are found in areas that were at one time worked by human labor (such as farming and mining) or have undergone modification in the past as the result of certain human practices (such as sheep grazing or woodcutting). Such an ecosystem may now have returned to a natural condition simply because it has been left alone for a long period of time. On the other hand, it may have resulted from intentional human efforts aimed at restoring it to approximately the condition it was in before it was changed by humans.

For both types of ecosystems, what makes them "natural" in the sense meant here is the fact that the biological and environmental factors determining the structure of relationships holding among their constituent species-populations take place without human intervention. I shall analyze in this study how the order of living things in a natural ecosystem is explained as the outcome of certain evolutionary processes and environmental conditions. When that explanation does not make reference to human purposes or to the effects of human actions, the ecosystem in question is here designated a "natural" one.

Doubts might be raised as to whether any genuinely natural ecosystems now exist on our planet. The impact of human civilization in the contemporary world appears inescapable. Certainly it is the case that wild biotic communities are rapidly disappearing, to say nothing of the accelerating rate of extinction of whole species. Directly correlated with these phenomena is the sharp decline in the number and variety of natural ecosystems. The effects of human culture and technology on the planetary biosphere are becoming ubiquitous. Due to the emergence of large-scale industrialization in the past century, the recent rise in the growth rate of human population, and the expansion of economies that stimulate and depend on high levels of consumption, our human presence is now felt throughout the Earth. It is not only where we have taken over land areas to grow our food crops and to build our towns and cities that ecological changes have been brought about; the physical, chemical, and biological concomitants of modern civilization can be found everywhere. Unless these dominant trends of our age are brought under control, we will see the natural environment of our planet turned into a vast artifact. A massive transformation has already begun not only of the entire land surface of the Earth but also of the open oceans and the very atmosphere itself.

Nevertheless, there still remain at present areas that are ecologically natural to some degree. At least in comparison with those environments that are now deliberately controlled and manipulated by humans or those that are undergoing extensive changes due to human influences, these areas have escaped severe ecological damage and their biotic communities still exist in a relatively wild state.

What we must recognize is that no sharp line can be drawn between natural ecosystems and those that are not natural. Perhaps the most appropriate method for making the distinction is to think of natural ecosystems as belonging at one end of a continuum that extends from ecosystems similar in all essential respects to those in existence before humans appeared on Earth, through a gradation of degrees of increasing human influence, to the opposite end of the spectrum, where ecosystems are completely regulated and even produced by humans. Examples of the latter are farms, golf courses, landscaped parks, gardens, and the plantation forests of timber companies. We might call these "artificial ecosystems," since they are instruments created and used by humans for human ends.

In some artificial ecosystems the very organisms themselves are a human product. Many varieties of plants have been created by hybridization, and through carefully manipulated breeding programs new subspecies of animals have been developed. Recently the emergence of genetic engineering enables humans to create species, greatly enlarging the power to use living things for human benefit. By way of contrast with artificial ecosystems, the biota of natural ones are made up of organisms that have evolved independently of human interference in the course of nature.

To the extent that an ecosystem belongs to the "natural" end of the continuum, its constituent species-populations, their patterns of ecological interdependence, and the range of habitats they occupy are all changing—sometimes rapidly, sometimes slowly. These changes take place without human intervention. According to biologists' current understanding of evolutionary ecology and population genetics, the structure of relationships among species-populations in a natural ecosystem, as well as the size, growth rate, age distribution, and other characteristics of each population are determined by the workings of natural selection at the level of individual organisms. This process, which has been true of natural ecosystems throughout the history of life on our planet, is explained by reference to two factors: changes in environmental conditions and genetic variation. Together these affect the reproductive success of individuals and thereby shape the order of the ecosystem as a whole.

If we start with genetic variation and assume a constant environment, the explanatory scheme can be summarized thus:

gene mutation (genotypic variation)
↓
new physical traits of individuals (phenotypic variation)
↓
increased or decreased competitive ability in the given environment
(augmented or diminished powers of adaptation)

↓

increase or decrease in survival of genes in future individuals
(greater or lesser reproductive success)

↓

changes in the species-population
(the new traits found in larger or smaller numbers of
individuals in the given population)

↓

changes in the distribution and size of species-populations throughout the ecosystem.

Another mode of biological explanation of evolutionary
processes in ecosystems, which supplements the foregoing, starts with environmental changes and assumes no genetic variation initially. Here the pattern may be repre-
sented thus:

change in environmental conditions

↓

increased competitive ability of some individuals and
decreased competitive ability of others

↓

increased reproductive success of some and less reproductive success of others

↓

some populations grow, others decline, and a new pattern of ecological niches develops in the system.

In each mode of explanation the decisive factor determining the outcome is the fitness of individual organisms,
where "fitness" is measured by an organism's ability to reproduce its own genes in future individuals. This is what it
means to say that the changes among species-populations
in an ecosystem, as well as the makeup of its biotic community at any given time, are finally the result of the workings of natural selection on the individual level.[1]

[1] That natural selection functions on the individual level and is the basic
determinant of population structures in ecosystems is fully argued in

One point of philosophical importance in this way of looking at ecosystems and their biota is that what has been called "the balance of nature" can no longer be assumed as a kind of basic norm built into the order of the natural world. "The balance of nature," as it was conceived in the nineteenth century both before and after Darwin, was taken to be evidence of overall design in the realm of living things. According to this idea the species-populations of each biotic community, and ultimately all species encompassed by the Earth's biosphere, were understood as forming an integrated order of harmonious relationships among themselves. The steady equilibrium of this system as a whole worked to the mutual benefit of living things. A biotic community was itself conceived of as a kind of supraorganism whose well-being is preserved by harmony among its parts, much as the well-being of an individual living thing is furthered when all its organs and tissues are performing their various biological functions in the proper manner.

Given the way modern biology looks at ecosystems and their component biota, however, this organicist or holistic conception of the order of life on Earth is not necessary for establishing any scientific explanation. Nor is it a useful paradigm for interpreting data or directing research. Whatever elements of equilibrium and stability may hold among the species-populations of an ecosystem *at a particular time*, these must be seen as general features resulting from natural selection as it occurs among individuals competing in their attempts to survive and reproduce. Whether humans *ought* to maintain or strengthen the stability and equilib-

George C. Williams, *Adaptation and Natural Selection: A Critique of Some Current Evolutionary Thought* (Princeton, N.J.: Princeton University Press, 1966). For the analysis of biological explanation in evolutionary ecology, I am indebted to two unpublished papers by Professor James P. Collins of the Department of Zoology at Arizona State University: "A Review of Some Historical Aspects of the Development of Evolutionary Ecology" and "Evolutionary Ecology and the Changing Role of Natural Selection in Ecological Theory."

rium of any of our planet's natural ecosystems as they happen to be structured at present is a question central to the concerns of environmental ethics. But to answer that question we can no longer simply appeal to the notion that the natural world has itself provided us with a guide to follow: preserve "the balance of nature" and so live in accordance with the design built into the very nature of things. As I shall point out later, we humans as moral agents must search for our own principles to guide us when we try to determine how to live in right relation to the natural world. This requires us to engage in ethical inquiry and not simply "read off" moral norms from a certain way of conceiving of the order of living things.

It was necessary to discuss the foregoing points in order to clarify what a theory of environmental ethics, as it is to be conceived here, is designed to do. Put briefly, it is an attempt to establish the rational grounds for a system of moral principles by which human treatment of natural ecosystems and their wild communities of life ought to be guided. This overall aim requires systematic examination of a broad range of problems. As we read on, we shall see that when the full implications of a theory of environmental ethics are explored in depth, our subject of concern will encompass nothing less than the place of human civilization in the natural world.

There are four basic, distinct areas of inquiry, each of which is presented here by means of a set of closely connected questions.

1. Is human conduct in relation to natural ecosystems properly subject to moral constraints, or are such constraints only applicable to the ways human beings treat one another? Are there *any* ethical principles that we should follow in our treatment of the natural environment? Does the fact that some of our actions affect the lives of wild animals and plants for better or worse have any ethical significance

at all? Does such a fact in and of itself give us any reason, not necessarily a conclusive one, to perform or refrain from performing the actions in question? Do we have duties and obligations with regard to the natural world independent of our duties and obligations with regard to humans?

2. If the answer to any of the foregoing questions is yes, what are the moral constraints involved, and how do they differ from those that govern our actions in relation to other human beings? If we have duties toward nonhumans independent of our duties toward humans, on what ground do those duties rest? What standards of good character and what rules of right conduct apply in that ethical domain?

3. How would one justify those standards and rules? Can a moral commitment to follow principles of environmental ethics be shown to rest on rational grounds? Can we establish that there are *valid* principles of environmental ethics, binding upon everyone alike?

4. Finally, how are our obligations and responsibilities toward the natural world (supposing we have them) to be weighed against human values and interests? Do the duties of environmental ethics ever require us to act in ways that may be contrary to human ends, and if so, when (if ever) do those duties override the fulfillment of human ends?

Any systematic and thoroughgoing attempt to answer these questions is what I shall call a theory of environmental ethics. The views set forth and defended in this book are one such attempt. I shall argue that, quite independently of the duties we owe to our fellow humans, we are morally required to do or refrain from doing certain acts insofar as those acts bring benefit or harm to wild living things in the natural world. I shall further argue that these moral requirements have to be weighed against certain things valued by humans. To fulfill the duties of environmental ethics does involve at times a sacrifice of at least some human interests.

In order to understand how such a view can be rationally justified, it is helpful to make a distinction between two types of environmental ethics, human-centered (or anthropocentric) and life-centered (or biocentric). A human-centered theory of environmental ethics holds that our moral duties with respect to the natural world are all ultimately derived from the duties we owe to one another as human beings. It is because we should respect the human rights of everyone, or should protect and promote the well-being of humans, that we must place certain constraints on our treatment of the Earth's natural environment and its non-human inhabitants.

A typical human-centered argument goes as follows. Future generations of people have as much right to live a physically secure and healthy life as those of the present generation. Each of us is therefore under an obligation not to allow the natural environment to deteriorate to such an extent that the survival and well-being of later human inhabitants of the Earth are jeopardized. We also have a duty to conserve natural resources so that future generations will be able to enjoy their fair share of benefits derived from those resources. Even our present responsibility to protect endangered species of wildlife is linked to human values. Thus it is sometimes argued that a varied gene pool of plant and animal species is needed for developing new ways to protect humans from diseases, to get rid of harmful bacteria, to learn how to control certain insects and other "pests," and to produce new sources of food through genetic engineering. We also have a duty, the argument continues, to preserve the beauty of wild nature so that those of future generations can have as much opportunity to experience and appreciate it as we do. It would be unfair of us to destroy the world's natural wonders and leave only ugly trash heaps for others to contemplate. Thus a whole system of standards and rules governing our present conduct in relation to the Earth's natural environment can be grounded on human needs and interests alone.[2]

[2] The two most complete and systematic human-centered theories of environmental ethics are: John Passmore, *Man's Responsibility for Nature: Ecological Problems and Western Traditions* (New York: Charles Scribner's Sons,

From the standpoint of a life-centered theory of environmental ethics, on the other hand, our duties toward nature do not stem from the duties we owe to humans. Environmental ethics is not a subdivision of human ethics. Although many of the same actions that are right according to a human-centered view may also be right according to a life-centered theory, what it is that makes such actions right is in each case a totally different set of considerations. The moral principles involved are fundamentally separate and distinct. And as we shall see later, the two views do not always yield the same results. It makes a practical difference in the way we treat the natural environment whether we accept an anthropocentric or a biocentric system of ethics.

When a life-centered view is taken, the obligations and responsibilities we have with respect to the wild animals and plants of the Earth are seen to arise from certain moral relations holding between ourselves and the natural world itself. The natural world is not there simply as an object to be exploited by us, nor are its living creatures to be regarded as nothing more than resources for our use and con-

---

1974) and H. J. McCloskey, *Ecological Ethics and Politics* (Totowa, N.J.: Rowman and Littlefield, 1983).

There is considerable dispute in human-centered approaches to environmental ethics about whether or not we can owe duties to future generations of humans. Since they do not yet exist, can they be harmed or benefited? And if their existence or nonexistence is contingent upon our present decisions, can we make sense of talk about harming or benefiting them as identifiable individuals? The position I shall take here is that, if there will be future beings, both human and nonhuman, that can be harmed or benefited by what moral agents now do, then we can have duties that are owed to future beings. Although they are not identifiable individuals until they are brought into existence, their *basic interests* can be identified and this is sufficient for making sense of the claim that they deserve our moral consideration. A good overall defense of this position, with critical discussion of opposing views, is: Annette Baier, "For the Sake of Future Generations," in Tom Regan, ed., *Earthbound: New Introductory Essays in Environmental Ethics* (New York: Random House, 1984), pp. 214-245. Baier does not include plants or nonconscious animals among those future beings to whom we have obligations, but for reasons to be presented in this book I would include them. Since we know what *kind* of beings plants and animals are, we know in general what their basic interests will be if and when they come into existence.

sumption. On the contrary, wild communities of life are understood to be deserving of our moral concern and consideration because they have a kind of value that belongs to them inherently. Just as we would think it inappropriate to ask, What is a human being good for? because such a question seems to assume that the value or worth of a person is merely a matter of being useful as a means to some end, so the question, What is a wilderness good for? is likewise considered inappropriate from the perspective of a biocentric outlook. The living things of the natural world have a worth that they possess simply in virtue of their being members of the Earth's Community of Life. Such worth does not derive from their actual or possible usefulness to humans, or from the fact that humans find them enjoyable to look at or interesting to study.

The general thesis to be defended in this book is in line with this life-centered viewpoint. It may be put this way. In addition to and independently of whatever moral obligations we might have toward our fellow humans, we also have duties that are owed to wild living things in their own right. (This is not to say that they are to be thought of as bearers of moral rights in the same sense in which human persons are said to have such rights. I shall explore this point in Chapter Five.) Our duties toward the Earth's nonhuman forms of life are grounded on their status as entities possessing inherent worth. They have a kind of value that belongs to them by their very nature, and it is this value that makes it wrong to treat them as if they existed as mere means to human ends. It is for *their* sake that their good should be promoted or protected. Just as humans should be treated with respect, so should they.[3]

[3] The claim that all living things, both human and nonhuman, are deserving of moral consideration is defended in Kenneth E. Goodpaster, "On Being Morally Considerable," *Journal of Philosophy* 75/6 (June 1978): 308-325. Goodpaster is careful to distinguish this claim from the assertion that all living things have rights. One can deny that nonhumans have rights and still hold that they are proper moral subjects (or "patients") toward whom agents have duties and responsibilities. For reasons to be set out in this book, I agree with Goodpaster on this point.

The full defense of this general thesis depends on a systematic and detailed construction of a whole biocentric theory of environmental ethics. It is only when such a theory is seen in its entirety and all its elements are carefully examined that its rational acceptability will be made evident. We shall find that the grounds on which its rational acceptability is established are at the same time grounds for rejecting all human-centered theories.

2. Moral Agents and Moral Subjects

The distinction between human-centered and life-centered theories of environmental ethics can be further clarified by focusing attention on the two concepts of moral agent and moral subject. While both types of theories agree about which beings in the world are moral agents, they have incompatible views concerning which entities are moral subjects. A moral agent, for both types of ethics, is any being that possesses those capacities by virtue of which it can act morally or immorally, can have duties and responsibilities, and can be held accountable for what it does. Among these capacities, the most important are the ability to form judgments about right and wrong; the ability to engage in moral deliberation, that is, to consider and weigh moral reasons for and against various courses of conduct open to choice; the ability to make decisions on the basis of those reasons; the ability to exercise the necessary resolve and willpower to carry out those decisions; and the capacity to hold oneself answerable to others for failing to carry them out.

One might at first think that these are all *human* capacities, and that we can therefore simply equate the class of moral agents with the class of human beings. It is important to see why this would be a mistake. The reason is twofold. First, not all humans are moral agents, and second, there may exist moral agents who are not human.

In the first category are human beings who are not moral agents because, either temporarily or permanently, they lack the capacities listed above. A three-day-old infant, a brain-damaged child, a man or woman who is incurably insane, and those who are mentally or emotionally retarded to an extreme degree are examples. These are all human beings in the biological sense. All belong to the species *Homo sapiens*. Yet they are clearly not moral agents, as is shown by the fact that we do not hold them responsible or blame them when they do things that violate ordinary moral rules. In judging them we do not use the moral norms that we use in judging the conduct of others because we believe their actions simply fall outside the range of application of those norms.

The second category includes beings who are moral agents but are not members of the human species. Whether there actually exist such beings, either on our own planet or elsewhere in the universe, is left an open question here. It may be the case that among the Earth's nonhuman species are animals that have a sufficiently developed sense of their own identity and a sufficient understanding of their relationship to other members of their social group that they can see themselves as bearing responsibilities toward their fellows. Perhaps dolphins, whales, elephants, and the primates possess such understanding. For my purposes it will not be necessary to decide this issue. In order to show what standards and rules of a system of environmental ethics validly apply to moral agents, we do not need to settle the empirical question of whether the only beings who are moral agents, and consequently the only ones who are morally obligated to comply with those standards and rules, are members of our own species.

Why is it that valid moral rules apply only to beings having the capacities of moral agents? The reason is that, if a moral rule does apply to an agent (one who intentionally acts or refrains from acting), the agent must be able to use the rule as a normative guide to its own choice and conduct. This requires having the capacity to make moral judgments on the basis of the rule, as well as the capacity to consider it a reason-for-action that an action open to choice is in accordance with the rule (or consider it a reason-against-action that it is in violation of the rule). The agent to whom the rule applies must also be able to perform the action for that reason, doing it *because* it is required by the rule (or to refrain from performing it *because* it is prohibited by the rule). These are capacities that moral agents alone possess.

The same considerations hold for standards of virtue and vice as well as for rules of right and wrong conduct. Such standards apply only to beings who are moral agents. This is because it must be possible for a being intentionally to strive to fulfill the standard by exemplifying a trait of good character or by getting rid of a trait of bad character. Such a being must have the capacity to know what a standard of character is and to use such a standard in making judgments regarding its own virtues and vices, its moral merits and deficiencies. Finally, the entity to which a standard of character applies must be able to set goals for itself and perform actions in the pursuit of those goals *for the reason that* it will more fully realize in its nature the ideal of good character specified in the standard. All of these capacities can only belong to moral agents.

Turning now to the concept of a moral subject as distinct from that of a moral agent, the first thing to notice is that human beings who are moral agents may at the same time be moral subjects. This means that they not only have duties and responsibilities toward others, but are themselves beings with regard to whom others have duties and responsibilities. In the role of moral *agents* they can treat others rightly or wrongly. In the role of moral *subjects* they can be treated rightly or wrongly by others (who are then moral agents with respect to them). Thus one person can be both a moral agent and a moral subject.

The class of moral subjects, however, is broader than the class of moral agents. All moral agents are moral subjects, but not all moral subjects are moral agents. This is because a moral subject may lack the capacities of a moral agent but nevertheless have the status of being an entity toward which moral agents have duties. For example, we may have duties not to harm or mistreat the insane and the severely retarded, who are then in the position of being moral subjects in relation to us.

We may define a moral subject as any being that can be treated rightly or wrongly and toward whom moral agents can have duties and responsibilities. Now it must be possible for such beings to have their conditions of existence be made better or worse by the actions of agents. It must make sense to treat them well or poorly. For it would be nonsensical to say that a moral agent has a duty toward something that cannot possibly be treated well or poorly by an agent. If it is impossible to do harm to an entity we cannot be responsible for not harming it, nor take responsibility to protect it from harm. If it is impossible to benefit something, we can have no duty to do so. Moral subjects must be entities that can be harmed or benefited.

When agents intentionally act to benefit a being, their aim is to better the conditions of that being's existence. They act benevolently toward it. To intend to harm a being is to aim at worsening its conditions of existence; it is to act malevolently toward it. Benevolent actions are those directed by the desire to do good to another or to further another's well-being. Malevolent actions are motivated by the desire to do evil to another by acting in a way detrimental to another's well-being. It follows that it is of the nature of a moral subject that good or evil can be done to it. Perhaps the most ethically significant fact about moral subjects is that it is always possible for a moral agent to *take a moral subject's standpoint and make judgments from its standpoint about how it ought to be treated*. The standard implicit in such judgments is the furtherance or preservation of the well-being of the subject, not of the one who does the judging.

In the next chapter I will show that all the above statements concerning moral subjects are true because moral subjects are entities that have a good of their own. Such entities include all living organisms as well as certain groups of organisms. Inanimate objects (stones, grains of sand, puddles of water, snow, fire, ice, air) are not themselves moral subjects. They have no good of their own and so cannot be treated rightly or wrongly, benevolently or malevolently.

Since inanimate objects are not moral subjects, the purely physical conditions of a natural environment must, from a moral point of view, be sharply separated from the animals and plants that depend on those conditions for their survival. Although we owe no duties to a river, we may yet have duties to the fish and other aquatic organisms in it not to pollute it. In other words, despite the fact that the river itself is not a moral subject it may still be the case that moral agents should treat it in a certain way in order to fulfill a duty to a moral subject. Similarly, we may be morally required by the principles of a life-centered system of environmental ethics to remove toxic chemicals from a waste disposal site, prevent the erosion of sand dunes, or preserve the rocky habitat of a canyon. In these cases it is not the waste disposal site, the sand dunes, or rocks themselves that are entitled to such treatment. No obligations *to them* are involved. But actions that are intentionally directed toward having an effect on them, that are aimed at either preserving them or changing them in some way, may be necessary steps to be taken by moral agents in fulfilling their obligations to moral subjects. Thus the fact that inanimate objects in the natural environment can be modified, destroyed, or preserved by moral agents is a significant ethical consideration. But it has this significance because such treatment of inanimate objects affects the well-being of moral subjects.

It is now easy to see why all moral agents are moral subjects but not all moral subjects are moral agents. There are many living things that lack the capacities necessary for being a moral agent. We saw this to be true even within the human species. The insane and the severely retarded are deemed by most people to be moral subjects. Their well-being is thought to be deserving of our concern and consideration. But no one regards them as moral agents. For a life-centered theory of environmental ethics, the same holds true of animals and plants. With the possible exception of a few mammals, nonhuman organisms are not moral agents. They cannot act rightly or wrongly, they have no duties or obligations, and they are not morally responsible beings. Yet they are beings who can be treated rightly or wrongly by moral agents. This is because animals and plants are creatures whose lives can intentionally be made better or worse by our conduct. We can deliberately act so as to protect and promote their well-being, or we can act in ways we know to be detrimental or damaging to their well-being. It is possible for us imaginatively to look at the world from their standpoint, to make judgments about what would be a good thing or a bad thing to happen to them, and to treat them in such a way as to help or hinder them in their struggle to survive. It therefore makes sense to think of them as having the status of moral subjects.

We must distinguish here between the *conceptual* claim that animals and plants can meaningfully be thought of as moral subjects and the *normative* claim that they are to be considered moral subjects. If the normative claim is correct, that is, if it is true that animals and plants are to be considered moral subjects, then we do have duties and obligations to them, which we are normally required to fulfill. However, if only the conceptual claim is correct, all that follows is that it makes sense to talk of having duties and obligations to animals and plants. Whether we do in fact have such duties and obligations is a further question, to be answered by finding out whether the normative claim is true or false. To put the point in simple terms, if the *conceptual* claim is correct then we *can* treat animals and plants either rightly or wrongly. If the *normative* claim is correct then we *ought* to treat them rightly and refrain from treating them wrongly.

Now, a life-centered theory of environmental ethics holds that both the conceptual and the normative claims are correct. Not only is it intelligible to speak of owing duties to animals and plants, but it is the case that we humans who are moral agents do have such duties, just as we have duties to our fellow humans. A human-centered theory, on the other hand, could accept the conceptual claim but would reject the normative one. Indeed, what makes such a theory human-centered is that it does consider the normative claim to be incorrect. Thus the issue between biocentric and anthropocentric theories centers on the question whether the normative claim is correct or incorrect.

The biocentric position may at first sight appear very odd. To some people it might seem obviously false, especially when all animals and plants are included in the class of moral subjects. How could it be that we humans have duties and responsibilities to mosquitoes and earthworms? Even if we can make sense of such an assertion (that is, even if the conceptual claim were true), what reasons could possibly justify it? Is it really meaningful to talk about treating such things as trees and mushrooms rightly or wrongly? And supposing it to be meaningful, on what grounds could it ever be established that we are under a moral obligation to act toward such things in certain ways and not in others?

Furthermore, if all animals and plants are to be considered proper moral subjects, then it is possible for our duties toward them to conflict with the duties we owe to our fellow humans. To fulfill the one set of duties will often involve failing to fulfill the other. This raises the question of which duties are to take priority. For if the normative assertion is correct and we do have duties and responsibilities toward animals and plants, these will frequently compete against the legitimate moral claims of humans. How could the dilemmas arising from such competing claims ever be

20

resolved? It would appear impossible to find a rational way to deal with these ineluctable conflicts.

Exactly how it can be shown that the normative claim is correct and that moral dilemmas arising from conflicts between humans and nonhumans are rationally resolvable is a task that will take the entire argument of this book to accomplish. At this point, however, certain considerations will be helpful in response to at least some of the doubts that may have arisen.

In the first place, we should observe that whenever a conflict occurs between the well-being of nonhuman organisms and human well-being, a decision must be made as to whose well-being is to be furthered at the expense of the other. This decision, as I shall eventually show in the last chapter of this book, can be arrived at on the basis of a set of priority principles governing the fair resolution of conflicts between humans and nonhumans. If we were to accept the theory of human ethics presented later in this chapter and the theory of environmental ethics defended throughout the remaining chapters, the conflict would be understood as one occurring between two kinds of entities, both of which are deserving of moral consideration. The well-being of each living organism, whether human or nonhuman, is recognized as making an initial claim to fulfillment, a claim whose moral legitimacy must be taken into account. For this is what follows when animals and plants as well as humans are regarded as proper moral subjects.

So the normative assertion that all living things are moral subjects does not render nonsensical or impractical a life-centered theory of environmental ethics. Rather, such a theory and the normative assertion entailed by it transform any situation of conflict from a brute battle of opposing forces in a blind struggle for self-preservation to an ethical problem requiring a fair resolution among competing moral claims. Each party to the conflict is acknowledged as making a legitimate demand for consideration, and settling the conflict becomes an ethical issue to be dealt with by appeal to objective moral principles. (In Chapter Six a number of these priority principles will be discussed.)

A second point that needs to be made here has to do with our "intuitive" moral judgments. It may seem to some that our moral intuition tells us that it is erroneous to consider such organisms as clams and pokeweeds moral subjects, the treatment of which can be right or wrong. We may intuitively feel that it is wrong to hurt animals that can experience pain, but no such intuitive feelings are aroused by the sight of people digging clams or pulling weeds out of their gardens. If a thing is incapable of feeling pain, how can it be wrong to kill or injure it? So it *seems* perfectly obvious to us, something self-evident to our intuitive moral sense, that there can be nothing wrong in the way we treat plants or those animals that cannot feel pain. Thus the appeal to practically everybody's moral intuition is enough to refute the idea, central to a life-centered theory of environmental ethics, that every living thing is a moral subject.

It is important to see why this sort of argument is not sound. In particular, it cannot be used against a life-centered theory of environmental ethics such as the one set forth in this book. Our moral intuitions regarding how the living things of the natural world should be treated are psychologically dependent on certain basic attitudes toward nature that we were imbued with in childhood. What attitudes were given to us early in life reflect the particular outlook on animals and plants accepted by our social group. Extreme variations are to be found in the outlooks of different groups even within Western culture, to say nothing of other cultures throughout the world. Consider how sport hunting is accepted as good, clean, healthy recreational activity among some people in our society while others consider it a cruel, vicious, contemptible practice. Feelings and convictions are often intense on these matters. Here is where people will have strong "intuitions" about what is right and wrong. It will seem self-evident to them that it is wrong, for example, to be cruel to birds, and it will seem equally self-evident that there is nothing wrong with trapping bobcats for their fur.

Since our intuitive judgments in matters of ethics are in this way strongly affected by our early moral conditioning and since different societies will imbue children with different attitudes and feelings about the treatment of animals and plants, we cannot use either our own or anyone else's moral intuitions as grounds for accepting or rejecting a theory of environmental ethics. For suppose we used our own intuitions. How could we justify choosing them as the basis for accepting or rejecting a theory of environmental ethics rather than the intuitions of others whose attitudes toward nature disagreed with ours? By choosing our own intuitions we would be assuming that ours were correct and that those of others were incorrect. But unless we could show why ours were correct and theirs incorrect, we could produce no reason for anyone to accept a system of environmental ethics based on *our* intuitions and for rejecting a system based on *their* intuitions. Thus intuitions cannot be used as rational, objective grounds for any theory of environmental ethics.

Reliance on moral intuitions is at bottom an appeal to our most strongly held inner convictions. Such an appeal has no relevance to the truth or falsity of what is felt and believed so deeply. Indeed, the search for truth in these matters is *seriously hindered* by the tendency to rely on our intuitive judgments. We want to think that the moral beliefs we hold with certainty are correct and that the opposite beliefs of others are mistaken. But they hold their beliefs with as much certainty as we do ours. Unless we can give good, adequate reasons that justify our beliefs, we cannot simply reject the intuitive convictions of others as erroneous. Reference to what seems intuitively to be so is no substitute for thinking things through to their foundations.

The conclusion I wish to draw from these remarks concerning our moral intuitions is that the burden of proof for establishing the rational acceptability of a theory of environmental ethics rests equally on everyone alike, no matter what particular views each might wish to defend. We cannot assume that any one position is initially more acceptable than another. In particular, we cannot assume that the position most in keeping with our own intuitions is most likely to be the correct one. All who engage in this area of ethical inquiry must carry out their investigations with a completely open mind. They must make every effort to achieve objectivity of judgment and be willing to accept the outcome of philosophical reflection even when that might mean giving up the convictions they have hitherto held with the greatest confidence.

In the domain of environmental ethics we may find that as we pursue our thought as far as reason can take us, our presently held beliefs and attitudes will come to appear inadequate. Indeed, our whole outlook on the natural world and the place of humans in it may be radically transformed. The moral concerns we now feel may expand and take new directions, and the awareness of our own responsibilities in relation to our planet's natural environment and its wild communities of life may be subject to profound and far-reaching changes. Only the most careful and critical reflection, carried through with total openness and honesty, can bring us nearer to whatever truth the human mind can attain in this domain of thought.

Now it happens that our own society's ethical outlook on nature is predominately human-centered. Thus the basic principles of a life-centered theory of environmental ethics will at first appear to many to be mistaken. But this should not be allowed to bias our judgment. We must strive for objectivity, and this requires a certain detachment from our immediate intuitions in this area so that we can consider without prejudice the merits of the case for a life-centered view.

3. *Formal Conditions for Valid Moral Principles*

In this and the next sections I set forth the conditions that any rule or standard must satisfy if it is to be included in a normative ethical system that can correctly be said to be valid. By "valid" I mean that the rules and standards of the system are in truth binding upon (lay down moral requirements for) all moral agents.

I shall divide the conditions into formal and material ones.[4] The formal conditions, which are now widely accepted in contemporary ethics, may be thought of as defining what is meant by describing or classifying a rule, standard, or principle as a moral one, that is, as belonging to the category of morality or ethics. If a rule, standard, or principle is known to satisfy the formal conditions, then it is understood to be a certain *type* of norm. Hence the formal conditions are the same for both human ethics and environmental ethics, and to accept them is simply to conceive of a moral norm in a certain way. In this book I shall proceed on the assumption that, to be a moral rule, standard, or principle at all—whether validly binding or not—the formal conditions must be satisfied.

With regard to the material conditions, on the other

[4] The distinction between formal and material conditions is set forth in Kurt Baier, *The Moral Point of View: A Rational Basis of Ethics* (Ithaca, N.Y.: Cornell University Press, 1958), chapter 8, and in John Rawls, *A Theory of Justice* (Cambridge, Mass.: Harvard University Press, 1971), especially Section 23, "The Formal Constraints on the Concept of Right." The distinction has also been discussed by William K. Frankena in "The Concept of Morality," *Journal of Philosophy* 63 (1966) 688-696, and in "On Defining Moral Judgments, Principles, and Codes," *Etyka* 2 (1973) pp. 45-56. Both articles are reprinted in K. E. Goodpaster, ed., *Perspectives on Morality: Essays by William K. Frankena* (Notre Dame, Ind.: University of Notre Dame Press, 1976). The most detailed and comprehensive study of the distinction is to be found in a recent analysis of moral reasons for action: Stephen L. Darwall, *Impartial Reason* (Ithaca, N.Y.: Cornell University Press, 1983).

hand, not only are they different for the norms of human ethics and of environmental ethics, but some justification must be given for accepting these as necessary conditions for the validity of moral norms that satisfy them. To establish the validity of any rule, standard, or principle that belongs to the category of morality, it is not enough to show that it fulfills the material conditions. One must also show that these conditions do determine the moral validity of the norms that satisfy them.

The material condition for human ethics, which I shall call "respect for persons," will be explained and analyzed later in this chapter and in Chapter Five. I shall give a brief account of the grounds for its justifiability, but the argument will not here be fully elaborated. My aim in this book is to focus attention on the area of environmental ethics, and although I shall be considering the relation of human ethics to environmental ethics, a detailed examination of the foundations of human ethics as such will not be needed for this purpose.

The material condition for valid moral norms in the domain of environmental ethics is *respect for nature*. Exactly what this phrase means and why it does provide the correct test for moral validity in this area are matters that will be our primary preoccupation throughout this book.

I turn now to a consideration of the formal conditions that must be satisfied by any rule of conduct or standard of character if it is to be included in the category of morality. A condition is formal when a complete statement of it entails no description of the empirical properties of actions or character traits to which the rule or standard applies. From the formal conditions alone one could not know what sorts of actions are right or wrong, or what sorts of character traits are virtues or vices. This additional information must be supplied by the material conditions. Thus both formal and material conditions are needed if the rules and standards are to function normatively, that is, as practical guides for moral agents to strive to fulfill in their choice and conduct.

The formal conditions are five in number. For any set of rules and standards to constitute a valid normative ethical system, the rules and standards

(a) must be general in form;

(b) must be considered to be universally applicable to all moral agents as such;

(c) must be intended to be applied disinterestedly;

(d) must be advocated as normative principles for all to adopt; and

(e) must be taken as overriding all nonmoral norms.

We may think of these conditions as specifying properties of rules and standards, but it should be noted that the way the rules and standards are intended to be applied and how they are viewed by those who accept them are included as such properties. I shall now explain each condition in the order given.

(a) A rule or standard is general in form when it does not contain any reference to particular persons or actions but only mentions *kinds* of things in terms of their properties. Thus a valid moral rule never states that a specific individual or group must perform a certain action at a certain time and place. It simply states that a kind of action must be done by anyone (that is, anyone who is a moral agent) in certain generally described circumstances. For example, it might state that anyone who has made a promise to someone is under an obligation to that person to keep the promise. Although the roles of promisor and promisee are referred to, no particular individuals in those roles are mentioned. The rule, "Do not harm another," to take a second example, is perfectly general in form. It lays down a prohibition upon all actions of a certain type, prescribing that *any* moral agent refrain from *any* action of that type.

Similarly, a moral standard of good character (such as

"Honesty is a virtue" or "One should be honest") makes no mention of specific people, times, or places for the cultivation of honesty in one's character.

Note that the formal condition we are discussing is the generality of moral rules and standards. References to keeping promises, not harming, and being honest are made here only for the purpose of providing examples. From the mere fact that a rule or standard is general in form we cannot infer any kinds of action or any types of character to be right or wrong, good or bad. Thus generality itself is a purely formal condition.

(b) A valid moral rule or standard must be a normative principle that *can* be applied universally to all beings who are moral agents, and it must be *conceived to be* universally applicable by those who subscribe to it as a validly binding moral norm. (Whether it is *correctly* applied in any given case is a further question that requires showing why a norm satisfying this condition is correctly considered to be valid.)

An important implication of the condition of universal applicability is that a whole system of valid moral rules and standards must be such that it is possible for everyone (all moral agents) to live in accordance with it. No rule prescribing conduct that annuls or defeats itself when everyone attempts to comply with it can be included.[5]

When one adopts a rule as one's own moral principle, one conceives it to be binding upon others as well as oneself. It is thought of as being universally applicable within the class of all moral agents. Rules not considered to be universally applicable are nonmoral rules. These may be perfectly useful rules, justifiable in terms of their practical functions. But they are not part of a person's moral system. A few examples of such nonmoral rules are the following:

(i) The rules agreed to by the members of a voluntary as-

---

[5] Kant's case of a lying promise is the most famous example. See Immanuel Kant, *Foundations of the Metaphysics of Morals*, section 1. This formal condition is stated in contemporary terms in Kurt Baier, *The Moral Point of View*, pp. 195-200.

sociation, such as a hiking club or a professional organization like the American Association for the Advancement of Science. The rules are understood to be applicable only to those who choose to be members.

(ii) The rules of a contest or game, applicable only to the contestants or players.

(iii) The "how-to" rules given as the best way to achieve a certain goal, applicable only to those who seek that goal.

(iv) A society's customs and rules of etiquette when understood as applying only to its own members. ("When in Rome, do as the Romans do.")

(v) The laws of a state, binding only upon its own citizens and those who reside in it.

None of these rules belong to a normative ethical system, and they may or may not be consistent with valid moral rules. If they are consistent with them, then there is nothing wrong in following these nonmoral rules. If they are not consistent with valid moral rules, then actions done in accordance with them are morally wrong. In that case, since valid moral rules (by the fifth condition below) take priority over all other types of rules, the actions in question should not be done.

(c) The third formal condition has to do with the manner in which moral rules and standards are applied, not with their scope or range of application. They must be intended to be applied disinterestedly, as matters of principle. They serve as "categorical imperatives," in one of Kant's senses of that term. If a rule or standard is a valid moral norm, it is subscribed to as a principle that is to be followed by each agent independently of that agent's particular ends and interests. One is under a requirement to comply with it whether or not such compliance in any given situation happens to be to one's advantage. This means that acting in accordance with a valid moral rule is acting on principle. It is to do what is right because that is what is morally required of one, not because it is in one's interest.

The same holds for standards of good character. Suppose, for example, that the standard of always being scrupulously fair to people is a valid standard of good moral character. Insofar as we sincerely hold this standard as one of our own moral norms, we strive to develop in ourselves the trait of fairness (or to strengthen it in us, if it is already present). We do this independently of whether we find ourselves naturally inclined in this direction and regardless of whether developing the steady disposition to be fair to others makes them like us or approve of us. Our relations with people may indeed go more smoothly and pleasantly when we are fair to them, and we may also benefit if they reciprocate by being fair to us. But if we try to be fair *only because* it has these results, then fairness is not functioning as a moral standard in our lives. We are not applying it to ourselves disinterestedly.

The reason why all valid moral rules and standards must be understood to apply to everyone disinterestedly is this. If they were considered to be morally binding only when they were expected to help an agent achieve some personal end or satisfy some particular interest (even an interest in furthering the good of others), no moral requiredness would attach to them unless the end or interest in question was first judged to be morally acceptable. In order to make a correct judgment about *this*, valid moral principles would have to be applied. If these principles were in turn used only as a way to achieve some further end or satisfy some further interest, again the end would have to be judged a morally desirable end to pursue or the interest a morally worthy one to fulfill. So we cannot ultimately avoid the necessity of relying on standards and rules that are applied as matters of principle.

It is not implied that there must be a conflict between morality and self-interest in every particular situation. It is frequently the case that a person has both moral reasons and reasons of self-interest for carrying out a certain action. To obey the law, for instance, is both morally right (assuming the law is just) and is a way to avoid being fined or imprisoned. All that the disinterestedness criterion entails is that, if we correctly judge an act to be morally right, it is because it is in accordance with a rule that applies to everyone as a matter of principle. The rule must be thought to be binding upon every agent *whether or not* the act required by it also serves the agent's interests.

(d) The fourth condition adds something to the first three (generality, universal applicability, and disinterestedness) by stipulating that a moral rule or standard is valid only if those who adopt it as their own normative guide have an attitude of approval toward its being adopted by all others. In Kant's terms, the standard or rule must be willed to be a universal law for all rational beings. Thus it is not enough that a moral norm be considered universally applicable (the second condition) and be intended to be applied disinterestedly (the third condition). It must be such that a moral agent who subscribes to it gives sincere assent to its being likewise subscribed to by every other being to which it is understood to be applicable, namely to every other moral agent.

From the point of view of each agent, a normative ethical system is understood to be meant for everyone. Its rules and standards are expected to function as guiding principles for the conduct of life and the development of character of all who fall within their scope. We might call this the public aspect of morality. It precludes the idea that there could be a private morality belonging only to a particular individual or group, like the secret rules of a club known only to its members.

A valid moral rule or standard, then, is intended to be a publicly recognized principle, openly acknowledged by everyone as a morally binding principle to be used by all as a guide to choice and conduct. In an actual society, not everyone may be willing to acknowledge a certain standard or rule. But this is beside the point, as far as the validity of the standard or rule is concerned. What this fourth condition requires is that, if a rule or standard is to be valid, it must be advocated as a principle for all to follow. Anyone who does accept it must be *willing* to have others accept it also and must *approve of* its becoming a publicly recognized norm acknowledged by everyone to be validly binding.

(e) The last formal condition is that a moral rule or standard can be valid only if those who accept it give it supreme weight and advocate that all others give supreme weight to it. To say that a moral standard or rule is given supreme weight is to say that it is assigned priority over all other types of norms. A valid moral consideration overrides (outweighs, takes precedence over) all nonmoral considerations. Nonmoral considerations are reasons-for-action determined by norms that lack any or all of the properties stated in conditions (a), (b), (c), and (d). These include both social norms (such as customs, laws, institutional regulations, and rules of a game) and individual norms (those used when one is deciding how best to achieve one's goals in life).

Although accepting a moral rule or standard as validly binding means that one regards it as legitimately overriding all other concerns, this should not be taken as a psychological claim that the one who so accepts it will in fact always be motivated to follow it when it conflicts with other interests and purposes. Rather, it is a logical claim about normative priorities in a well-ordered system of practical reasoning. One might believe that a moral rule takes precedence over any consideration of self-interest when the pursuit of self-interest is not compatible with following the rule, yet act in one's self-interest nevertheless. This would be an instance of weakness of will. The moral rule is still regarded as having priority, although one does not act consistently with one's considered judgment in this instance.

This completes my account of the five formal conditions that must be satisfied by any rule or standard if it is correctly to be included in a valid normative ethical system. They are all formal conditions because they do not tell us what the content of any rules and standards that satisfy them might be. They only state that, whatever the content, the rules and standards must be general in form and must be considered by those who adopt them to be universally applicable, disinterested, public, and overriding norms meant for everyone.

In order to understand fully what a valid normative ethical system is, it is clear that some material condition or conditions must be added to the formal conditions already stated. What must be the *content* of a rule or standard if it is to be validly binding on all moral agents?

Answering this question necessitates separating human ethics from environmental ethics. Both domains of ethics are governed by rules and standards that satisfy the five formal conditions. As far as these conditions go, no distinction can be made between the two. The differences between them lie in the content of their respective systems of norms. I shall therefore discuss material conditions of a valid normative ethical system first under the heading of human ethics, putting aside for the moment consideration of the content of environmental ethics. This procedure will allow us to make comparisons between the two domains of ethics without confusing them with one another.

4. *Material Conditions for Valid Moral Principles: The Content of Human Ethics*

With reference to the domain of human ethics, the content of valid moral rules and standards has to do with human beings as persons. A human being is here defined biologically as any member of the mammalian species, *Homo sapiens*. A person, on the other hand, is to be understood as *a center of autonomous choice and valuation. Persons are beings that give direction to their lives on the basis of their own values*. They are entities that not only have interests and purposes, but also have the capacity to set long-range and short-range goals for themselves in the light of those interests and purposes. They have the power to decide for themselves what ends to seek in life and they can make up their own minds about the best means to take toward those ends. They have the ability to impose order on their various activities and projects, determining what purposes are more important than others and choosing not to take steps to accomplish one purpose if that will prevent them from achieving a more important purpose. Finally, persons are beings who place value on things according to how they judge each thing's contribution to their overall well-being and happiness.

Some experiences of life are valued by persons as ultimate or final ends, being considered significant and worthwhile in themselves. Other experiences are found to be worthless, empty, meaningless. Persons also develop their own "life styles," or ways of living that they judge to be desirable and rewarding as expressions of their deepest needs and aspirations. Because they have different value-systems, persons vary in their conceptions of what makes for a truly good life, the kind of life they would judge to be most worth living.

A person's value-system, as that term is being used here, is not to be thought of as a mere set of personal preferences. Nor is it a simple unstructured series of likes and dislikes, of desires and aversions, of positive and negative responses to the world. One does not have a value-system of one's own if one simply finds oneself aiming to satisfy certain wants and needs, or simply experiencing various satisfactions and dissatisfactions in daily life. To have a value-system of one's own is to be disposed to judge certain things to be *preferable* to others in the light of one's total view of oneself and one's conception of what constitutes a worthwhile and meaningful life. To judge one thing to be preferable to another is to judge that it is better than the other because it makes a larger or more fundamental contribution to the major components of a good life. As distinct from merely feeling a stronger liking for X than for Y, one's judgment (a genuine value judgment) that X is preferable to Y is a judgment that X has *greater value or worth* than Y when taking into account the relation each bears to the goodness of one's life as a whole.

Just as preference can in this way be distinguished from preferability, so desire can be distinguished from desirability. Instead of simply having desires and being disposed to aim at their satisfaction, an individual with a value-system adopts certain standards for judging the desirability or undesirability of satisfying those desires and even for judging the desirability or undesirability of having those desires in the first place. Such desirability-judgments, like preferability-judgments, are grounded on principles of rational choice, and these principles are adopted by persons according to their conceptions of their own true good. Different sets of principles make up what have been called people's "plans of life," which are the different ways of ordering means and ends by which people endeavor to realize their true good as far as they can do so in the circumstances in which they find themselves. What is desirable, then, is not what is in fact desired, but what one has good reason to desire. And one has good reason to desire something when it has a valuable place in the total ordering of means and ends that constitutes one's plan of life as a whole.

To make preferability-judgments and desirability-judgments in the foregoing way presupposes that people have a sense of their own identity over time. For they must be able to conceive of themselves as having a future, and this means that they believe they will be the same persons later in life as the persons they are now, however different may be their external circumstances. To have a vision of one's life as a unified whole and to make judgments in the light of that vision requires a sense of personal identity. Only beings with that kind of self-awareness can be persons.

With this analysis in mind of what it means to be a person, we can see that an entity that has the potentiality for becoming a person may not have the opportunity to develop into full personhood. By "full personhood" I mean the most complete actualization of the powers of autonomy and rationality required for choosing one's own value-system and for directing one's life on the basis of that value-system. People can realize different degrees or levels of personhood, depending on how they were treated as children, what opportunities for the development of autonomy and rationality were given to them, the extent to which they are free of serious mental and emotional disorders, and so on.[6] In general, whether an entity is a person depends on how completely it exemplifies the characteristics of full personhood, and this is a matter of degree. This is not true of the humanity of an entity, where "humanity" is used in the strictly biological sense of being a member of the species *Homo sapiens*.

I shall use the term "personhood," then, to mean the set of properties in virtue of which an entity is a person. Personhood is what *makes* a being a person, or in other words, what it is about an entity that we would point out to explain why we consider it a person. The properties in question may be exemplified by an individual in varying degrees at different times in its life, and a being who is a person can lose personhood (cease to be a person), either temporarily or permanently, at some moment in its existence. Thus a person might become totally insane or, through illness or a sudden accident, suffer severe brain damage and become mentally a "vegetable." Such an individual may or may not be able to return to personhood before death.

In discussing the idea of personhood the question might be raised whether only human beings can be persons. As was the case with the concept of a moral agent, I wish to leave this question open in this book. Perhaps some levels

---

[6] I am here indebted to Robert Young's studies of autonomy and the conditions for its development: Robert Young, "Autonomy and the 'Inner Self'," *American Philosophical Quarterly* 17/1 (January 1980): 35-43; and "Autonomy and Socialization," *Mind* 89/356 (October 1980): 565-576.

of personhood are realized by chimpanzees, monkeys, gorillas, and other primates. Dolphins and whales may also exemplify some aspects of personhood. And there may be beings on other planets in other solar systems and galaxies who are persons. These issues are all empirical matters that need not be settled here. For convenience I shall speak as if all persons were biological humans, but this manner of speaking is not to be taken as acceptance of a fact. If some nonhumans are also persons (whether they exist on our planet or elsewhere in the universe) and if they have the capacities of moral agents, then what I am calling "human ethics" will apply to them as much as it does to us.

I turn now to the connection between the idea of personhood and the content of a valid system of human ethics. Human ethics has to do with the moral relations holding among persons as persons. In such an ethical system we are to think of everyone not only as a moral agent but also as a center of autonomous choice, living (or potentially capable of living) a way of life according to his or her own value-system, and morally related to every other person in accordance with a set of standards and rules. We are not considering their relations to each other in various social roles, such as employer and employee, nor are we concerned with differences among them due to the particular set of values each is trying to realize in life. We are abstracting from these differences and considering only their relations to one another as persons and moral agents.

Now these relations must be determined by rules and standards that satisfy the five formal conditions, since we are here dealing with an ethical system that will qualify as a valid one. Thus the relations among all persons simply as persons are to be thought of as being governed by rules and standards that do not refer to any specific individuals and at the same time are understood to be applicable to everyone. What is more, they apply to everyone in a categorical way, having no regard for the particular value-systems of each person. We are also to think of everyone accepting these rules and standards as taking priority over all other values, including those that each pursues as an autonomous person. Finally, each individual as a moral agent must be willing to advocate that all use these disinterested and overriding norms as the supreme principles defining their duties and obligations to one another.

What sort of rules and standards would be so advocated by each individual? In answering this we must keep in mind that in advocating the universal adoption of these norms the individual is acting as a moral agent, not as a unique self pursuing a particular set of values. Being general and disinterested, the norms in question will not favor the value-systems of any specific individuals or groups. Being overriding, they will outweigh any values that come into conflict with them. Since all are persons as well as moral agents, each is seeking to realize his or her own value-system. Yet all must adopt the same set of norms to be morally binding on themselves as their supreme principles. Thus it is only if the norms *give equal weight to every person's value-system and at the same time make it possible for each to pursue the realization of his or her own value-system in ways compatible with everyone else's similar pursuit* that such norms would be acceptable to all.

The conclusion to be drawn from this line of reasoning may be stated in the following way. Rational and autonomous persons acting as moral agents will unanimously adopt rules and standards satisfying the five formal conditions if and only if those rules and standards embody the principle that each person's autonomy in living according to his or her chosen value-system be respected. *A valid system of human ethics, therefore, is a set of moral rules and standards that embody the principle of respect for all persons as persons*.

What relations among persons are such that the principle of respect for each individual's personhood is adhered to? To respect others as persons is, in the first place, to give recognition to their personhood by regarding them as centers of autonomous choice. One looks at them as having a life of their own to live, just as one views oneself in the same way. To recognize them as persons is to see them as one sees oneself. Secondly, it is to consider their personhood as having a worth or value in itself, just as one values one's own personhood as something good in itself. And just as the sense of our own worth as a person means that we believe we should be allowed to live our own life and pursue the conception of our own true good that we have chosen for ourselves, so our acknowledgment of the worth of others as persons means that we believe they should be allowed to pursue their true good as they conceive of it. To respect others as persons is to consider them worthy of being given control over their own destinies. It is to let their futures be in their own hands. Respecting them involves a commitment on our part not to interfere with them in the pursuit of their values as long as they are not violating anyone else's autonomy.

Exercise of autonomous choice, having control over one's destiny, living a life of one's own, and being free from interference in the pursuit of one's values are all impossible unless one has been able to develop certain capacities. To allow a being to *exercise* autonomy in choosing its own way of living presupposes that it has already developed the *capacity* for autonomous choice. To grant it control over its own destiny is to assume that it can envision a future of its own, which in turn implies that it has an awareness of self-identity over time. To refrain from interfering with its freedom to pursue its values assumes that it has the ability to set goals for itself and to direct its conduct in the light of its "plan of life." Such capacities and powers are possible only when an individual has been given the opportunity to develop them. The principle of respect for all persons as persons, then, imposes both requirements for the development of certain capacities in individuals and requirements for the free exercise of those capacities. The rules of a valid system of human ethics must provide for the fulfillment of both requirements.

The most fundamental rules needed to meet these requirements are the rules against killing persons and against harming them in ways seriously damaging to their personhood. Further, since the personhood of individuals cannot be developed or respected unless certain of their basic needs are satisfied, there must be a rule about making available a fair share of resources to meet those minimal needs. In addition there must be a rule of freedom from interference, and rules of fidelity, nondeception, and reciprocity. These rules can be thought of as defining a social order which at one and the same time makes it possible for persons to realize their personhood and gives public expression to the attitude of respect for persons. The full compliance of moral agents in conducting their lives in accordance with these rules creates a social world where acknowledgment is made of each individual's worth by the actions of others. In that world each is given the same opportunity to pursue ends and goals of her or his own choosing within the constraints set by the rules. Every person is viewed by every other as an independent, self-directed being possessing inherent worth. Thus the autonomy and integrity of all are accorded equal value.

When the content of human ethics is analyzed this way, the principle of respect for persons is built into the very structure of the moral community and serves as the ultimate ground of the rules of duty within the domain of human ethics. (In Chapter Five I will show how the principle of respect for persons serves as the foundation for universal human rights.)

This completes the account of human ethics I wish to use as a basis for comparison with environmental ethics. I proceed now to compare human ethics with environmental ethics, making special reference to certain similarities between them. In particular, I wish to show that there is a symmetry or isomorphism of structure holding between a theory of human ethics based on respect for persons and a life-centered theory of environmental ethics based on respect for nature. Although the two systems of ethics differ from one another as far as their normative content is concerned, the internal ordering of their main components discloses interesting and significant parallels. This study will also serve to provide a preliminary overall account of the theory of environmental ethics to be set forth in detail in subsequent chapters.

5. The Structural Symmetry between Human Ethics and Environmental Ethics

The theory of human ethics outlined above has three main components. First, there is the acceptance of a *belief-system* within which each moral agent conceives of others in a certain way. One's fellow humans (when not insane or severely retarded) are perceived as persons like oneself. Each is understood to be a subjective center of conscious existence with the capacity to choose its own value-system and live a self-directed life. Thus each is seen to exemplify the same traits of personhood found in oneself.

The second component is the *attitude* of respect for persons. This attitude is both a moral one and an ultimate one. It is a moral attitude because it is universalizable and disinterested. That is, each moral agent who sincerely has the attitude advocates its universal adoption by all other agents, regardless of whether they are so inclined and regardless of their fondness or lack of fondness for particular individuals. As a moral attitude it is considered binding upon everyone alike. For the one who has the attitude of respect, each person is deemed worthy of *everyone's* respect, not just of one's own respect. The attitude is an ultimate one because its justifiability does not consist in being derivable from any more general or more fundamental attitude. It sets the

41

most basic framework within which all moral relations among persons are to be determined.

The third component is *a system of rules and standards* considered valid in the domain of human ethics. These norms (the most important of which are the rules mentioned earlier) are understood to satisfy all the five formal conditions for valid moral principles. In addition their content must meet the material condition of embodying the attitude of respect for persons.

These three components—the belief-system, the ultimate moral attitude, and the set of rules and standards—are related to each other as follows. When a moral agent accepts the belief-system and conceives of others as persons, she or he takes up a certain outlook on the social world. Others are seen as belonging to a community of which one is also a member on equal terms with them. The community itself is so ordered as to make it possible for all individuals to live self-directed lives according to value-systems of their own choosing, subject only to those constraints needed to give each an equal chance.

This belief-system *supports* and *makes intelligible* the attitude of respect for persons. It provides the conceptual background against which it makes sense to adopt that attitude as an ultimate moral one to take toward all persons. The belief-system helps us to understand not only why people would take up that attitude for themselves but also why they would adovocate that others take up the attitude. For once we know the belief-system, we know how and why the attitude comes to be seen as an appropriate or morally fitting one to have toward persons as persons.

It was shown above that the belief-system provides a conception of a social world in which each individual, in virtue of his or her personhood, is recognized to be an equal among equals. Now, if one has self-respect and so regards oneself as possessing inherent worth, then given the belief-system in question one will understand one's relations with others in terms of *equality of worth*. Others will be conceived as persons like oneself and on the ground of their personhood alone they will be perceived as bearers of the same inherent value one ascribes to oneself out of self-respect. When one perceives others in this light, acknowledging the personhood of each to be something as valuable as one's own, all will be thought of as deserving equal consideration. The preservation of their existence as persons as well as their chance to develop into full personhood will be held to make the same claim-to-fulfillment as the preservation and development of one's own personhood. And this means that one will have adopted the attitude of respect for persons. What is more, one will have adopted it as a moral attitude. For it will be seen as the only appropriate or fitting attitude to take toward persons and thus an attitude that ought to be taken toward persons by everyone.[7]

The relation between the second component (the attitude of respect) and the third (the system of moral norms) is now easy to see. Insofar as one has the attitude as an ultimate moral attitude one will be committed to fulfilling whatever rules of conduct and standards of character embody the principle of respect for persons. This is what is practically entailed by adopting that attitude and advocating that all moral agents adopt it, too. We can say that conduct and character that fulfill those rules and standards give concrete expression to the attitude in practical life. To adhere to the rules and standards as matters of principle is to *show* respect for all persons as persons. It is to give public recognition to their inherent worth and to accord to everyone equal consideration.

[7] The connection between self-respect and respect for persons as a basic component in a valid system of human ethics goes back to Kant's doctrine of humanity (or rational being) as an end in itself. Immanuel Kant, *Foundations of the Metaphysics of Morals*, section 2. The idea of humanity as an end in itself is interpreted as "respect for personality" in H. J. Paton, *The Categorical Imperative: A Study in Kant's Moral Philosophy* (London: Hutchinson and Co., 1947), chapter 16. A contemporary system of ethics using these concepts in a Kantian way is set forth in Alan Donagan, *The Theory of Morality* (Chicago: University of Chicago Press, 1977), especially chapters

Let us now take an overall view of the theory of environmental ethics which is to be propounded and defended in this book. Like the theory of human ethics just outlined, it is made up of three components: a belief-system, an ultimate moral attitude, and a set of moral rules and standards. These elements stand in relation to each other in the same way that the three components of human ethics are interrelated. The belief-system supports and makes intelligible the adopting of the attitude, and the rules and standards give concrete expression to that attitude in practical life. A brief summary of each component will bring out this parallel with human ethics.

The belief-system, which will be explained in detail in Chapter Three, constitutes a philosophical world view concerning the order of nature and the place of humans in it. I call this world view "the biocentric outlook on nature." When one conceives of oneself, one's relation to other living things, and the whole set of natural ecosystems on our planet in terms of this outlook, one identifies oneself as a member of the Earth's Community of Life. This does not entail a denial of one's personhood. Rather, it is a way of understanding one's true self to include one's biological nature as well as one's personhood. From the perspective of the biocentric outlook, one sees one's membership in the Earth's Community of Life as providing a common bond with all the different species of animals and plants that have evolved over the ages. One becomes aware that, like all other living things on our planet, one's very existence depends on the fundamental soundness and integrity of the biological system of nature. When one looks at this domain of life in its totality, one sees it to be a complex and unified web of interdependent parts.

The biocentric outlook on nature also includes a certain way of perceiving and understanding each individual or-

---

2 and 7. Donagan claims that these concepts are rooted in "the Hebrew-Christian Moral Tradition."

ganism. Each is seen to be a teleological (goal-oriented) center of life, pursuing its own good in its own unique way. This, of course, does not mean that they all seek their good as a conscious end or purpose, the realization of which is their intended aim. Consciousness may not be present at all, and even when it is present the organism need not be thought of as intentionally taking steps to achieve goals it sets for itself. Rather, a living thing is conceived as a unified system of organized activity, the constant tendency of which is to preserve its existence by protecting and promoting its well-being.

Finally, to view the place of humans in the natural world from the perspective of the biocentric outlook is to reject the idea of human superiority over other living things. Humans are not thought of as carrying on a higher grade of existence when compared with the so-called "lower" orders of life. The biocentric outlook precludes a hierarchical view of nature. To accept that outlook and view the living world in its terms is to commit oneself to the principle of species-impartiality. No bias in favor of some over others is acceptable. This impartiality applies to the human species just as it does to nonhuman species.

These are the implications of accepting the biocentric outlook. A full argument justifying the acceptance of that outlook will be presented in Chapter Three. For the moment we shall simply assume its justifiability and consider how its acceptance supports and makes intelligible a moral agent's adopting the attitude of respect for nature. It can be seen from the foregoing account that insofar as one conceives of one's relation to the whole system of nature through the conceptual framework of the biocentric outlook, one will look at members of nonhuman species as one looks at members of one's own species. Each living thing, human and nonhuman alike, will be viewed as an entity pursuing its own good in its own way according to its species-specific nature. (For humans this will include not only an autonomous, self-directed pursuing of one's good, but also the self-created conception of what one's true good is.) No living thing will be considered inherently superior or inferior to any other, since the biocentric outlook entails species-impartiality. All are then judged to be equally deserving of moral concern and consideration.

Now, for a moral agent to be disposed to give equal consideration to all wild living things and to judge the good of each to be worthy of being preserved and protected as an end in itself and for the sake of the being whose good it is means that every wild living thing is seen to be the appropriate object of the attitude of respect. Given the acceptance of the biocentric outlook, the attitude of respect will be adopted as the only suitable or morally fitting attitude to have toward the Earth's wild creatures. One who takes the attitude of respect toward the individual organisms, species-populations, and biotic communities of the Earth's natural ecosystems regards those entities and groups of entities as possessing inherent worth, in the sense that *their value or worth does not depend on their being valued for their usefulness in furthering human ends* (or the ends of any other species). When such an attitude is adopted as one's ultimate moral attitude, I shall speak of that person as having *respect for nature*.

The third component of this theory of environmental ethics is the set of standards and rules considered to be morally binding upon everyone who has the capacities of a moral agent. These norms are principles that guide a moral agent's conduct with regard to how such an agent should or should not treat natural ecosystems and their wild communities of life. They are valid norms, according to the present theory, because they embody the attitude of respect for nature. To say that a rule or standard embodies that attitude is to say that a moral agent's complying with the rule or fulfilling the standard is a genuine manifestation of that attitude in conduct or character. Indeed, sincerely adopting that attitude as one's ultimate moral attitude *means* (among other things) that one is disposed to use those rules and standards as normative directives upon one's choice and conduct.

Thus we see how a structural symmetry holds between the two theories, one of human ethics and one of environmental ethics, with respect to their three main components and the way those components are related to each other.

6. Biology and Ethics

When a biocentric system of environmental ethics is understood in the way outlined above, the logical gap between the is-statements of the biological sciences and the ought-statements of ethics is maintained. Although it is correct to say that, according to biocentrism, moral principles governing our conduct in relation to nature are "based on" the modern biological account of living things, this must not be taken to mean that the findings of the biological sciences function as premises from which it is possible validly to deduce moral conclusions. Many connections between biology and ethics will be brought to light in this book as the biocentric theory of respect for nature is set forth and defended. But throughout this inquiry it will be noticed that the autonomy of ethics is preserved. No logical entailment is shown to hold between biological descriptions and explanations on the one hand and moral principles on the other.

The reason for the existence of such a logical gap may perhaps best be brought out by considering the relation between two different but equally correct conceptions of human beings: as biological organisms and as moral agents. In particular, we must try to understand our relationship to the natural world without denying either of these conceptions. Not only is there the question of how the biological way of looking at ourselves can be compatible with our thinking of ourselves as morally responsible beings, there is also the question: What bearing does the biological view of ourselves have on our moral commitment to principles of environmental ethics?

47

The first thing to notice is that, from a strictly biological point of view, human beings are animals. Like all other species, we have evolved from earlier forms of life according to the laws of genetics and natural selection. Taxonomically we fit into the scientific classifications of the zoological order, being members of the kingdom *Animalia*, the phylum *Chordata*, the class *Mammalia*, the family *Hominidae*, and the species *Homo sapiens*. Furthermore, as biologically functioning organisms we must be able successfully to adapt to our physical environment if we are to preserve our existence as a species. Our survival also requires that we maintain a certain ecological balance in our relations with other living things. It is a basic fact of the human condition that we are biologically dependent upon a sound, stable order in the Earth's natural ecosystems. We share this aspect of reality with all nonhuman species.

Although these things are true of us, they contain only a partial picture of the human condition. We also exist in a world where, unlike other creatures, we must *decide* how to live. Any number of possibilities are open to our choice. This holds not only for the many alternative ways it is possible to create a human civilization, but also for how we define our relationship to the natural world. For human beings there simply is no escape from the ultimate necessity to make choices. We can and do guide those choices by following normative principles, but on a deeper level those principles themselves are set by human choice. The norms by which we bind ourselves are laws of our own legislation. No rules of conduct or standards of character can impose constraints upon us unless we decide to make them our own normative guides by committing ourselves to following them and by holding ourselves accountable for failing to fulfill them.

This fundamental duality between our biological nature and our moral autonomy gives rise to the question, "Is our biological nature at all relevant to the choices we must make as moral agents, and, if it is, in what ways is it relevant?" To

48

put it another way, *"What is the ethical significance of our being members of the Earth's Community of Life?"* This is the question I wish to explore here.

A study of the geological time scale along with a knowledge of the evolution of mammalian vertebrates reveals the original emergence of the human species as a very recent event on our planet. Whether this newcomer will be able to survive as long as other species remains to be seen.

From an evolutionary point of view, we perceive ourselves as sharing with other species a similar origin as well as an existential condition that includes the ever-present possibility of total extinction. If we now move to an ecological point of view, our animal nature makes itself evident in another way. We see ourselves subject to the inexorable constraints of biological necessity. We find that our physical survival as living organisms is explainable by the same laws and theories that account for the physical survival of other species. Our ecological relations with nonhuman animals and plants and our need for an environment free of pollution are not at bottom any different from what has been found to be true of other forms of life on Earth. Like them we are an integral part of the natural universe.

Understanding ourselves as biological entities, however, does not provide us with any particular directives as to how we should conduct our lives.[8] Our proper role as moral

[8] In particular, we cannot conclude from the fact that humans are part of the natural world that we should *imitate* other species and act as they do in nature. Nothing in the biocentric outlook entails that humans ought to "follow nature" in the sense of using what happens in the natural world as a model for our behavior. This mistake is to be found, for example, in Richard A. Watson's attack on biocentrism. Richard A. Watson, "A Critique of Anti-Anthropocentric Biocentrism," *Environmental Ethics* 5/3 (Fall 1983): 252-256.

The sociobiologists also try to derive ethical assertions directly from statements about conditions that make it possible for genes to be preserved. See Edward O. Wilson, *Sociobiology: The New Synthesis* (Cambridge, Mass.: Harvard University Press, 1975). This attempt to use biological findings as a guide to life is thoroughly examined and criticized by Michael Ruse in *Sociobiology: Sense or Nonsense* (Dordrecht: D. Reidel, 1979), especially chapter 9, "Sociobiology and Ethics."

agents is not deducible from the facts about our biological nature. Nor can we draw from knowledge gained in the biological sciences alone any conclusions about what specific standards and rules should be adopted as our normative principles. Even the goal of self-preservation cannot be shown to be an end that humans *ought* to seek as moral beings. As far as biology is concerned, humans might make themselves extinct by their own free actions. Nothing in evolutionary theory says this is either impossible or undesirable; the process of evolution has included the extinction of many species. If the extinction of humanity is undesirable, it is undesirable for reasons that transcend biological science or any other science. We may well go the way of other species now extinct. The enlightenment that scientific knowledge can give us is no guarantee that humans will use it rationally!

How humans should live with other species, and even whether humans should live at all, are matters that require the making of normative and evaluative judgments. The biological sciences can give us the relevant factual knowledge, but those sciences cannot provide the standards on which our normative and evaluative judgments are grounded. As long as humans in their role of moral agents have the capacity to use biological knowledge for purposes of their own choosing, the question of how they *should* use it and *for what purposes* is an ethical question, not a scientific one.

These considerations apply with special force to a branch of biology that has become a popular source of persuasive appeals: the science of ecology. The claim is frequently made that ecology shows us how to live in relation to the natural environment. Thus it is held that ecological stability and integrity themselves constitute norms for environmental ethics. The very structure and functioning of the Earth's ecosystems, it is said, make known to us the proper relationships that should hold between ourselves and the natural world. The ecological balance holding among organisms and between organisms and environment in a healthy ecosystem should be our guide in shaping a human culture that fits harmoniously into the order of nature. The conclusion drawn from these considerations is that the science of ecology provides us with a model to follow in the domain of environmental ethics.[9]

This line of reasoning is not sound from a logical point of view. It confuses fact and value, "is" and "ought." The ecological relationships among organisms and between organisms and environment in healthy ecosystems are matters of biological fact. It is the task of the science of ecology to discover and explain those relationships. But the ethical question, "How *should* human culture fit into the order of nature?" is not a question of biological fact. It is a question that confronts humans as moral agents, not as biological organisms, since it asks which way of relating ourselves to nature, among the various alternatives open to our choice, is the ethically right one to adopt.

It is quite true that if environmental pollution and degradation reach a certain point, or if damage to the Earth's biosphere goes beyond a certain limit, the physical conditions for our continued existence will be irreversibly undermined and we will be doomed to extinction. But within the limits set by these ecological constraints there are many alternative modes of living by which humans can relate to nature, and ecology cannot tell us which of these possibilities ought to be chosen by us as moral agents. Nothing in ecology, for example, can tell us that it is wrong to have a wholly *exploitative* attitude toward nature. As far as ecology is concerned it is perfectly possible for humans to choose not to adopt the attitude of respect for nature, but rather to consider wild living things as so many objects that are there to be used for

[9] This way of thinking is to be found in Aldo Leopold, *A Sand County Almanac* (New York: Oxford University Press, 1966), and in Paul Shepard and Daniel McKinley, eds., *The Subversive Science: Essays toward an Ecology of Man* (Boston: Houghton Mifflin Co., 1969). A philosophically sophisticated statement of the position is presented in Holmes Rolston III, "Is There an Ecological Ethic?" *Ethics* 85/2 (1975), 93-109.

the exclusive benefit of humans. From that ethical standpoint nature is *rightly* controlled, transformed, and consumed in the service of human interests alone. The value that other living things have is purely instrumental. Aside from their actual or potential usefulness to humans, they lack all worth. The science of ecology itself cannot judge that such a way of looking at and valuing other creatures is inappropriate, wrong, or undesirable.

One further point is to be noted in connection with this distinction between our animal status and our moral status. This has to do with what might seem to many to be a self-evident truth: that human survival is a good. Isn't the goodness of human life a basic presupposition for all ethical thinking? Any theory of ethics that did not accept it would appear to be obviously wrongheaded. Yet I shall contend in this book that, from a certain perspective, the preservation of the human species may not be a good. I will argue that, once we are willing to view the natural world from a standpoint that is not anthropocentric, the desirability of human life is a claim that needs rational substantiation. It cannot just be assumed without question. Indeed, to assume it without question is already to commit oneself to an anthropocentric point of view concerning the natural world and the place of humans in it, and this is to beg some of the most fundamental issues of environmental ethics. As long as we keep clearly in mind the difference between humans as animals and humans as moral agents, we will recognize that although as animals we *want* to survive and reproduce, as moral agents we can ask ourselves whether we *ought* to survive and reproduce. Our biological needs and wants do not take away the freedom we have to decide whether to satisfy those needs and wants or not to satisfy them. Nor do our biological needs and wants present us with final, conclusive, logically unchallengeable reasons for deciding one way rather than another. It is not inconsistent for a human to believe in all sincerity that the world would be a better place if there were no humans in it. Whether such a judgment, though consistent, is rationally acceptable is a question that must wait until the foundations of an adequate theory of environmental ethics are thoroughly examined. It would be premature for us at the beginning of our inquiry to assume without argument the answer to *any* normative or evaluative question, even that of the desirability of human survival itself.

7. *A Note on the Ethics of the Bioculture*

The scope of environmental ethics as it is conceived of here will be better understood if it is distinguished not only from human ethics but also from what I shall refer to as the ethics of the bioculture. Although I shall not give further consideration to this third area of ethics beyond the present section, a general characterization of its main features will help us get a clearer grasp of the distinctive concerns of environmental ethics.

While human ethics has to do with the moral relations holding among human beings themselves and environmental ethics with the moral relations between humans and the natural world, the ethics of the bioculture is concerned with the human treatment of animals and plants in artificially created environments that are completely under human control. The bioculture is a set of social institutions and practices. It is that aspect of any human culture in which humans create and regulate the environment of living things and systematically exploit them for human benefit. The bioculture thus includes all organized activities in which humans make use of animals and plants to further human ends. Not only does it cover the manipulation of environmental conditions, but also the manipulation of the organisms themselves. By means of hybridization, breeding programs, and other methods of genetic control, humans produce the kind of animals and plants that will best serve human purposes.

In the bioculture, then, the total conditions of life and

death for nonhuman organisms and the very organisms themselves are in human hands. Environment and heredity are both subject to human contrivance and direction. Here is a list of some of the social institutions and practices that may be contained in a society's bioculture.

Agriculture (grain, vegetable, and fruit farming).

Raising and slaughtering animals for food and clothing (for example, chicken farming, sheep raising, pig farming, and cattle ranching).

Cultivated forests for timber production.

Plant nurseries for raising garden flowers, shrubs, and trees.

Breeding and training animals for various tasks (work horses, racing horses, hunting dogs, watchdogs, circus animals).

The pet trade and all activities involved in the private ownership of pets.

Raising, collecting, and using animals and plants for scientific experiments.

Zoos, animal exhibition parks, aquariums, and "marineland" establishments.

Sports that depend on the use of animals (horse racing and dog racing, rodeos and horseback riding, bullfighting and cockfighting).

Some wildlife management practices aimed at the benefit of humans, not the good of the animals being "managed" (raising pheasants and other birds on game farms, to be released for sport hunting. Stocking lakes and streams with game fish, and raising those fish in hatcheries).

When we look at these practices from an ethical viewpoint, two characteristics immediately stand out. First, they all depend on total human dominance over nonhuman living things and their environment. Second, they all involve treating nonhuman living things as means to human ends (though, as in the case of pets, this does not always mean that nonhuman things are being harmed). It is the moral relevance of these characteristics that gives rise to the ethics of the bioculture. Let us consider these two features in this light.

The social institutions and practices of the bioculture are, first and foremost, exercises of absolute, unconditioned power. They are examples of the way humans "conquer" and "subdue" nature. (The conquest of nature has often been seen as a key to the progress of civilization.) When we humans create the bioculture and engage in its practices we enter upon a special relationship with animals and plants. We hold them completely within our power. They must serve us or be destroyed. For some practices their being killed by us is the very thing necessary to further our ends. Instances are slaughtering animals for food, cutting timber for lumber, and causing laboratory animals to die by giving them lethal dosages of toxic chemicals.

Now it is a truth of fact and *not* a value judgment that all the living organisms being used in any society's bioculture are entities that have a good of their own. They can be benefited or harmed. In this matter they are exactly like wild animals and plants in natural ecosystems. Thus it makes sense to inquire whether there are any obligations and responsibilities on the part of humans with regard to the proper exercise of their power over living things in the bioculture. Might, after all, does not make right. That we have power over living things does not give us license to do what we wish with that power. In the case of having an animal as a pet, people do willingly accept certain responsibilities for the animal's well-being. This is because they care about it and want to help it lead a healthy, happy life. The pet owner's sense of responsibility is concomitant with her or his love for the pet. The fact that one has power over the animal's life does not mean there are no moral constraints upon the exercise of that power.

The central ethical issue regarding the treatment of living things in the bioculture as a whole focuses on those situations where there are no personal feelings of love or affectionate caring. Does the absence of such feelings mean that human moral agents have no responsibilities with respect to those animals and plants they use for their own ends? This certainly does not follow. As was pointed out in connection with human ethics, our duties toward other persons do not depend on our feeling love or affection for them, but hold regardless of such personal contingencies. Therefore, just as our *power* over other living things does not absolve us from all responsibilities regarding their welfare, so our *lack of personal caring* about them does not entail freedom from all moral constraints on how we treat them.

Can any ethical principles be found to guide us in this area? Before attempting an answer, let us look at the second morally relevant characteristic of any society's bioculture. This is the fact that the social institutions and practices that make up a bioculture are all aimed at benefiting humans. Both organisms and their environments are developed, managed, and controlled for the purpose of making life better for people in some way—more enjoyable, more interesting, healthier, or more secure. Living things then come to be thought of primarily as having instrumental value. A *good* watchdog, circus animal, laboratory rodent, variety of hybrid corn, or the like is one which can be cheaply and easily used for some human end. Aside from those animals and plants for which people happen to have affectionate feelings, nonhuman organisms are given the same status as machines, buildings, tools, and other human artifacts.

Still, they are not like machines, buildings, and tools in one crucial respect (even though in some cases they are human artifacts). In this one crucial respect they share a fundamental characteristic with humans themselves: they have a good of their own, with all that that entails. Thus their lives can be made better or worse by the way humans treat them, and it is possible for humans to take their standpoint and judge what happens to them in terms of *their* well-being. Such judgments take the form of asserting what is good or evil for the organism from whose standpoint the judgment is being made, and this is a matter that is quite independent of whatever usefulness the organism might have to humans. So the fact that the animals and plants being dealt with in a society's bioculture are valued instrumentally does not settle the ethical question of how they should be treated. There always remains the further issue of whether they should be regarded as having a kind of worth additional to and independent of their instrumental value.

If the animals and plants of the bioculture *were* viewed as having a kind of worth additional to and independent of their usefulness to humans, then the question of how they ought to be treated could not be decided simply by seeing what sort of treatment of them most effectively brings about the human benefit for which they are being used. On the contrary, certain constraints on their treatment would be imposed as moral requirements, such as minimizing their pain (in the case of sentient animals). These moral constraints could mean that proper treatment of living things in the bioculture involves more expensive, less efficient, and more difficult ways of dealing with them. Some sacrifice of human interests (such as maximum profit-making in commercial enterprises) would then be entailed.

The ethical question of deciding what shape the bioculture of a society should take cannot be avoided. Moral agents, here as elsewhere, are confronted with alternatives among which to choose. It is possible to have a bioculture that serves human needs and at the same time is held within certain moral bounds. The fact that the entire practice exists for the benefit of humans does not justify a totally laissez faire policy with regard to the way animals and plants are treated. It becomes a major responsibility of moral agents in this domain of ethics to work out a balance between effectiveness in producing human benefits, on the one hand, and proper restraint in the control and manipulation of living things, on the other. It is not my purpose here to develop or defend a system of principles for carrying out that responsibility. But giving due concern and consideration for the well-being of the creatures that are held within human power would be a fundamental element in choosing a morally justifiable way to organize and operate a bioculture.[10]

[10] One issue that is becoming of increasing concern among many people is the question of vegetarianism versus meat eating. This is an area in which environmental ethics has some bearing on the ethics of the bioculture. I will take up this matter in the last chapter of the book, where I discuss priority principles governing conflicts between human interests and the interests of other living things.

T W O

THE ATTITUDE OF RESPECT
FOR NATURE

1. Introduction

In this and the following two chapters the three main components of the theory of environmental ethics which I call "Respect for Nature" will be considered in turn. The first component is the moral attitude of respect itself. In the present chapter I shall offer an analysis of what it means for moral agents to adopt such an attitude toward the natural world and make it their own ultimate moral attitude. The second component consists of the biocentric outlook on nature. In the next chapter this belief-system, which constitutes a unified, coherent view of the world and of the place of humans in it, will be examined in detail. After its various elements and its internal order are presented, I will show how the biocentric outlook supports and makes intelligible the moral commitment involved when rational, autonomous agents take the attitude of respect for nature. The third component, to be considered in Chapter Four, is the ethical system of standards and rules that normatively governs the character and conduct of moral agents insofar as they have the attitude of respect for nature and accordingly are disposed to give concrete expression to it in their practical, everyday living.

In order to grasp what it means for rational, autonomous agents to take (or to have) the attitude of respect for nature as their own ultimate moral attitude, it is necessary to understand two concepts: the idea of the *good* of a being, and the idea of the *inherent worth* of a being. The first concept is logically independent of the second. That is, an entity may be recognized correctly as having a good of its own, but at the same time it may not be regarded as possessing inherent worth; this is perfectly consistent. However, we shall see that if rational agents adopt the attitude of respect toward a being that they understand to have a good of its own, they will also conceive of it as possessing inherent worth.[1]

2. The Concept of the Good of a Being

Some entities in the universe are such that we can meaningfully speak of their having a good of their own, while other entities are of a kind that makes such a judgment nonsense. We may think, for example, that a parent is furthering the good of a child by going on a camping trip with it. Our thinking this may be true or it may be false, depending on whether the child's good is actually furthered. But whether true or false, the idea of furthering the good of a child is an intelligible notion. The concept of entity-having-a-good-of-its-own includes in its range of application human children. Suppose, however, that someone tells us that we can further the good of a pile of sand by, say, erecting a shelter over it so that it does not get wet in the rain. We might be puzzled about what the person could mean. Perhaps we would interpret the statement to mean that, since wet sand is no good for a certain purpose, it should be kept dry. In that case it is not the sand's own good that would be fur-

[1] The idea of respect used here and throughout the book belongs to the type, "recognition respect." Stephen Darwall contrasts this kind of attitude with "appraisal respect," which is the respect we have toward things, actions, and persons that we judge high in merit or excellence. See Stephen L. Darwall, "Two Kinds of Respect," *Ethics* 88/1 (October 1977): 36-49. Still a third kind of respect is taken by persons toward whatever they regard as inherently valuable. The concept of inherent value, as distinct from that of inherent worth, will be discussed in Section Three of this chapter.

thered, but the purpose for which it is to be used. Presumably this would be some human purpose, so that if any being's good is furthered by keeping the sand dry, it is the good of those who have this purpose as one of their ends. Concerning the pile of sand itself, however, it is neither true nor false that keeping it dry furthers its good. The sand has no good of its own. It is not the sort of thing that can be included in the range of application of the concept, entity-that-has-a-good-of-its-own.

One way to know whether something belongs to the class of entities that have a good is to see whether it makes sense to speak of what is good or bad *for* the thing in question. If we can say, truly or falsely, that something is good for an entity or bad for it, without reference to any *other* entity, then the entity has a good of its own. Thus we speak of someone's doing physical exercise daily as being good for him or her. There is no need to refer to any other person or thing to understand our meaning. On the other hand, if we say that keeping a machine well-oiled is good for it we must refer to the purpose for which the machine is used in order to support our claim. As was the case with the pile of sand, this purpose is not attributable to the machine itself, but to those who made it or who now use it. It is not the machine's own good that is being furthered by being kept well-oiled, but the good of certain humans for whom the machine is a means to their ends.

Just as we speak of what is good for an entity, so we speak of what does an entity good. Concerning an elderly couple who have moved to a warm climate, we might say things like, "The change was good for them" or "It did them a lot of good."[2]

It is easy to see how the good of a being is connected with what is good for it and with what does it good. What is

[2] The connections between the good *of* a being, what is good *for* a being, and doing good *to* a being are derived from G. H. Von Wright, *The Varieties of Goodness* (New York: Humanities Press, 1963). The general concept of the Human Good (the good of a human being as such) was central to the ethical thought of both Plato and Aristotle.

good for a being or what does it good is something that promotes or protects its good. Correspondingly, what is bad for a being is something damaging or detrimental to its good. These ideas can equally well be expressed in terms of benefit and harm. To benefit a being is to bring about or to preserve a condition that is favorable to it, or to avoid, get rid of, or prevent from occurring a condition that is unfavorable to it. To harm it is either to bring about a condition unfavorable to it or to destroy or take away a condition favorable to it. The terms "favorable" and "unfavorable" apply to something whose well-being can be furthered or damaged, and this can meaningfully be said only of an entity that has a good of its own. Indeed, an entity's well-being can ordinarily be taken as synonymous with its good.

To promote a being's good is either to bring about a state of affairs not yet realized in its existence that is conducive to its good, or to get rid of a condition in its existence that is detrimental to its good. Protecting an entity's good can be done in any number of ways: by avoiding causing it harm (that is, by refraining from doing what would be contrary to its good), by preventing the loss of something needed for the preservation of its good, and by keeping it safe from danger, thereby enabling it to escape harm that might otherwise come to it. All these ways of promoting and protecting a being's good are, by definition, beneficial to it.

In the light of these considerations, what sorts of entities have a good of their own? At first we might think that they are entities that can be said to *have interests* in the sense of having ends and seeking means to achieve their ends. Since piles of sand, stones, puddles of water, and the like do not pursue ends, they have no interests. Not having any interests, they cannot be benefited by having their interests furthered, nor harmed by having their interests frustrated. Nothing gives them either satisfaction or dissatisfaction. It would perhaps be odd to hold that they are indifferent to everything that happens to them or to say that nothing matters to them, for we ordinarily speak this way about people who are in special circumstances (such as being in a severe state of depression), and we are thus contrasting their present state of mind with their normal condition. But inanimate objects are never in a condition where things that happen to them *do* matter to them.

Although having interests is a characteristic of at least some entities that have a good of their own, is it true of all such entities? It seems that this is not so. There are some entities that have a good of their own but cannot, strictly speaking, be described as having interests. They have a good of their own because it makes sense to speak of their being benefited or harmed. Things that happen to them can be judged, from their standpoint, to be favorable or unfavorable to them. Yet they are not beings that consciously aim at ends or take means to achieve such ends. They do not have interests because they are not interested in, do not care about, what happens to them. They can experience neither satisfaction nor dissatisfaction, neither fulfillment nor frustration. Such entities are all those living things that lack consciousness or, if conscious, lack the ability to make choices among alternatives confronting them. They include all forms of plant life and the simpler forms of animal life.

To understand more clearly how it is possible for a being to have a good of its own and yet not have interests, it will be useful to distinguish between an entity having an interest in something and something being in an entity's interest. Something can be in a being's interest and so benefit it, but the being itself might have no interest in it. Indeed, it might not even be the kind of entity that can have interests at all. In order to know whether something is (truly) in X's interests, we do not find out whether X has an interest in it. We inquire whether the thing in question will in fact further X's overall well-being. We ask, "Does this promote or protect the good of X?" This is an objective matter because it is not determined by the beliefs, desires, feelings, or conscious interests of X.

It is clear that what an entity has an interest in obtaining or doing may not be in its (overall, best, long-range) interest to have or do. In human life this is the basis for the classic distinction between one's apparent good and one's true good. One's apparent good is whatever one values because one *believes* it to be conducive to the realization of one's good. One's true good is whatever *in fact* contributes to the realization of one's good. It is in this way that people often make mistakes in their subjective values. They place value on things that later turn out to be contrary to, or at least not to be instrumental to, their own true good. They aim at ends they come to judge worthless when achieved. What is subjectively valued by them is not objectively valuable to them. Their apparent good does not always coincide with their true good.

In addition to the idea of what people value, then, there is also the idea of what contributes to the realization of their overall good. In order to refer to the objective value concept of a human person's good, I shall use the term "the Human Good," letting the term "human values" designate whatever people value subjectively.

What is the Human Good? Philosophers have struggled with this question since the time of Socrates. Many different answers have been proposed. We might think of these various answers as *particular conceptions* of the Human Good, as distinct from *the general concept* of it. Other particular conceptions are found in the ways of life of different cultures and in the value systems of individuals.

The general concept has a number of approximate synonyms, such as "human flourishing," "self-actualization," and "true happiness." Our grasp of the concept, however, is not helped by simply equating it with one of these terms, since their meaning is as obscure and indeterminate as the idea of "the good of humans" itself. Perhaps the clearest way to define it is to say that it is the kind of life one *would* place supreme value on *if* one were fully rational, autonomous, and enlightened. No one's valuation is ever actually made under these conditions. They define an ideal choice of a whole way of life made under the most favorable circumstances. We can say, however, that to the extent a given choice approximates these ideal conditions, to that extent the individual who makes the choice gains a more adequate and clearer understanding of his or her true good. As the person's rationality, autonomy, and factual knowledge increase, the choice of the kind of life most worth living becomes less subject to revision or abandonment, and the individual in question becomes less subject to regret and disillusionment. Under these conditions the system of valued ends that one considers to be worth pursuing as ultimate goals in life is more likely to constitute one's true good than one's apparent good only.[3]

What about nonhuman animals? Can we say that the idea of entity-having-a-good-of-its-own also applies to them? With regard to *subjective* value concepts, it is always possible, of course, to raise questions about the behavioral criteria used in applying subjective value concepts to such creatures. One can doubt whether an animal finds anything to be good or bad, desirable or undesirable, worth seeking or worth avoiding. But whatever may be our questions and doubts in this area, they need not bother us as far as developing an adequate life-centered system of environmental ethics is concerned. Disputes about the applicability of *subjective* value concepts to nonhuman animals are simply not relevant to the ethics of respect for nature. It is the *objective* value concept of a being's good which is presupposed by that theory, not the various subjective concepts that have been mentioned. Once we make the distinction between the two sorts of value concepts, it is no longer necessary to

[3] This "enlightened preference" view of the Human Good is analyzed with care by G. H. Von Wright (*ibid.*, chapter 5). A similar view is the "rational plan of life" definition of the good of a human individual propounded by John Rawls. See John Rawls, *A Theory of Justice* (Cambridge, Mass.: Harvard University Press, 1971), sections 63 and 64. In Part II of his book *Impartial Reason*, Stephen Darwall has shown how this way of conceiving the Human Good is relevant to the logical structure of practical reason.

be concerned with the questionable applicability of the subjective ones. For the theory of respect for nature only assumes that animals are beings to which it is correct to apply the objective concept of entity-having-a-good-of-its-own. It is, indeed, one of the fundamental principles of the theory that *all animals, however dissimilar to humans they may be, are beings that have a good of their own*. A second principle, equally fundamental, is that *all plants are likewise beings that have a good of their own*. The reasoning behind both principles will now be set forth.

Consider any doubtful case regarding the applicability of subjective value concepts to an entity. Concerning a butterfly, for example, we may hesitate to speak of its interests or preferences, and we would probably deny outright that it values anything in the sense of considering it good or desirable. But once we come to understand its life cycle and know the environmental conditions it needs to survive in a healthy state, we have no difficulty in speaking about what is beneficial to it and what might be harmful to it. A butterfly that develops through the egg, larva, and pupa stages of its life in a normal manner, and then emerges as a healthy adult that carries on its existence under favorable environmental conditions, might well be said to thrive and prosper. It fares well, successfully adapting to its physical surroundings and maintaining the normal biological functions of its species throughout its entire span of life. When all these things are true of it, we are warranted in concluding that the good of this particular insect has been fully realized. It has lived at a high level of well-being. From the perspective of the butterfly's world, it has had a good life.

Even when we consider such simple animal organisms as one-celled protozoa, it makes perfectly good sense to a biologically informed person to speak of what benefits or harms them, what environmental changes are to their advantage or disadvantage, and what physical circumstances are favorable or unfavorable to them. The more knowledge we gain concerning these organisms, the better are we able

66

to make sound judgments about what is in their interest or contrary to their interest, what promotes their welfare or what is detrimental to their welfare.

We can now understand how it is possible for a human being *to take an animal's standpoint* and, without a trace of anthropomorphism, make a factually informed and objective judgment regarding what is desirable or undesirable *from that standpoint*. This is of considerable importance since, as we shall see later, being willing to take the standpoint of nonhuman living things and to make informed, objective judgments from that standpoint is one of the central elements of the ethics of respect for nature. Once we acknowledge that it is meaningful to speak about what is good or bad for an organism as seen from the standpoint of its own good, we humans can make value judgments from the perspective of the organism's life, even if the organism itself can neither make nor understand those judgments. Furthermore, we can conceive of ourselves as having a duty to give consideration to its good and to see to it that it does not suffer harm as the result of our own conduct. None of these ways of thinking and acting with regard to it presupposes that the organism values anything subjectively or even has an interest in what we may do for it.

All of the foregoing considerations hold true of plants as well as animals. Once we separate the objective value concept of a being's good from subjective value concepts, there is no problem about understanding what it means to benefit or harm a plant, to be concerned about its good, and to act benevolently toward it. We can intentionally act with the aim of helping a plant to grow and thrive, and we can do this because we have genuine concern for its well-being. As moral agents we might think of ourselves as under an obligation not to destroy or injure a plant. We can also take the standpoint of a plant and judge what happens to it as being good or bad from its standpoint. To do this would involve our using as the standard of evaluation the preservation or promotion of the plant's own good. Anyone who has ever taken care of flowers, shrubs, or trees will know what these things mean.

Nothing in the above ways of responding to and dealing with plants implies that they have interests in the sense of having conscious aims and desires. We can deny that subjective value concepts apply to vegetative life and yet hold that plants do have a good of their own, which can be furthered or damaged by our treatment of them.[4]

The particular conditions that make up the *content* of an animal's or plant's good will depend on the kind of animal or plant it is. What furthers the well-being of one species of organism will not necessarily further that of another, and indeed may be harmful to it. In order to know what a particular organism's good consists in, as well as what is good or bad for it, it is necessary to know its species-specific characteristics. These characteristics include the cellular structure of the organism, the internal functioning of its various parts, and its external relations to other organisms and to the physical-chemical aspects of its environment. Unless we learn how the organism develops, grows, and sustains its life according to the laws of its species-specific nature, we cannot fully understand what promotes the realization of its good or what is detrimental to its good.

Throughout the foregoing discussion of the good of living things, the sort of entity having a good of its own has al-

[4] Joel Feinberg has argued that since plants do not have desires and interests, they do not have a good of their own. However, to make this argument hold he must say: "[W]e speak even of weeds flourishing, but . . . this way of talking is a plain piece of irony. . . ." See J. Feinberg, "The Rights of Animals and Unborn Generations," in W. T. Blackstone, ed., *Philosophy and Environmental Crisis* (Athens, Ga.: University of Georgia Press, 1974), p. 55n. This seems to be seriously misleading. Once we distinguish between having interests and the good of a living thing, we can quite literally speak of weeds flourishing, meaning thereby that their good is being realized to an exceptionally high degree. That weeds can and do flourish is no irony, but a plain truth of nature, much to the dismay of farmers and gardeners.

ways been understood to be an individual organism. Now, if individual organisms have a good that can be furthered, then *statistically* it is intelligible to speak of furthering the good of a whole species-population. The population has no good of its own, independently of the good of its members. To promote or protect the population's good, however, does not mean that the good of every one of its members is also promoted or protected. The level of a species-population's good is determined by the median distribution point of the good of its individual members. The higher this median, the better off is the species-population as a whole (when considered as an isolated unit). To benefit a whole species-population is to further the good of its individual members in such a way that the median level of their good-realization is raised. To cause this level to go down is to harm the species-population. Thus whenever the good of an entire species-population is referred to, we must always keep in mind that it is individual organisms that alone comprise the actual entities that have a good definable independently of the good of any other entities. Their good, unlike the good of species-populations, is not analyzable into the good of any other kind of thing.[5]

[5] It should be noted that although a species-population can be benefited or harmed, a species itself cannot. The species Polar Bear (*Thalarctos maritimus*) is a classification of a certain mammal, not an actual mammal or group of actual mammals. The term "species" is a class name, and classes themselves have no good of their own, only their members do. This is why I use the term "species-population" to refer to a group of organisms belonging to the same species.

Lawrence Johnson has suggested that a species, when construed as a particular genetic lineage, can be taken as a single entity having a good of its own. A genetic lineage, he says, is what ties a species together, being "sequentially embodied in different organisms." It is not simply a collection of organisms (a species-population). See Lawrence E. Johnson, "Humanity, Holism, and Environmental Ethics," *Environmental Ethics* 5/4 (Winter 1983): 345-354.

In response to this suggestion I would raise the question of whether it makes sense to speak of the well-being of a genetic lineage. Such a lineage will continue to exist until the last organism whose gene structure embodies it dies. Then it will cease to exist. In common parlance, the species will become extinct. Does this mean that the interests of the genetic lineage

Just as it makes sense to speak of the good of a whole species-population, so it makes sense to talk about the good of a whole biotic community. It should be emphasized that there is no individual physical entity referred to by the term "a whole biotic community." There is only a set of organisms, each a physical reality, related to one another and to their nonliving environment in various ways. The good of a biotic community can only be realized in the good lives of its individual members. When they fare well, so does the community. Nevertheless, what promotes or protects the good of an individual organism may not promote or protect the good of the community as a whole, and what harms an individual may not harm but actually benefit the community. Consider, for example, the predator-prey relationship in a well-functioning ecosystem. The fact that individual members of the prey species are killed and consumed by individual predators is consistent with the good of the whole life community in the given ecosystem. Indeed, such destruction of some individuals by others is an integral aspect of the realization of the community's good. To try to protect the prey from the predator would, in a soundly functioning ecosystem, cause harm to the predator and this in turn would have bad effects on the prey population, bringing harm to many of its members. Thus the reality of a community's good, like that of a species-population, can be found nowhere but in the lives of individual organisms, even though when we speak of the good of the community we are not referring to the good of each individual member

---

have been frustrated, or that it has suffered harm? This seems to confuse the preserving and furthering of the well-being of an entity with the continued occurrence of instances of the entity. This is not at all like the well-being of a species-population, which is an actual group of entities. The well-being of the group is a function of the *well-being* of the individuals that compose it. A genetic lineage, on the other hand, remains unchanged in its characteristics, whether the organisms that embody it have their well-being furthered or damaged. Thus it can make sense to think of a species-population as having a good of its own. It is questionable whether a genetic lineage can be thought of in the same way.

taken separately. The good of the community is a statistical concept.

This completes my account of the concept of a being's good. The range of application of the concept includes every living thing. It applies directly and primarily to individual organisms, and statistically to populations and communities. It is now time to examine the second concept necessary for understanding what it means to have the attitude of respect for nature. This is the concept of a being's inherent worth.

3. The Concept of Inherent Worth

To have the attitude of respect for nature is to regard the wild plants and animals of the Earth's natural ecosystems as possessing inherent worth. That such creatures have inherent worth may be considered the fundamental value-presupposition of the attitude of respect. The same point can be made concerning the attitude of respect for persons in human ethics. Unless we deem persons to be possessors of inherent worth (as distinct from considering them only in terms of their merits, or their instrumental value as contributors to some social goal, or their personal likableness), we will not have respect for them simply in virtue of their being persons. And when we do regard them as having inherent worth we deem them appropriate objects of the attitude of respect and so take that attitude toward them. What is of special interest here is that it is possible to take the same attitude toward nonhuman living things because it makes sense to regard them as possessors of inherent worth. (Whether we are rationally justified in so regarding them is a further question to be dealt with later.)

The concept of inherent worth must not be confused with the concept of the good of a being. To bring out the difference between them, consider the logical gap between the fact that a being has a good of its own (an is-statement) and the claim that it should or should not be treated in a certain way (an ought-statement). One can acknowledge that an animal or plant has a good of its own and yet, consistently with this acknowledgment, deny that moral agents have a duty to promote or protect its good or even to refrain from harming it. One does not contradict oneself by saying, "Yes, I know that this action of mine will adversely affect the good of living things, but nevertheless there is no reason why I shouldn't do it." There may in truth *be* a reason against doing the act, and that reason may be the fact that the act will be detrimental to the good of living things, but we cannot just assert this to be the case on the ground that the living things in question have a good of their own.

If the fact that an entity has a good of its own does not logically entail that moral agents ought or ought not to treat it in a certain way, the problem arises: What relationship holds (if any) between an entity's having a good and the claim its good makes upon moral agents? I shall argue that, if a moral agent is to recognize or acknowledge such a claim, the entity in question must not only be thought of as having a good of its own; it must also be regarded as having inherent worth. When so regarded, the entity is considered to be *worthy of respect* on the part of all moral agents. The attitude of respect is itself then seen to be the only suitable, appropriate, or fitting attitude to take toward the entity. In taking that attitude, one commits oneself to following, as one's own moral norm, the principle that living things ought not to be harmed or interfered with in nature, other things being equal.

To be clear about exactly what it means for an entity to possess inherent worth, we should carefully separate in our minds that idea from two other value-concepts with which it might be confused, namely, the concept of *intrinsic value* and the concept of *inherent value*. Neither is identical with *inherent worth*. The terms being used to designate the three concepts are not uniformly agreed upon, either in everyday language or in technical philosophical discourse. I am not assuming that these are the only correct terms for expressing the three ideas. The important thing is to have a clear comprehension of the differences among the ideas themselves.

(a) *Intrinsic value.* When humans or other conscious beings place positive value on an event or condition in their lives which they directly experience to be enjoyable in and of itself, and when they value the experience (consider it to be good) *because* of its enjoyableness, the value they place on it is intrinsic. The experience is judged to be intrinsically good. Intrinsic value is likewise placed on goals that conscious beings seek to bring about as ends in themselves, and also on interests they pursue as intrinsically worthwhile. Experiences, ends, and interests may be valued not only intrinsically but also as means to further ends. They would in that case have both intrinsic and instrumental value for the beings concerned. Thus a person's vocation may involve work that is satisfying in itself, as well as yielding a good income. But as long as any activity is carried on for its own sake or as an end in itself, whether or not it is also valued for its consequences, it has intrinsic value for those who find satisfaction in it.

(b) *Inherent value.* This is the value we place on an object or a place (such as a work of art, a historical building, a battlefield, a "wonder of nature," or an archaeological site) that we believe should be preserved, not because of its usefulness or its commercial value, but simply because it has beauty, or historical importance, or cultural significance. When an object or place is valued in this way, it is considered wrong to destroy or damage it, or to allow it to deteriorate through neglect. Efforts are made to preserve it in good condition and to protect it from vandalism. It is something precious to people, something they hold dear. Quite aside from whatever practical usefulness or commercial value it might have, it is held in high esteem and considered important because it is the kind of thing it is. An individual might thus value some small trinket, knowing that it is worthless on the market, since it was given to him or her by someone loved.

Besides works of art, natural wonders, historical monuments, and other inanimate objects, living things themselves can be judged to have inherent value. Most people value their pets this way, and some may so value houseplants, the flowers in their gardens, or a favorite tree in a park. Wild animals and plants may also have inherent value to people. But it is to be observed that, whatever the basis of the inherent value placed on something may be, whether aesthetic, historical, cultural, or a matter of personal sentiment, wonder, or admiration, *the inherent value of anything is relative to and dependent upon someone's valuing it*. If people did not want to preserve a work of art, did not care about it, admire it for what it is, it would lack all inherent value, no matter what might be its aesthetic merits. Similarly, if historical landmarks, unusual scenic areas, or the ruins of ancient civilizations were not *considered* significant or valuable in themselves, they would lack inherent value. And the same holds for living things taken only as objects having inherent value. It is people who, as it were, *endow* those animals and plants with inherent value. In the absence of subjective valuing on the part of persons who value them for what they are, such animals and plants would have no inherent value. Their value is "inherent" only in the sense that they are valued because of their noncommercial importance, and independently of any practical use to which they could be put. Thus a cow that is valued only for its worth as a milk producer has no inherent value. For those things that are inherently valuable, their value is not "inherent" in the sense of belonging to them independently of how they happen to be valued by people. (In this respect inherent value is similar to intrinsic value. Both must be relativized to the subjective valuings of conscious beings. Neither kind of value is properly attributable to anything outside its relation to beings who value it in a certain way.)[6]

---

[6] This concept of inherent value and its relation to intrinsic value ("the immediately valuable") were originally set forth by C. I. Lewis in *An Analysis of Knowledge and Valuation* (La Salle, Ill.: Open Court, 1946), chapters 13 and 14.

(c) *Inherent worth.* As I shall use it here, the term "inherent worth" is to be attributed only to entities that have a good of their own. To say that such an entity X has inherent worth is to assert the following:

A state of affairs in which the good of X is realized is better than an otherwise similar state of affairs in which it is not realized (or not realized to the same degree), (a) independently of X's being valued, either intrinsically or instrumentally, by some human valuer, and (b) independently of X's being in fact useful in furthering the ends of a conscious being or in furthering the realization of some other being's good, human or nonhuman, conscious or nonconscious.

If it is true that a living thing has inherent worth, then it possesses such worth regardless of any instrumental or inherent *value* it may have and without reference to the good of any other being.

The assertion that an entity has inherent worth is here to be understood as entailing two moral judgments: (1) that the entity is deserving of moral concern and consideration, or, in other words, that it is to be regarded as a moral subject, and (2) that all moral agents have a prima facie duty to promote or preserve the entity's good as an end in itself and for the sake of the entity whose good it is.[7] Suppose, now, that we do conceive of a wild animal or plant as having in-

---

[7] Although I developed my views on inherent worth independently of Tom Regan's fine book *The Case for Animal Rights* (Los Angeles: University of California Press, 1983), his concept of "inherent value" and my "inherent worth" are essentially identical. (I shall refer to some of Regan's ideas in Chapters Five and Six.) Regan has applied his concept of "inherent value" to the field of environmental ethics in his article, "The Nature and Possibility of an Environmental Ethic," *Environmental Ethics* 3/1 (Spring 1981): 19-34. A suggested metaethical analysis of Regan's concept is offered by Evelyn B. Pluhar in "The Justification of an Environmental Ethic," *Environmental Ethics* 5/1 (Spring 1983): 47-61. The first published account of my own theory, including my views on the justification of the claim that all wild animals and plants have inherent worth, was "The Ethics of Respect for Nature," *Environmental Ethics* 3/3 (Fall 1981): 197-218.

herent worth. Then not only are we disposed to give respectful consideration to its existence in nature as a wild creature, but we also see ourselves as bearing a moral relation to it such that we acknowledge the claim-to-be-respected which its existence makes upon us.

Within the class of entities that have a good of their own, whether human or nonhuman, the idea of inherent worth should be separated from the concept of merit. As applied to human persons, the distinction between merit and inherent worth may be brought out as follows.[8] We often judge how good a person is at some activity or how well a person performs in a certain role or position. "He is a fairly good dentist." "She is an excellent tennis player." "The city has a first-rate symphony orchestra." We also compare two or more people by ranking one as better or worse than another or as the best or worst of the group. Just as the grading of an individual as excellent, good, fair, or poor is done according to certain criteria of merit, so is the ranking of one as better or worse than another. Thus whenever judgments of this kind are made, we are evaluating (grading or ranking) people on the basis of their merits.

How do we determine the merits of people? The answer lies in the *criteria* of merit that are being applied to them. These criteria are standards of evaluation, according to which certain properties of people are good-making properties (merits) and others are bad-making properties (defects). Thus the standards for judging the merits of a tennis player are the criteria anyone would use for deciding who was a good player. Such criteria include speed, accuracy, stamina, and any other characteristics that make for excellence in playing tennis. It might be noted here that standards of good character in a normative ethical system are one type of criteria of merit. Indeed, we can think of virtues and vices as moral merits and defects.

[8] For the distinction between merit and inherent worth as applied to humans, I am indebted to Gregory Vlastos, "Justice and Equality," in R. B. Brandt, ed., *Social Justice* (Englewood Cliffs, N.J.: Prentice-Hall, 1962), pp. 47-61.

It is part of the idea of merit that individuals vary in their merits. A may be a better tennis player than B, but B may be a better poet than A, and both may be very poor carpenters. This kind of variation, by way of contrast, does not occur in respect of the inherent worth of people. This is one of the fundamental ways in which the concept of merit differs from that of inherent worth. If we regard persons as possessing inherent worth as persons, then they all possess the same worth, since it is their simple personhood itself which is the ground of their worth.

Animals and plants may also be judged according to their merits as determined by grading or ranking criteria. When the judgment is human-centered, an animal (wild or domesticated) or plant (natural or cultivated) is considered to have merits insofar as it furthers some human interest or end. Thus the merits of "game" fish or mammals are those characteristics that make them suitable objects for sport fishing and hunting. From the sportsman's point of view some species make much better "game" than others. Similarly, some trees are much better (have many more merits) than others from the timber company's point of view. When a nonhuman standpoint is taken, the merits of an animal or plant are those characteristics in virtue of which it contributes either to the good of some other animal or plant or to the good of a whole biotic community. If a certain kind of prey is a much better food source for a predator than another prey-species, for example, the properties that make the first better than the second are merits from the predator's standpoint. And a predator-population of a certain species may itself have merit in relation to the biotic community of which it is a part. This would occur when it has characteristics that help maintain ecological stability that is instrumental to the community's overall well-being.

The distinction between merit and inherent worth has consequences of the greatest importance both for human ethics and environmental ethics. Consider, first, the consequences for human ethics. The idea that all persons are bearers of inherent worth just in virtue of their being persons is, as we saw in Chapter One, the ultimate ground of all duties in a moral community. Some of the implications of this principle are the following.

In the first place, everyone is understood to have the same status as a moral subject to whom duties are owed. No one is considered inherently (that is, aside from merits) superior to another, and so the good of each is recognized as making the same claim-to-fulfillment. As persons, all are deemed to deserve equal concern and consideration.

A second implication is that no one is to be treated as a mere means to someone else's ends. The principle of humanity as an end in itself is an entailment of the proposition that all persons as persons have inherent worth.

Third, if all persons are considered to possess inherent worth, the promotion or protection of each individual's good is accepted as an ultimate end, to be brought about for the sake of the person whose good it is.

A fourth implication is that the good of persons is to be promoted or protected as a matter of moral principle. If persons have inherent worth, then there is a duty binding upon all moral agents to respect their personhood by giving recognition to their good as something that, other things being equal, ought to be realized. This duty holds, whether or not a moral agent is inclined to fulfill it and regardless of any personal feelings the agent might have or might lack toward another person. Here again we have a case of the independence of inherent worth from the subjective valuings of particular individuals.

When we turn to the domain of environmental ethics and consider the consequences of regarding all wild animals and plants as having inherent worth (as distinct from merit), a close parallel with the foregoing implications in the field of human ethics can readily be drawn.

First, if inherent worth is attributed to any wild creature just in virtue of its being a member of the biotic community of a natural ecosystem, then each wild animal or plant is understood to have the same status as a moral subject to which duties are owed by moral agents. Whatever its species may be, none is thought to be superior to another and all are held to be deserving of equal consideration.

Second, each is never to be treated as a mere means to human ends, since doing so would contradict—would amount to a denial of—its status as a bearer of inherent worth.

Third, the promotion or protection of each one's good is taken as an ultimate end, to be brought about for the sake of the being whose good it is.

Fourth, it is a matter of principle that moral agents are required to give consideration to the good of such a being. They owe it the duty of respect regardless of their having (or lacking) a love for the creature and so being inclined (or disinclined) to fulfill the duty.

It is clear from the foregoing account of the concept of inherent worth that our whole conception of the moral universe in which we act is profoundly shaped by it. In particular, the range of application of that concept determines what sorts of beings we take to be proper moral subjects. At this point the question inevitably arises: How can we know that an entity has inherent worth?

As we saw in Chapter One, it is possible to establish the truth of the claim that a person has inherent worth by showing that *only this way of regarding persons is coherent with the conception of every person as a rational, valuing being—an autonomous center of conscious life.* To see ourselves as such an entity and to assert our own inherent worth out of self-respect, while at the same time denying that worth to others whom we conceive to be persons like ourselves, is incoherent.

The same type of argument will also hold for the claim that all animals and plants in the natural world have inher-

ent worth. We can establish the truth of that claim by showing that *only this way of regarding them is coherent with how we
must understand them when we accept the belief-system of the biocentric outlook on nature.* Assuming that that belief-system
can itself be shown to be well-grounded, we have every reason to take the attitude of respect, along with its presupposition of the inherent worth of its objects, toward all wild
living things. (This argument will be fully set out in the next
chapter.)

Putting aside the problem of justification here, our next
subject for investigation is what it means to *take* or *have* the
attitude of respect for nature and what it means to *express* or
embody it in our conduct and character.

4. *Having and Expressing the Attitude of Respect for Nature*

The central tenet of the theory of environmental ethics that
I am defending is that actions are right and character traits
are morally good in virtue of their expressing or embodying
a certain ultimate moral attitude, which I call respect for
nature. When moral agents adopt the attitude, they
thereby subscribe to a set of standards of character and
rules of conduct as their own ethical principles. Having the
attitude entails being morally committed to fulfilling the
standards and complying with the rules. When moral
agents then act in accordance with the rules and when they
develop character traits that meet the standards, their conduct and character express (give concrete embodiment to)
the attitude. Thus ethical action and goodness of character
naturally flow from the attitude, and the attitude is made
manifest in how one acts and in what sort of person one is.

The attitude of respect for nature is a set of dispositions
of moral agents. These dispositions can be classified into
four types, each type constituting one aspect or dimension
of the attitude. I shall name these the valuational, the conative, the practical, and the affective dimensions. The valuational dimension is the disposition to make certain value

judgments or judgments of worth; the conative dimension is the disposition to have certain ends or to want to achieve certain goals; the practical dimension is the disposition to act for certain reasons, as well as the disposition to consider those reasons as good reasons for action; the affective dimension is the disposition to have certain feelings. I consider each dimension in turn.

The valuational dimension of the attitude of respect for nature is the disposition to regard all wild living things in the Earth's natural ecosystems as possessing inherent worth. We have seen that this entails the disposition to think of their good as deserving moral concern and consideration on the part of all agents, and the disposition to deem their wild existence to be worthy of being preserved as an end in itself and for their sake. For a moral agent to be so disposed is one aspect of having the attitude of respect for nature. Indeed, we shall now see that it is the central aspect. All the other dispositions that make up the attitude stem from this one.

The conative dimension is the disposition to aim at certain ends and to pursue certain purposes. Given these ends and purposes, one has a set of wants or desires. One is accordingly disposed to set goals for oneself to accomplish the ends and purposes in question and so to obtain what one wants and satisfy one's desires. The general ends and overall purposes of one who has respect for nature are twofold: the purpose of avoiding doing harm to or interfering with the natural status of wild living things, and the purpose of preserving their existence as part of the order of nature. Taking steps to accomplish these ends involves adopting policies and engaging in practices that are aimed at specific ways of preserving natural ecosystems and of ensuring a physical environment on our planet that is beneficial to a great variety of biotic communities.

The disposition to seek such ends and pursue such purposes stems from the fundamental valuational disposition to consider wild creatures as beings having inherent worth.

It is *because* moral agents look at animals and plants in this way that they are disposed to pursue the aforementioned ends and purposes.

The practical dimension is that aspect of the attitude that has to do with a moral agent's practical reason. Practical reason is the capacity to think through and decide upon reasons for or against action and to act or abstain from acting for those reasons. It encompasses powers of evaluative judgment and deliberation, of decision making and the exercise of will. An agent's capacities of practical reason come into play whenever a choice has to be made among alternative possibilities of action. One *judges* (evaluates) different alternatives as to whether, and why, they ought or ought not be done. One *deliberates* by weighing the reasons for and against each alternative being considered. A *decision* is then arrived at concerning the alternative which has the strongest reasons in its support, and the *will* is exercised in carrying out that decision in practical life.

Practical reason is involved in having the attitude of respect for nature since having that attitude means being disposed to perform or refrain from certain kinds of actions *because they are of those kinds*. The reasons for performing or refraining from the actions are certain facts about them, concerning either their qualities or their future consequences, which are taken to be morally relevant considerations in judging whether, and why, such actions ought or ought not to be performed. In the case of actions that ought to be done, when there are no countervailing reasons, or when these reasons outweigh all countervailing ones, the actions are regarded as morally justified. The same structure of practical reasoning applies to decisions about actions that agents ought not to perform. In these cases the morally relevant considerations are facts about the actions that provide reasons against doing them. If there are no countervailing reasons in support of the actions, or if these reasons against them outweigh in importance any countervailing reasons, then the conclusion follows that the action is morally unjustified.

What are the properties and consequences of actions that are taken to be good moral reasons for or against doing them, if one has the attitude of respect for nature? They are the properties and consequences which make them effective ways of achieving the ends, or which make them hindrances to achieving those ends, toward which one is disposed under the conative dimension of the attitude. They are facts about the actions that show that one would, or would not, be able to accomplish one's purposes if one did them. Given those purposes, one has good reason to perform actions insofar as one has good reason to believe that one will thereby successfully achieve one's ends, and one has good reason to refrain from them if one has good reason to believe they would prevent one from achieving one's ends. When moral agents have the ends mentioned in connection with the conative dimension, and when they do things or abstain from doing things for the reasons just given, they have the attitude of respect for nature.

The fourth and final dimension is the affective. It is the disposition to have certain feelings in response to certain events in the world. These feelings are closely linked with the valuational, conative, and practical dimensions. When one has respect for nature one is disposed *to feel pleased about* any occurrence that is expected to maintain in existence the Earth's wild communities of life, their constituent species-populations, or their individual members. The occurrences in question may be either the intended and unintended results of human actions, or events in nature. One will also be disposed *to feel displeased about* any occurrence that does harm to living things in the Earth's natural ecosystems. One is disposed to experience these positive and negative reactions because one has the valuational, conative, and practical dispositions already described. The reactions are a sign that one does regard wild living things as possessing inherent worth, that one has the appropriate ends and purposes, and that one is disposed to act for the relevant reasons. The feelings go along with these other dispositions, and all of the dispositions together comprise the unified attitude of respect for the natural world.

At the beginning of this section I formulated the central tenet of the theory of environmental ethics being defended in this book in the following words: "Actions are right and character traits are morally good in virtue of their expressing or embodying a certain ultimate moral attitude, which I call respect for nature." We have been considering what it means to *have* that attitude, and now we must turn to what it means to *express* or *embody* the attitude in conduct and character.

With regard to conduct, it is easy to see how and in what sense the actions of moral agents can express the attitude of respect for nature. The relevant dimensions are the conative and the practical. Whenever moral agents perform actions or intentionally refrain from them in order to achieve the ends of the conative dimension, and whenever they perform or refrain from actions for the reasons given in the practical dimension, their conduct expresses the attitude. We saw that having the attitude means having certain dispositions. With reference to the two dimensions we are considering, having the attitude means being disposed to act or refrain from acting with certain ends in view and for certain reasons. When one actualizes these dispositions by performing or refraining from actions because one has the relevant ends and reasons, one exemplifies the attitude in one's practical life. It is in this way that moral agents can give concrete embodiment to the attitude.

It follows that people show genuine respect for nature only when they act or decline to act *out of consideration and concern for the good of wild living things*. Such respect is not exhibited by actions or omissions that have the same effect on wild creatures but are not motivated in that way. To express in practical life one's respect for nature, one's intentions and aims must be directed toward not interfering with or harming animals and plants in natural ecosystems and to preserving their wild status for their sake. Having those aims and intentions as one's ultimate ends is essential to having true respect for nature.

People who have an exclusively human-centered viewpoint in environmental matters may at times perform actions that in fact further the good of wild creatures. But their actions do not express the attitude of respect for nature because they are not done for the sake of the wild creatures themselves. The underlying aim is to benefit humans, either immediately or in the long run. What is absent from their motivation is the holding of nonhuman forms of wildlife as possessors of inherent worth. Without this valuational element, their conduct cannot be considered an expression of respect for nature.

One further aspect of conduct is needed, however, for it to be a fully adequate expression of the attitude in practical life. The actions must be done as a matter of moral principle. Although one's aim is to preserve and protect the good of wild living things, one must conceive of acting with this aim in mind as something morally required of one and not as the fulfillment of a particular interest one happens to have at the moment. The end of action, in other words, must be thought of as an ethically obligatory end and consequently as an end that is to be pursued disinterestedly, whether or not one is so inclined. If one seeks that end solely or primarily from inclination, the attitude being expressed is not moral respect but personal affection or love.

It is not that respect for nature *precludes* feelings of care and concern for living things. One may, as a matter of simple kindness, not want to harm them. But the fact that one is so motivated does not itself indicate the presence of a moral attitude of respect. Having the desire to preserve or protect the good of wild animals and plants for their sake is neither contrary to, nor evidence of, respect for nature. It is only if the person who has the desire understands that the actions fulfilling it are ethically obligatory, and that they would be obligatory even in the absence of the desire, that the person has genuine respect for nature. In order to express that respect the actions must be aimed at the protection or preservation of a wild organism's good (or the good of a group of such organisms) as an end in itself. This is part of the conative dimension of the attitude of respect. That aim, however, must be *made* the agent's end of action by his or her moral commitment to the principle that the animals and plants of the natural world are possessors of inherent worth and accordingly *deserve* to have their good preserved and protected for their own sake. They are understood to deserve this treatment whatever personal interest may or may not be taken in them by the agent concerned. Only when the aim of such treatment has this ethical significance is it a matter of respect for nature.

I have been examining how the attitude of respect for nature can be expressed in a person's actions and intentional refrainings from action. Let us now consider how that attitude can be expressed in a person's character. Whether we focus on the idea of good character in general (being an overall morally good agent) or on the idea of particular virtues (an agent's having this or that morally good character trait, such as honesty, benevolence, or fair-mindedness), a person's character has two aspects, one deliberative and the other practical.[9] Concerning the deliberative aspect, good character consists in having the developed ability and the steady disposition to think rationally and clearly about what action one ought or ought not to do in a situation of choice where there is a tendency for one to become confused or irrational due to the influence of one's nonmoral

[9] Sources of this view of character and virtue are mentioned in note 3, Chapter Four.

interests, wants, needs, and emotions (including one's wishes, hopes, and fears). A particular virtue, in its deliberative aspect, is the capacity of a moral agent consistently to avoid confusion of mind and distorted thinking about duties, obligations, and responsibilities of a certain specific ethical type. For example, an honest person is one who not only aims at being honest in his or her conduct but also has the ability to see clearly what is the honest thing to do in a situation where one's motives and desires, needs and interests have a tendency to cause one to indulge in duplicity, rationalization, special pleading, wishful thinking, or to succumb to other forms of evasion, biased judgment, self-deception, and deception of others. People who have cultivated the virtue of honesty have the power of deliberative rationality so that, given the relevant factual knowledge, they regularly arrive at the correct conclusion about what honesty requires of them in any circumstances where obligations of honesty are involved.

Concerning the second aspect of virtue, the practical element, a person of good character is one who has the capacity to act in accordance with one's deliberative reasoning and judgment in circumstances where, unless one places restraints upon the influence of one's nonmoral interests, needs, desires, and emotions, they will deprive one of the power to carry out one's moral decision or will seriously weaken one's power to do so. The practical aspect of virtue, in other words, is the counterweight to weakness of will. Taking the example of honesty once more, to possess that character trait is to have the capacity to perform honest actions and abstain from dishonest ones in situations where the exercise of willpower and self-mastery are needed to successfully conduct oneself in that manner.

We are now in a position to see how a person's character in matters of environmental ethics can express or embody the attitude of respect for nature. A person's character will be said to express that attitude to the extent that, in all situations of choice to which the rules of the ethics of respect for nature apply, the person consistently exemplifies those virtues that enable him or her to deliberate correctly about what action ought to be done and to carry out the decision resulting from that deliberation. Thus good character expresses the attitude in the sense that it is the agent's possessing such character that accounts for his or her regularly performing the actions that express the attitude in the way indicated earlier. Virtues give one the steady ability to do the right thing with the right aim and for the right reasons in situations where moral failure due to confusion of mind and weakness of will are not uncommon. In such circumstances the virtues are *needed* for doing what is right and refraining from what is wrong.

As far as our duties, obligations, and responsibilities toward the Earth's wild living things are concerned, our character expresses respect for nature when it enables us to see clearly what those duties, obligations, and responsibilities are and to carry out their requirements in difficult and complex situations. In Chapter Four I shall discuss some of the basic virtues in the ethics of respect for nature. They are determined by the specific standards of character which, in conjunction with a set of rules of conduct, comprise a valid system of environmental ethics.

The foregoing discussion has shown how the attitude of respect for nature can be expressed in the conduct and character of moral agents. I now wish to point out that it is also possible for that attitude to be expressed or embodied in the moral rules and standards of a system of environmental ethics. Indeed, if the system is *valid*, its rules and standards will embody the attitude.

How the attitude can be embodied in a set of moral norms (standards and rules) is easy to understand in light of what has been said about the way a person's conduct and character can express the attitude. All that is necessary is to link up ethical conduct and character with the normative principles that govern them. A person's conduct will then be seen to express respect for nature insofar as it meets the requirements laid down in a certain set of rules. These rules themselves can accordingly be said to embody the attitude. Similarly, a person's character expresses the attitude just to the extent that it fulfills certain standards of virtue. These standards can then be said to embody the attitude. Thus respect for nature is embodied in that set of moral norms which, when adopted and adhered to by moral agents, serve to guide them in the performance of actions and in the development of character traits that express the attitude in the manner indicated earlier. Those norms define a "possible world" where respect for nature is fully expressed in the character and conduct of all moral agents.

Given this way in which the attitude of respect for nature can be embodied in moral norms themselves, we can then simply *identify* a valid system of environmental ethics as one whose constituent rules of conduct and standards of character embody the attitude. There is a parallel here with human ethics. In Chapter One I mentioned that the standards and rules of a valid system of human ethics embody the attitude of respect for persons. The relation between respect for persons and those norms of human ethics is symmetrical with the relation between respect for nature and the norms of a valid system of environmental ethics. The rules and standards of human ethics were held to be those that must be followed by all moral agents if they are to perform actions and cultivate virtues that express respect for persons as persons. The parallel with environmental ethics should now be clear. The rules and standards of a valid system of environmental ethics are those that must be followed by all moral agents if the requirements for giving due recognition to the inherent worth of wild living things are to be met. Such norms must be fulfilled, in other words, if the actions and character traits of all moral agents are adequately to express respect for nature.

This completes the first part of my analysis of the attitude of respect for nature and my account of what it means to express or embody the attitude in practical life. I shall now take up the second part of the study of the attitude. This part will focus our attention on what it means to describe the attitude as an ultimate one.

5. *Respect for Nature as an Ultimate Attitude*

The sense in which respect for nature is an ultimate attitude must be examined with some care, since its ultimacy gives rise to a special problem concerning its justification. The practical life of moral agents insofar as they express the attitude in their conduct and character is not the result of their having adopted another, higher-level moral attitude from which their respect for nature can be derived. Nor is there a broader, more general attitude toward the natural universe under which respect for nature could be subsumed as a special case. Adopting the attitude of respect for nature cannot, therefore, be justified by being shown to be grounded on a more fundamental moral commitment. It is itself the most fundamental kind of moral commitment that one can make.

In order to see clearly what the problem of justification is, it is necessary to consider certain aspects of respect for nature as a *moral* attitude. The first thing to notice is the fact, pointed out earlier in this chapter, that respect for nature is quite different from the love of nature. Being a moral attitude, respect is not a matter of simple personal affection or caring in the way the love of nature is. The feelings one might have for animals and plants make one concerned about their well-being. One may have a special fondness for a particular species-population in a wild area (for example, all the ponderosa pines on a mountainside) or for a whole biotic community (such as all the flora and fauna found in a favorite stretch of woodland), and accordingly experience feelings of care and concern about these creatures. When concern and caring in this way stem from personal affection, they are part of one's love of nature. But they do not give evidence that one has respect for nature unless they are understood to be a matter of moral commitment. The attitude of respect is not a private relationship between the person who has the attitude and that toward which the attitude is taken, as the love of nature is.

This contrast between respect and love has fundamental significance for our understanding of what is required for the attitude of respect to be rationally justified. Since the ground of respect does not lie in the emotional appeal that living things might have for us, the fact that an animal or plant is attractive to us is not relevant to our adopting the attitude of respect toward it or to our expressing such an attitude in the way we treat it. Some things in the natural world may be more beautiful, more interesting, or more pleasing to us than others. Some may be unattractive, uninteresting, and even repulsive to us. But if we have respect for nature their attractiveness or unattractiveness in no way affects our impartial concern for their well-being.

Taking the attitude of respect for nature is like adopting a set of moral rules and standards as valid ethical norms. Indeed, it actually involves the making of a commitment to abide by those ethical norms that embody the attitude in the sense explained earlier. Now, when we adopt certain norms because we think they are morally binding upon us, we at the same time believe that they are binding upon all other moral agents. This was pointed out in Chapter One, where one of the formal conditions for ethically valid norms stipulated that any agent who adopts them as his or her own moral principles also advocates that they be universally adopted by all moral agents. So it is with the attitude of respect for nature. Being a moral attitude, one who sincerely takes it also considers it an attitude all others should take. To have the attitude ourselves is at the same time to believe it is a legitimate or justified attitude for every moral agent to have.

This universal aspect of respect for nature is connected logically with the valuational dimension of the attitude. We have seen that this consists in the fact that all who have the attitude regard wild living things as possessing inherent worth, a worth that does not depend on the subjective interests and ends of humans. As possessors of inherent worth those creatures are deemed to be deserving of the concern and consideration of everyone. Regardless of whatever personal affection people might or might not feel toward them, every person as a moral agent is understood to be obligated to give due recognition to their inherent worth. Thus one who takes the attitude of respect advocates its universal adoption.

The attitude of respect for nature is not only a moral one, but an ultimate one. In order to be clear about what this means, let us consider two ways in which attitudes can be higher-level or lower-level. The first way contrasts moral with nonmoral attitudes, the second distinguishes among levels of moral attitudes themselves.

Besides the moral attitude of respect, many other kinds of attitude can be taken toward nature. The attitude of scientific curiosity, the aesthetic attitude of appreciation for nature's beauty, and the hedonistic attitude of enjoying the pleasures of the out-of-doors are examples. Now, if we have any of these other attitudes as well as that of respect for nature, whatever conduct furthers the interests connected with these other attitudes never supersedes or overrides conduct expressing respect. The reason is that, as was pointed out in Chapter One, moral norms always take priority over any other norms. We have not adopted a rule as one of our moral principles if we think it is ever justifiable for someone to transgress the rule in order to fulfill some nonmoral norm. Actions inconsistent with respect for nature can never be justified on nonmoral grounds. So if the pursuit of scientific knowledge, the appreciation of natural beauty, or the enjoyment of outdoor recreational activities involve doing harm to wild creatures, a more basic or higher-level principle has been violated.

Suppose, however, that certain kinds of scientific research and experimentation are necessary for discovering how to avoid or prevent grave dangers to the physical well-being of humans. Such practices might then be justified on *moral* grounds by reference to the norms of the human ethics of respect for persons. This would be a case of one ultimate moral attitude (respect for persons) being in conflict with another (respect for nature). Full consideration of this kind of conflict will be given in the last chapter of this book, after the complete system of environmental ethics based on respect for nature has been set forth and defended. At this point we will be concerned with other types of conflict.

The scientific, the aesthetic, and the hedonistic attitudes may be incompatible with respect for nature in many sorts of circumstances. Scientists, for example, may endanger the lives of the few remaining individuals of a rare species when they carry out a research project. The desire to have a beautiful scenic view from a resort hotel might lead to building the hotel in an ecologically sensitive area. The hedonistic attitude toward nature may involve considerable harm to wild communities of life. The construction and use of ski slopes and marinas, campsites for recreational vehicles and lakeside bathing facilities, golf courses and hiking trails can all interfere in a damaging way with the functioning of natural ecosystems. Large numbers of people pursuing an outdoor way of life may involve the destruction of wilderness habitats needed by many species-populations of animals and plants.[10] Since these human practices are nonmoral, their incompatibility with respect for nature makes them at least prima facie unjustified. Unless some compelling moral reason can be given for them, no one who has genuine respect for nature can consider them permissible from an ethical point of view. The moral requirements of re-

[10] A deservedly famous study of changing attitudes toward wilderness in the context of the history of the American conservation movement is Roderick Nash, *Wilderness and the American Mind* (New Haven, Conn.: Yale University Press, 1967; revised edition, 1973). In the revised edition Nash has added an epilogue titled "The Irony of Victory," in which he considers how in recent decades Americans are "loving the wilderness to death."

spect for nature cannot be outweighed by whatever non-moral values are realized by those activities.

The scientific, aesthetic, and hedonistic attitudes, however, are not *necessarily* incompatible with respect for nature. There are ways of carrying on scientific research, of experiencing the beauty of nature, and of enjoying the out-of-doors that do not seriously harm wild creatures or damage natural ecosystems. We can make special efforts to arrange things so that, at least as far as the good of whole species-populations and communities of life is concerned, no real harm is done. This involves placing careful constraints on human activity in ecologically sensitive areas, and sometimes simply prohibiting the pursuit of certain practices (such as driving off-road vehicles into a wild desert habitat, or motorboating on a natural lake).

It is worth noting that some interference with or manipulation of the natural world by humans is compatible with respect for nature and may actually constitute an expression of that attitude. This would be the case, for instance, when a polluted river, lake, or marshland is cleaned up. Another example would be the effort to reintroduce a species (such as the Peregrine Falcon in the northeastern United States) which had been extirpated from one of its original habitats. Still other cases are such activities as putting up nesting boxes for Eastern Bluebirds, having animal hospitals where sick or injured wild mammals, birds, and reptiles are restored to health and then set free in their proper habitats, and returning to its (approximate) original natural condition an area where coal mines were once operating but have now been abandoned. In all circumstances of this sort, however, the final end of the human practices involved must be to promote or protect the good of wild creatures themselves. If human interference with or manipulation of nature is to be a genuine expression of the attitude of respect, the actions in question must be done for the sake of animals and plants living in a natural state and not for the benefit of humans alone.

There is one general attitude toward nature, on the other hand, that is *necessarily* incompatible with the attitude of respect. This is the exploitative attitude which, in Western civilization at least, is now and has always been the dominant attitude taken by most humans toward the natural world. The exploitative attitude is taken whenever nature is thought of as nothing more than a vast repository of resources, both physical and biological, to be developed, used, and consumed by humans for human ends. It is there for our sake, not for the sake of other creatures; we have exclusive entitlement to it as an instrument for our own use. The very advancement of civilization is a matter of "subduing" the wilderness, "conquering" nature, and putting it to the service of humanity so that a better life can be enjoyed by people.

That the exploitative attitude is necessarily in conflict with the attitude of respect is a logical consequence of its way of judging the worth of wild living things. From the exploitative point of view, animals and plants are valuable only because they can be used as means to human benefit or can be directly enjoyed as a source of human pleasure. Wild creatures therefore have either instrumental or inherent value, but do not possess inherent worth. They have instrumental value insofar as they can be manipulated, controlled, and consumed in such manner as to help humans bring about certain benefits for themselves. They have inherent value insofar as humans find satisfaction in observing them, learning about them, or interacting with them in some way. To see living things as so many instruments or objects in this manner is to deny that they have inherent worth. Thus the conception of wild creatures as possessors of inherent worth, which is at the heart of the attitude of respect, is in its very essence contrary to the exploitative attitude.

Is the exploitative attitude a moral one, not in the sense of being morally good, but in the sense of belonging to the category of morality? The answer depends on whether those who have the attitude commit themselves to following principles that satisfy the five formal conditions stated in Chapter One. It is perfectly possible for this to be the case. The exploitative attitude is general in form (not mentioning any particular individuals, human or nonhuman); it can be universally applied to all moral agents; it can be accepted disinterestedly (not merely serving the particular interests of those who take it); it can be advocated for all to adopt; and it can be considered as overriding any nonmoral attitude. Thus the exploitative attitude, no less than the attitude of respect, can be viewed as a supreme moral commitment that takes priority over all other norms and values, as far as the treatment of the natural world is concerned. The choice between these two ultimate, incompatible attitudes must then be based on whatever sound arguments can be given to show that adopting one and not the other *as* an ultimate moral attitude is justified on rational grounds.

Let us turn, then, to the problem concerning the justification of the attitude of respect for nature when understood as an ultimate moral attitude. In approaching this problem we must first distinguish between two kinds of *moral* attitudes, derivative and ultimate. The distinction may be brought out as follows. If we have adopted respect for nature as our own moral attitude, we will approve or disapprove of certain policies and actions taken by people (ourselves as well as others) regarding the natural world. These approvals and disapprovals constitute a set of moral attitudes themselves, but they are more specific than and are derivative from the general, ultimate attitude of respect for nature. Thus if people have respect for nature they will morally approve of such things as a government ban on DDT, the setting aside of a wilderness area, and the recycling of waste. Similarly, they will disapprove of social policies and practices, as well as the actions of individuals, which degrade the natural environment and are harmful to wild creatures. These specific positive and negative moral attitudes follow from respect for nature in the sense that one would be inconsistent if one believed that respect is the appropriate attitude to have toward the natural world but one did not experience these approvals and disapprovals with regard to social practices and individual actions. A person who condoned environmental ⸱ollution (in the absence of some special reason) could not be said to have respect for nature.

We can *explain* someone's approval of, say, the government ban on DDT by showing that the person sincerely has respect for nature. This attitude itself, however, cannot be explained by reference to a still more general or basic one held by the person. It is in this sense that respect for nature is a highest-level attitude. To take a highest-level moral attitude is to subscribe to the fundamental principles or the most basic norms of a whole ethical system. One adopts, as it were, a total normative framework for one's moral reasoning and one's specific moral attitudes. In the domain of environmental ethics, respect for nature is such a highest-level attitude. It sets the final criteria for what reasons are good reasons when actions that affect the natural world are justified or shown to be unjustified. At the same time it serves as the ground for all one's specific attitudes of approval or disapproval toward the various ways humans treat living things in the Earth's natural ecosystems.

When we give moral reasons for or against certain actions and thereby justify approving or disapproving of them, we apply certain rules and standards that we have accepted as our own normative principles in the domain of environmental ethics. If any of these rules and standards is brought into question, we can show that it is a constituent element of a certain ethical system and that it fits coherently into the system. It is then seen to be integral to a structure of moral principles that define a whole way of living in relation to nature. Now, in subscribing to or adopting that total structure of moral principles, we are taking a certain ultimate moral attitude and committing ourselves to expressing that attitude in our conduct and character. Our belief that the total system of principles constitutes a *valid* ethical system is identical with, and not a ground for, our belief that the ultimate moral attitude embodied in those principles is justified. Unlike the specific moral attitudes of approval and disapproval that we have toward human conduct and that follow from the ultimate attitude, the ultimate attitude itself does not follow from any more basic commitment.

It is for this reason that we cannot justify the attitude of respect for nature by giving *moral* reasons for taking it. All moral reasons are themselves determined by the principles of a valid ethical system. Now, taking an ultimate moral attitude involves committing oneself to a whole ethical system as a valid one. To show the validity of the whole system is to justify the attitude. The attitude cannot be justified simply by *using* the principles of such a system in one's moral reasoning, which is what we would be doing if we tried to give *moral* reasons for taking the attitude.

In order to justify the attitude, then, we must show that the whole ethical system that embodies it is a valid one. How can this be done? The only way is to set forth the *belief-system* that underlies and supports the attitude and show that it is acceptable to all who are rational, factually informed, and have a developed capacity of reality-awareness. In the case of the attitude of respect for nature, this involves examining the way of looking at nature and the place of humans in it which makes intelligible the taking of that attitude. We must first understand the outlook on nature that underlies the attitude. We then can see how the attitude has the proper "fit" in the context of that total outlook, so that taking the attitude is understood as being appropriate to a whole way of conceiving of the natural world and the place of humans in it. We must then show why every rational being who is factually informed and open to the reality of life would accept that outlook as part of their own total world view.

These are the tasks that will occupy us in the next chapter.

THREE

THE BIOCENTRIC OUTLOOK
ON NATURE

1. *The Biocentric Outlook and the Attitude of Respect for Nature*

The attitude we think it appropriate to take toward living things depends on how we conceive of them and of our relationship to them. What moral significance the natural world has for us depends on the way we look at the whole system of nature and our role in it. With regard to the attitude of respect for nature, the belief-system that renders it intelligible and on which it depends for its justifiability is the biocentric outlook. This outlook underlies and supports the attitude of respect for nature in the following sense. Unless we grasp what it means to accept that belief-system and so view the natural order from its perspective, we cannot see the point of taking the attitude of respect. But once we do grasp it and shape our world outlook in accordance with it, we immediately understand how and why a person would adopt that attitude as the only appropriate one to have toward nature. Thus the biocentric outlook provides the explanatory and justificatory background that makes sense of and gives point to a person's taking the attitude.

The beliefs that form the core of the biocentric outlook are four in number:

(a) The belief that humans are members of the Earth's Community of Life in the same sense and on the same terms in which other living things are members of that Community.

(b) The belief that the human species, along with all other species, are integral elements in a system of interdependence such that the survival of each living thing, as well as its chances of faring well or poorly, is determined not only by the physical conditions of its environment but also by its relations to other living things.

(c) The belief that all organisms are teleological centers of life in the sense that each is a unique individual pursuing its own good in its own way.

(d) The belief that humans are not inherently superior to other living things.

To accept all four of these beliefs is to have a coherent outlook on the natural world and the place of humans in it. It is to take a certain perspective on human life and to conceive of the relation between human and other forms of life in a certain way. Given this world view, the attitude of respect is then seen to be the only suitable, fitting, or appropriate moral attitude to take toward the natural world and its living inhabitants.

If we now ask, "Why *should* moral agents accept the four beliefs that make up the biocentric outlook?" the answer lies in showing that, to the extent that moral agents are rational, factually informed, and have developed a high level of reality-awareness, they will find those beliefs acceptable. The acceptability of the beliefs is linked with the rationality, factual enlightenment, and reality-awareness of moral agents in such a way that moral agents who have those properties accept the beliefs *because* they are rational, informed, and aware of reality. The full line of reasoning that leads to this conclusion will be given in the last part of this chapter. We must first examine the four beliefs themselves and the grounds on which they rest. Each will be considered in the four sections that follow.

2. *Humans as Members of the Earth's Community of Life*

From the perspective of the biocentric outlook on nature we see human life as *an integral part of the natural order of the Earth's biosphere*. We thus conceive of the place of humans in the system of nature in the same way we conceive of the place of other species. There is a common relationship to the Earth that we share with wild animals and plants. Full awareness of this common relationship gives us a sense of true community with them. Let us see how this sense of community develops.

The first thing we do when we accept the biocentric outlook is to take the fact of our being members of a biological species to be a fundamental feature of our existence. We do not deny the differences between ourselves and other species, any more than we deny the differences among other species themselves. Rather, we put aside these differences and focus our attention upon our nature as biological creatures. As far as our relation to the Earth's ecosystems is concerned, we see ourselves as but one species-population among many. Thus we keep in the forefront of our consciousness the characteristics we share with all forms of life on Earth. Not only is our common origin in one evolutionary process fully acknowledged, but also the common environmental circumstances that surround us all. We view ourselves as one with them, not as set apart from them. We are then ready to affirm our fellowship with them as equal members of the whole Community of Life on Earth.

Recognition of our membership in that universal Community of Life is rooted in five realities: (a) We as well as they must face certain biological and physical requirements for our survival and well-being. (b) They as well as we have a good of their own, the realization of which depends on contingencies that are not always under either our or their

101

control. (c) Although the concepts of free will, autonomy, and social freedom apply only to humans, there is a fourth sense of freedom that holds equally of them and of us, and this kind of freedom is of great importance in any living thing's struggle to realize its good, whether human or non-human. (d) As a species we humans are a recent arrival on our planet, a relative newcomer to an order of life that had been established for hundreds of millions of years before we came into existence. (e) Finally, there is the fact that, while we cannot do without them, they can do without us. I shall now consider each of these points in turn. We shall see that our full awareness and acknowledgment of them as fundamental truths about our existence constitute the basis for our conceiving of ourselves to be but one small part of the total membership of the Earth's Community of Life.

(a) The physical requirements for survival impose on all living things, human and nonhuman alike, the constant necessity to adjust to environmental changes and to the activities of other organisms in their surroundings. It is as true of a human being as it is true of any plant or animal that, in order to preserve its existence as a functioning organism, it must be able constantly to respond to environmental contingencies and to maintain certain relationships with members of other species.

If we move from considerations of simple survival to conditions that promote and enhance the well-being of living things, we find again certain biological and physical circumstances that are essential to both humans and nonhumans. Both must have the capacity to relate themselves in certain ways to other living organisms, as well as to events and processes taking place in their physico-chemical environments, if they are to grow and develop in an optimal manner. In order to live a long, healthy life at their fullest biological capacities and thus realize their good at a high level of biological flourishing, it is necessary that they carry

102

on their life functions in ways that allow successful ecological coexistence with other organisms.

All this applies equally to humans and nonhumans. In the case of the species *Homo sapiens*, however, since its population has extended itself in vast numbers throughout the globe, adaptation to many different sorts of physical conditions, as well as maintaining a balanced coexistence with the biotic communities of many diverse ecosystems all over the surface of the Earth, is necessary for optimum, biologically healthy human life. No doubt we humans have purposes in life other than simple biological survival and physical well-being. But survival itself and at least a certain minimal level of health and strength are necessary conditions for the pursuit of those other human values.

These similarities between ourselves and other species do not entail a denial of our free will and autonomy. Unlike other species, we have the freedom to choose how we shall carry on our existence and even whether to continue our existence at all. Unlike them, we have the independence of self-directed beings. We can set ends for ourselves and shape our own future. This freedom and autonomy include the power to bring harm to ourselves as well as to further our good. As free and autonomous beings we have the capacity to make our environment a place of beauty and security, but we also have the capacity to make it a place of ugliness and danger. We can likewise seek to enhance our well-being and that of future generations, or we can terminate our individual lives and even our existence as a species. Our free will and autonomy only mean that whether we use our powers for the realization of our values or for self-destructive ends is entirely up to us. We must decide for ourselves what we shall do with our lives. This is not true of other species.

The point we are concerned with here, however, is this. *If* we want to preserve our existence and live at an optimum level of well-being, the biological requirements of survival and physical health must be made our normative guides.

We must follow biologically enlightened principles that ensure the conditions essential to life.

(b) A second respect in which humans share with all other species the role of being fellow members in the Earth's Community of Life was tacitly assumed in the foregoing discussion under (a). This is the fact that the concept of entity-having-a-good-of-its-own includes both humans and nonhumans in its scope. As we saw in Chapter Two, everything that is alive can be correctly said to have a good. That one might fare well or poorly, be benefited or harmed, achieve or fail to achieve one's own good—these things so central to the meaning of our everyday existence can be asserted literally and without distortion about animals and plants as well as ourselves.

A further aspect of this link between ourselves and other species is the fact that the conditions required for survival and biological health for all of us are not always under our control. We are all, humans and nonhumans alike, subject to environmental changes that might harm us and that cannot be avoided. Our lives and well-being are dependent on contingencies and accidents, forces and processes, which we can neither predict nor direct to our advantage. No matter how much we humans believe we can successfully "subdue" nature and manipulate it for our own ends, we deceive ourselves if we fail to recognize the limits of our knowledge and our power. To think we have complete control over the environment, or that we will have such control some day, is a sign of arrogance and an illusion of grandeur. The results of that self-deception are all too evident in the world around us.[1]

Consider, for example, the unforeseen ecological and en-

---

[1] This point is brought out and elaborated with many examples in David Ehrenfeld, *The Arrogance of Humanism* (New York: Oxford University Press, 1978).

vironmental problems that have arisen from the building of the Aswan Dam in Egypt.

First, there is the residue problem of the large quantity of silt normally carried by the Nile. This silt is now settling out in the still waters of Lake Nasser behind the dam. . . . Second, the fertile silt accumulating in Lake Nasser was once spread over the Egyptian fields by the annual floods. This must now be replaced by expensive fertilizer. Third, the decreasing amounts of silt and fresh water now entering the eastern end of the Mediterranean Sea from the Nile have caused a reduction in marine fertility and an increase in salinity which have, in turn, destroyed the Egyptian sardine fishery. Fourth, the great increase in the number and length of Egyptian irrigation canals has caused the proliferation of the snails that spread the dread parasitic disease schistosomiasis. . . . And fifth, there is the problem of the salting of soils, which results from excessive evaporation of water at the surface of soggy fields, leaving behind heavy deposits of salts.[2]

By becoming aware of our human limits in dealing with the realm of nature, we come to see that we are in the same existential situation as are all other living things. Neither the realization of our good nor our very existence can be guaranteed. From this perspective we see the circumstances of other creatures as we see our own: we are all vulnerable.

(c) The third parallel between human life and the life of other creatures has to do with the idea of freedom. We saw above that, with respect to free will and autonomy, we are different from animals and plants. Only humans have the

[2] Ibid., pp. 109-110.

capacity to make decisions and choices among alternative courses of action based on their own reasons-for-choosing, and only they have the powers of self-governance and self-direction that enable them to set their own goals, shape their own future, and determine for themselves what values to strive for. There is also a third kind of freedom that can correctly be attributed only to humans, and then only to those humans who enjoy certain circumstances of life. This might be called "social" or "political" freedom. It is having the power to control basic conditions of one's life through participation in democratically structured institutions. To the degree that one has the opportunity to exert an influence on social practices and policies that affect one's life and well-being, to that degree one has a kind of freedom. One lacks this kind of freedom when one is under the domination of social forces one has had no role in shaping or directing.

In addition to free will, autonomy, and social freedom, there is a fourth sense in which human beings can be said to be free (or unfree). This meaning of freedom, unlike the others, applies equally to nonhuman living things. It is a concept of freedom that is of central importance for every creature which has a good of its own it is striving to realize. For being free in this sense is being in a position to be able to preserve one's existence and further one's good, and being unfree in this sense is being unable to do these things. Recognition of this kind of freedom and of its great value for every living thing is one of the major links between humans and nonhumans.

The sense of freedom concerned here makes it equivalent to *absence of constraint*. In order to assert that a being is free in this sense it is first necessary to specify some type of constraint from which the being is free. Secondly, one must specify what the being is free to do. For example, when one is released from prison one is *free from* the constraints of physical confinement as well as from the social constraints of the rules and regulations governing the daily life of prisoners. One is now *free to* go where one pleases and to do many things one was prevented from doing in prison.

Let us first consider this kind of freedom as it applies to human persons.[3] The types of constraints that must be absent if a person is to be free may be conveniently divided into two classifications, each independent of the other: external and internal constraints, and positive and negative constraints. The distinction between external and internal constraints lies in whether the constraint is something outside the person's body or mind (an external constraint) or is a condition of the person's body or mind (an internal constraint). The locks and bars of a prison, as well as its rules backed by punishment, are external constraints. On the other hand, if a person is driven to do something by an uncontrollable compulsion, whether emotional or physiological, he or she experiences an internal constraint upon action.

The distinction between positive and negative constraints rests on the difference between the existence and the nonexistence of some specifiable state of affairs. Both the external and internal constraints just mentioned are positive. It is the *existence* of the prison bars and regulations, and the *existence* of the inner compulsion, that are constraints upon the persons involved. Examples of negative constraints are the *absence* of enough money to buy food and the *lack* of skills one needs to get a job.

These two classifications can be combined so as to yield four types of constraints, as follows:

(i) *External positive*. Locked doors; barbed wire fences; having tear gas fired at one; being bound and gagged; being beaten or tortured.

(ii) *Internal positive*. Obsessive thoughts and feel-

[3] As applied to humans, this analysis of freedom is taken from Joel Feinberg, *Social Philosophy* (Englewood Cliffs, N.J.: Prentice-Hall, 1973), chapter 1. The original account of the concept was set forth in Gerald C. MacCallum, Jr., "Negative and Positive Freedom," *Philosophical Review* 76/3 (July 1967): 312-324.

ings; compulsive, uncontrollable cravings and desires; extreme physiological needs, such as the need to eat, to drink, to sleep, to eliminate.

(iii) *External negative*. Absence of money, food, potable water, medical services, heating fuel, electricity, transportation, tools (depending on what ends one wants to achieve).

(iv) *Internal negative*. Lack of knowledge, skills, health. Physical and mental disabilities.

In many cases, of course, no sharp dividing lines can be drawn among types of constraints. Thus the absence of food (an external negative constraint on those who are undernourished) is a counterpart to the presence of hunger (an internal positive constraint) and the various incapacities that accompany malnutrition (internal negative constraints). To be free from one is to be free from the others. Nevertheless, even in these cases each type of constraint draws attention to a different aspect of freedom or lack of freedom.

Common to all four classifications is the general idea of freedom as a condition of not being constrained (hindered or prevented) with respect to what one might want to do. To be free in this sense is to be able to pursue one's ends because no restrictions, obstacles, or forces frustrate one's attempt (absence of positive constraints) and because one has the necessary abilities, opportunities, and means to gain one's ends (absence of negative constraints). Now it is this general idea of freedom that applies to nonhuman living things as well as to persons. The examples given above in connection with each of the four kinds of constraints make clear what it means to speak of freedom as absence of constraint in the case of humans. What is meant by such freedom in the case of nonhumans?

The key to answering this question is found in the idea of an organism's being able to realize its good in a biologically normal way. An organism may be said to be free if it has the ability and opportunity to promote or protect its good according to the laws of its nature. To the extent that there are constraints that make it difficult or impossible for the organism to realize its good, to that extent it is unfree.

The constraints involved may be any of the four types we have considered. Sometimes an organism is prevented from realizing its good by the presence of some environmental condition (an external positive constraint); sometimes by the absence of a necessary means to the promotion or protection of its good (an external negative constraint). Other times its inability to preserve its existence or further its well-being is due to the presence of some abnormal bodily condition such as a disease, which impairs its proper functioning (an internal positive constraint); and still other times its inability is due to the absence of a certain capacity essential to its self-preservation, such as blindness caused by an accident (an internal negative constraint). When it is the case that, due to the *absence* of any or all such constraints, an organism can successfully adapt to its environment and so preserve its life and further its well-being, then it is free. Its freedom simply consists in the absence of those constraints.

Perhaps the most easily recognized instance of an animal's being unfree is the situation in which it is prevented from moving about in a normal way. Being in a cage, caught in a trap, or chained to a stake would be examples. The common notion of *freeing* an animal from such physical restrictions (external positive constraints) exemplifies this meaning of freedom.

Is it possible for a plant to be freed from constraints of this kind? An instance of this might indeed occur. Suppose a tree or shrub has been unable to grow normally because its roots have been held in a small concrete container. By transplanting it in the ground one frees it from a constraint (an external positive one) that had been preventing its normal development. A similar case could occur in the wild. A tree may be unfree to grow properly because a landslide has half-buried its trunk, or because it is being "strangled" by a vine.

Consider another type of external positive constraint upon animals, corresponding to the rules of a prison, backed up by punishment, in the case of humans. When lions and tigers undergo the discipline imposed by an animal trainer in a circus, an external constraint (or rather, a series of external constraints) is placed on them. Their behavior is no longer the result of normal development and adaptation. Other examples of this kind of unfreedom of animals occur when elephants are trained as work animals, wild horses are "broken," and monkeys, dogs, cats, mice, and other animals are made to give conditioned responses to artificially controlled situations in the experiments of behavioral psychologists.

Turning now to internal positive constraints, an animal's or plant's being unable to maintain healthy growth because of such bodily conditions as severe hunger, injuries, or diseases are cases in point. Whenever the state of an organism is such that it causes the organism to weaken or die, there is an internal positive constraint upon it. Its physical condition prevents it from adjusting to its circumstances in such a way as to further its good.

Constraints of the third sort (external negative constraints) occur in the lives of animals when, for example, there is lack of sufficient water or food needed by them. In the case of plants, soil that lacks certain nutrients and the absence of adequate moisture would be instances of external negative constraints upon plants.

Finally, internal negative constraints might be exemplified by the absence of a proper chemical balance in an organism due to deficiencies in its source of nourishment. When it is the case that, by correcting this chemical imbalance the organism is restored to health, we can say that a plant or animal is *free from* what had been a constraint upon it. It is now *free to* grow in a normal manner and cope successfully with the problems of survival.

I conclude that in one important sense of the word, "freedom" applies to animals and plants as much as it does to humans. Freedom in the sense of absence of constraints is an instrumental good for all living things. It is valuable to nonhumans for the same reason it is valuable to humans. For them as well as for us, to be free is to have a better chance to live the best kind of life we are capable of.

This, then, is the third reality in the conditions of existence shared by both humans and nonhumans. All are equally beings of whom the ideas of being free and being unfree can correctly be predicated in the sense analyzed above. We humans are united with other forms of life under this concept of freedom. Being subject to constraints upon our pursuit of the good is a characteristic of our common existential situation. And the great value for each of us to be free from such constraints is a value we all share. We constitute a community of beings in part because we have this value in common.

(d) The fourth respect in which we humans may be identified as members of the Earth's Community of Life concerns our common origin with other living things. A number of relevant considerations are brought to light when we look at our nature and our circumstances from the viewpoint of the theory of evolution. In the first place we see that it was the same order of evolutionary processes, governed by the same laws of natural selection and genetic transmission, that gave rise to our existence and to the existence of every other species. We have all emerged in fundamentally the same way, an effect of the same basic kinds of causes. We accordingly recognize that we are like other creatures as far as our beginnings are concerned. Evolution, as biological science has come to know it, offers a unified explanation for the existence of both human and nonhuman forms of life.

111

To understand how others came to be is to understand how we came to be.

In the second place, as was pointed out in Chapter One, from an evolutionary perspective the appearance of the species *Homo sapiens* is a very recent event in the history of life on Earth. We are a brand new arrival, having come upon the scene only a brief moment ago in geological time. Although the exact age of our species is currently a matter of dispute, it is generally estimated to be between 400,000 and 500,000 years. Thus the total span of our human existence is but an instant in comparison with the periods during which some plants and animals have been present on the planet.

A third aspect of the evolutionary picture, closely associated with the preceding, is the fact that long before our appearance on Earth there had already been established a system of relations among species that made for mutual adaptation and interdependence, allowed for genetic transmission and change, and operated according to the laws of natural selection. In order that there be such a thing as a human being, that system of life had to be there already. The conditions necessary and sufficient for our coming into existence were the outcome of an order of events going back millions of centuries. When viewed in this light we no longer see ourselves as special objects of creation. We are the product of a system that has also produced every other kind of living thing.

It is true that after we appeared we came to use our brains to form a civilization that has radically transformed the surface of the planet. Unlike any other species, we have disarranged much of the very order of nature that produced us. But apart from the disturbances wrought by our civilization, the evolutionary factors that governed our original emergence were not different from those that gave rise to all other creatures. It is in this sense that we and they are united by a common origin.

Taking these various facts into account, we can consider the theory of evolution to be a framework of thought that underlies one part of the biocentric outlook on nature. Within the conceptual, explanatory system set by that theory, we understand ourselves as beings that fit into the same structure of reality that accounts for every other form of life. To look at ourselves in this way is to have a vivid sense of our membership in the Earth's total Community of Life. What then shall we make of the claim, which humans are so often prone to advance, that their appearance on Earth was the final goal and culmination of the evolutionary process? We will see it for what it is—simply an expression of human vanity. It assumes that evolution has had an over-all direction, that this direction was toward ever higher forms of life, and that human life represents the highest type of existence.[4] Later I shall argue that the fundamental presupposition of this whole way of thinking, namely that humans are inherently superior (have greater inherent worth) to all other living things, is a totally groundless assumption. We shall find that there are reasons for considering it to be nothing more than an unfounded bias in our own favor.

(e) The vanity of the claim of human superiority strikes us forcefully when the fifth reality concerning the relation of

---

[4] A thoroughgoing critique of the idea that evolution has either a single direction or an overall purpose is presented in George Gaylord Simpson's classic study, *The Meaning of Evolution: A Study of the History of Life and Its Significance for Man* (New Haven, Conn.: Yale University Press, 1949). Simpson attacks, from a scientific point of view, the whole idea that evolution shows progress from earlier, lower forms of life to later, higher ones. He also criticizes the view (held by Lamarck) that there is a sequence of types of living things from less to more perfect. Only a self-centered criterion of progress, Simpson argues, makes the arrival of *Homo sapiens* the final culmination of the evolutionary process.

A more recent study, criticizing some contemporary interpretations of evolution, provides strong reasons for holding that evolutionary changes have no overall direction and that the concept of progress does not apply to them. Genetic variation and the workings of natural selection, it is argued, do not lend themselves to a purposive interpretation of nature oriented toward the emergence of human life. See Williams, *Adaptation and Natural Selection*, especially chapter 2.

our species to other members of the Earth's Community of Life is brought to the forefront of our minds. This is the fact that, from a biological point of view, humans are absolutely dependent upon the soundness and good health of the Earth's biosphere, but its soundness and good health are not in the least dependent upon humans. Indeed, it developed and maintained itself quite well for a period over ten thousand times as long as the total duration of human existence up to the present moment. We are, in other words, not only newcomers; we are also (like every other species taken by itself) needy dependents, unable to support ourselves without the aid of the rest of the natural order of life. As long as the Earth's biosphere as a whole is functioning well our own existence may continue. Should it disintegrate, however, or become seriously disordered, we will exist no more. Our dependence on the general integrity of the whole realm of life is absolute.

Consider, on the other hand, the reverse relationship. Suppose we humans were to destroy ourselves (without taking all other living things with us into oblivion!), or suppose that the human species became extinct from some natural cause such as an uncontrollable disease. The Earth's biosphere could still continue to exist; life would go on without us. Our demise would be no loss to other species, nor would it adversely affect the natural environment. On the contrary, other living things would be much benefited. The physical environment of the Earth would be greatly improved. It is perhaps worthwhile to dwell on the significance of this a bit further.

It seems quite clear that in the contemporary world the extinction of the species *Homo sapiens* would be beneficial to the Earth's Community of Life as a whole. The destruction of natural habitats by housing developments, industrial complexes, airports, and other large-scale projects would cease. The poisoning of soil and pollution of rivers would come to an end. The Earth would no longer have to suffer ecological destruction and widespread environmental degradation due to modern technology, uncontrolled population growth, and wasteful consumption. After the disappearance of the human species, life communities in natural ecosystems would gradually be restored to their former healthy state. Tropical forests, for example, would again be able to make their full contribution to a life-sustaining atmosphere for the whole planet. The lakes, oceans, and wetlands of the world would slowly become clean again. Spilled oil, plastic trash, and even radioactive waste, after many centuries, might finally cease doing their terrible work. Ecosystems with their plant and animal life would be subject only to the disruptions of natural events such as volcanic eruptions and glaciation. From these the Community of Life could recover, as it has so often done in the past. But the ecological disasters it is now undergoing at the hands of humans, from which it might never recover—these would no longer be inflicted upon it.

Given the total, absolute, and final disappearance of *Homo sapiens*, then, not only would the Earth's Community of Life continue to exist but in all probability its well-being would be enhanced. Our presence, in short, is not needed. And if we were to take the standpoint of that Life Community and give voice to its true interest, the ending of the human epoch on Earth would most likely be greeted with a hearty "Good riddance!"

Let us recapitulate the argument to this point. We have considered five general empirical truths which, when brought together and placed in the forefront of our awareness, give us a sense of oneness with all other living things and lead us to see ourselves as members of one great Community of Life. To face the realities of human existence expressed in these truths is to become cognizant of our status as members of the Earth's whole biotic community, a status we share with every other species. It is to raise our consciousness, as it were, to full awareness of the fundamental fact that we are animals. This awareness is the first of the four basic components of the biocentric outlook on nature. I turn now to the second component.

3. *The Natural World As a System of Interdependence*

To accept the biocentric outlook and regard ourselves and the world from its perspective is to see the whole natural domain of living things and their environment as an order of interconnected objects and events. The interactions among species-populations and between those populations and the physical environment comprise a tightly woven web. A particular change occurring in the conditions of a living population's existence or in the environmental situation will cause adjustments to be made throughout the entire structure.

As an illustration of a system of interdependence *within* the natural world we might consider some aspects of the ecology of the Everglades of Florida. In that ecosystem alligators make large depressions in marshy areas when they feed and rest. These depressions become permanent pools of water, containing a variety of forms of marine life nourished by the alligators' droppings and by bits of their food. During dry spells these pools are the only place where the marine organisms can survive. When rains come, they spread out over the Everglades, contributing to the whole grassland ecology in essential ways.

Female alligators are integral to the Everglades ecosystem in a special way. They build their nests by forming large piles of sticks and mud. These become the core of small islands of dry soil after many years, and trees begin to grow on them. The trees in turn support nesting birds which live on the fish, insects, and amphibia of the area, maintaining the balance between animal and plant life in the grasslands. Although the alligators sometimes eat nesting birds, they also protect the birds from predators.

When the alligators are trapped and killed (to supply

skins to the makers of expensive shoes and handbags), the whole Everglades ecosystem suffers. The pools dry up, the marine life disappears, and the balance of life in the watery grassland is destroyed. Certain species of fish die off and, during rainy seasons, other species intrude into the area in great numbers. They had formerly been kept in check by their natural predator, the alligators. Thus the entire area undergoes deep ecological changes which, if not reversed, will spell the end of the ecosystem itself.

When one accepts the biocentric outlook, the whole realm of life is understood to exemplify a vast complex of relationships of interdependence similar to that found in each ecosystem. All the different ecosystems that make up the Earth's biosphere fit together in such a way that if one is radically changed or totally destroyed, an adjustment takes place in others and the whole structure undergoes a certain shift. The biological order of the planet does not remain exactly what it was.

No life community associated with a particular ecological system is an isolated unit. It is directly or indirectly connected with other life communities. And the connections among them are similar to those that hold among populations within an ecosystem. What happens to one will have consequences for others. It is for this reason that the entire biosphere of our planet comprises a single unified whole, which I refer to in this book by the term "the natural world."

It follows that, if the biocentric outlook forms the basis of our perspective on *human* life, we will see ourselves as an integral part of the system of nature. We will then recognize that our faring well or poorly depends to a great extent on the role we choose to play in the web of life. We will realize that if we try to break our connections with that web, or if we disrupt too severely the ties that bind the fabric together, we will thereby destroy our chances for pursuing our uniquely human values. For it is the place we choose to occupy (our "niche," as it were) in the system of nature that sets the necessary conditions for the realization of the primary goods of life and health, without which all other human goods are unachievable.

In order to forestall at this juncture any mistaken impressions the above account might give rise to, I wish to emphasize that the biocentric outlook does *not* entail a holistic or organicist view of environmental ethics. We cannot derive moral rules for our treatment of the natural world from a conception of the Earth's biosphere as a kind of supraorganism, the furtherance of whose well-being determines the ultimate principle of right and wrong.

According to a holistic theory of environmental ethics, our conduct with regard to the natural world is right if it tends to preserve the ecological stability, integrity, and equilibrium of biotic communities, and wrong if it tends to destroy or disrupt such ecological balance.[5] Such a theory is not human-centered, since the norm of preserving the good of the whole system is taken to be an ultimate end having value in itself. Its status as an end at which we are morally obligated to aim is not grounded on its importance to human well-being. Nevertheless, such a position is open to the objection that it gives no place to the good of individual organisms, other than how their pursuit of their good contributes to the well-being of the system as a whole. This overlooks the fact that unless individuals have a good of their own that deserves the moral consideration of agents, no account of the organic system of nature-as-a-whole can explain why moral agents have a duty to preserve *its* good. Even if it is the case that the entire realm of life on Earth is

[5] It was Aldo Leopold in his work, *A Sand County Almanac*, who was the inspiration for many of the current holistic views. See especially the essay, "The Land Ethic," included in Aldo Leopold, *A Sand County Almanac* (New York: Oxford University Press, 1949). Examples of contemporary holistic theories are: Kenneth E. Goodpaster, "From Egoism to Environmentalism," in K. E. Goodpaster and K. M. Sayre, eds., *Ethics and Problems of the 21st Century* (Notre Dame, Ind.: University of Notre Dame Press, 1979), pp. 21-35; and Stephen R. L. Clark, "Gaia and the Forms of Life," in R. Elliot and A. Gare, eds., *Environmental Philosophy: A Collection of Essays* (University Park: Pennsylvania State University Press, 1983), pp. 182-197.

itself a quasi-organism, why should the well-being of that entity count ethically? As I shall point out in connection with the third component of the biocentric outlook, it is individual organisms (not supraorganisms or quasi-organisms) that, when fully understood and recognized for what they are, are seen to be entities having a good of their own, a good that is not reducible to the good of any other entity. Once we have rejected a human-centered ethics, it is only by reference to the particular lives of such beings as made better or worse by our actions that consideration for the natural world becomes morally relevant. If no benefits to those entities are valued as ends to be brought about for their sake, we are not given any nonhuman-centered reason to maintain the order of the whole system. The full argument in support of this claim, however, requires a complete explication of all four components of the biocentric outlook and an argument justifying our accepting that outlook in its entirety. This is precisely the task that occupies us in the present chapter.

4. Individual Organisms as Teleological Centers of Life

So far the biocentric outlook has been presented as a belief-system that sets a framework for viewing ourselves in relation to other species and for understanding how we and they alike fit into the whole natural environment of our planet. The third component of that outlook, in contrast with the first two, focuses our attention on the lives of individual organisms. The biocentric outlook includes a certain way of conceiving of each entity that has a life of its own. To accept the outlook is to sharpen and deepen our awareness of what it means to be a particular living thing.

Our knowledge of individual organisms has expanded rapidly with advances in the biological and physical sciences in the past century. Organic chemistry and microbiology have brought us close to every cell and every molecule that make up the physical structure of the bodies of organisms. We have greatly increased our understanding of how living things function as physical and chemical systems. We are acquiring ever more accurate and complete explanations of why organisms behave as they do. As we thus come to know more about their life cycles, their interactions with other organisms and with the environment, we become increasingly aware of how each of them is carrying out its life functions according to the laws of its species-specific nature. But besides this, our increasing knowledge and understanding also enable us to grasp the uniqueness of each organism as an individual. Scientists who have made careful and detailed studies of particular plants and animals have often come to know their subjects as identifiable individuals. Close observation over extended periods, whether in the laboratory or in the field, has led them to an appreciation of the unique "personalities" of their subjects. Sometimes a scientist develops a special interest in a particular animal or plant, all the while remaining strictly objective in the gathering and recording of data.[6]

Nonscientists may likewise experience this development of interest when, as amateur naturalists, they make accurate observations over a sustained period of close acquaintance with a plant or animal. As one becomes more and more familiar with the organism being observed, one acquires a sharpened awareness of the particular way it is living its life. One may become fascinated by it and even get to be involved with its good and bad fortunes. The organism comes to mean something to one as a unique, irreplaceable individual. Finally one achieves a genuine understanding of its point of view. One can then imaginatively place oneself in the organism's situation and look at the world from its standpoint.

This progressive development from objective, detached

[6] It is nowadays standard practice for biologists conducting research in the field to study organisms not only by observing natural differences by which to identify particular individuals but also by tagging or marking individuals for purposes of ready recognition.

knowledge to the recognition of individuality, and from the recognition of individuality to a full awareness of an organism's standpoint, is a process of heightening our consciousness of what it means to be an individual living thing. We conceive of the organism as a teleological center of life, striving to preserve itself and realize its good in its own unique way.[7] To say it is a teleological center of life is to say that its internal functioning as well as its external activities are all goal-oriented, having the constant tendency to maintain the organism's existence through time and to enable it successfully to perform those biological operations

[7] The concept of an organism's striving to preserve itself and realize its good is not identical with the more restricted concept of biological fitness, where fitness means the ability of an organism to ensure the continued existence of its genes in future individuals. (See Chapter One.) A case in which the distinction must be made between the individual's own good and the survival of its genes in future organisms is that which occurs among the so-called social insects, such as bees and ants. In these cases the individual's performing a particular function or role in the species-community, which may not further its own well-being or survival (for example, ants that defend the nest against intruders by sacrificing their lives), nevertheless enables the *siblings* of the individual to survive. In such a case the biological fitness of the organism increases the probability that its genes will continue to exist.

It should be noted, however, that even when the individual's own well-being takes second place to the preservation of its genes in future individuals, only a healthy and living organism can be biologically fit for this purpose. A weak, diseased, injured, or dying individual cannot perform well at the task of helping its offspring or siblings to survive. Thus the teleological concept of an individual's pursuing its own good in its own way includes the *tendency* of the individual to maintain or enhance its biological fitness.

In the case of humans another whole dimension of the relation between biological fitness and individual well-being must be taken into account. Biological fitness (as defined above) may or may not be included in a person's own good. Some people who are perfectly capable of having children prefer not to have them. Having children is simply not included in their conception of a good life, while for others the opposite is true. This is a matter of a person's autonomously chosen value-system, and the exercise of autonomy in making such a choice is part of the realization of the Human Good. No biological requirements for ensuring one's genes in future individuals *dictates* how a person must choose. This is one feature of human persons by which they are to be distinguished from other animals. A person's autonomous choice places a (conceptual or logical) boundary on what can be explained in *human* life by natural selection and adaptation.

121

whereby it reproduces its kind and continually adapts to changing environmental events and conditions. It is the coherence and unity of these functions of an organism, all directed toward the realization of its good, that make it one teleological center of activity. Physically and chemically it is in the molecules of its cells that this activity occurs, but the organism as a whole is the unit that responds to its environment and so accomplishes (or tends to accomplish) the end of sustaining its life.[8]

Understanding individual organisms as teleological centers of life does not mean that we are falsely anthropomorphizing. It does not involve "reading into" them human characteristics. We need not, for example, consider them to have consciousness. That a particular tree is a teleological center of life does not entail that it is intentionally aiming at preserving its existence, that it is exerting efforts to avoid death, or that it even cares whether it lives or dies. As we saw in Chapter Two, organisms like trees and one-celled protozoa do not have a conscious life. They are not aware of a world around them. They have no thoughts or feelings and hence no interest in anything that happens to them. Yet they have a good of their own around which their behavior is organized. All organisms, whether conscious or not, are teleological centers of life in the sense that each is a unified, coherently ordered system of goal-oriented activities that has a constant tendency to protect and maintain the organism's existence.

Under this conception of individual living things, each is seen to have a single, unique point of view. This point of view is determined by the organism's particular way of re-

---

[8] Three recent books have explored in depth the use of teleological concepts and explanations in biology. Although they are in sharp disagreement about the correct analysis to be made of such concepts and explanations, there is general acknowledgment that those concepts and explanations are integral to the biological sciences. See Michael Ruse, *The Philosophy of Biology* (London: J. M. Dent, 1973); Andrew Woodfield, *Teleology* (New York: Cambridge University Press, 1976); and Larry Wright, *Teleological Explanations* (Los Angeles: University of California Press, 1976).

sponding to its environment, interacting with other individual organisms, and undergoing the regular, lawlike transformations of the various stages of its species-specific life cycle. As it sustains its existence through time, it exemplifies all the functions and activities of its species in its own peculiar manner. When observed in detail, its way of existing is seen to be different from that of any other organism, including those of its species. To be aware of it not only as *a* center of life, but as *the* particular center of life that it is, is to be aware of its uniqueness and individuality. The organism is the individual it is precisely in virtue of its having its own idiosyncratic manner of carrying on its existence in the (not necessarily conscious) pursuit of its good.

This mode of understanding a particular individual is not possible with regard to inanimate objects. Although no two stones are exactly alike in their physical characteristics, stones do not have points of view. In pure fantasy, of course, we can play at performing the imaginative act of taking a stone's standpoint and looking at the world from its perspective. But we are then moving away from reality, not getting closer to it. The true reality of a stone's existence includes no point of view. This is not due to the fact that it lacks consciousness. As we have noted, plants and simple animal organisms also lack consciousness, but have points of view nonetheless. What makes our awareness of an individual stone fundamentally different from our awareness of a plant or animal is that the stone is not a teleological center of life, while the plant or animal is. The stone has no good of its own. We cannot benefit it by furthering its well-being or harm it by acting contrary to its well-being, since the concept of well-being simply does not apply to it.

This point holds even for those complex mechanisms (such as self-monitoring space satellites, chess-playing computers, and assembly-line "robots") that have been constructed by humans to function in a quasi-autonomous, self-regulating manner in the process of accomplishing certain purposes. Though such machines are understandable

123

as teleological systems, they remain in actual fact inanimate objects. The ends they are programmed to accomplish are not purposes of their own, independent of the human purposes for which they were made. This is not to deny that in certain contexts it is perfectly proper to speak of what is good or bad for them. These would be conditions that add to or detract from their effectiveness as instruments for bringing about the (human) ends they were made to serve. But it is precisely this fact that separates them from living things.

The goal-oriented operations of machines are not inherent to them as the goal-oriented behavior of organisms is inherent to *them*. To put it another way, the goals of a machine are derivative, whereas the goals of a living thing are original. The ends and purposes of machines are built into them by their human creators. It is the original purposes of humans that determine the structures and hence the teleological functions of those machines. Although they manifest goal-directed activities, the machines do not, as independent entities, have a good of their own. Their "good" is "furthered" only insofar as they are treated in such a way as to be an effective means to human ends.

A living plant or animal, on the other hand, has a good of its own in the same sense that a human being has a good of its own. It is, independently of anything else in the universe, itself a center of goal-oriented activity. What is good or bad for it can be understood by reference to its own survival, health, and well-being. As a living thing it seeks its own ends in a way that is not true of any teleologically structured mechanism. It is in terms of *its* goals that we can give teleological explanations of why it does what it does. We cannot do the same for machines, since any such explanation must ultimately refer to the goals their human producers had in mind when they made the machines.

I should add as a parenthetical note that this difference between mechanism and organism may no longer be maintainable with regard to those complex electronic devices now being developed under the name of artificial intelligence. Perhaps some day computer scientists and engineers will construct beings whose internal processes and electrical responses to their surroundings closely parallel the functions of the human brain and nervous system. Concerning such beings we may begin to speak of their having a good of their own independently of the purposes of their creators. At that point the distinction drawn above between living things and inanimate machines may break down. It is best, I think, to have an open mind about this. But for our present purposes we need not go into this matter. In working out a life-centered theory of environmental ethics that is applicable to the relations between humans and the natural world, we can use for practical purposes the distinction as it is made above. If mechanisms (organisms?) of artificial intelligence were ever to be produced, another system of ethics might have to be applied to the treatment of such entities by moral agents.

The fundamental difference between our current conception of living things (as beings belonging to the natural world) and of teleologically ordered machines may be further clarified by considering this difference in light of the first element of the biocentric outlook on nature. Our ability to understand and take the standpoint of individual organisms depends, we have seen, on our conceiving of them as teleological centers of life. Our disposition to conceive of them this way is supported by our looking at ourselves and them as fellow members of a community of life that includes both of us on equal terms. To the extent that we see ourselves to be one with other living things in the Earth's biosphere, to that extent we are able to achieve the frame of mind for having a full sense of the reality of their individual existences.

Turning now to a consideration of the state of awareness of individual organisms as teleological centers of life, two general features of that state are worthy of note: objectivity and wholeness of vision. Our heightened state of reality-awareness with regard to the life of a particular organism is *objective* because in that state we are "open" to the full existence and nature of the organism. We are ready to let the individuality of the organism come before us, undistorted by our likes and dislikes, our hopes and fears, our interests, wants, and needs. As far as it is humanly possible to do so, we comprehend the organism as it is in itself, not as we want it to be.

In most circumstances of everyday life, humans view animals and plants through the distorting lens of their feelings and desires. Our consciousness of another tends to be influenced by our taking it to be a friend or an enemy. This is true of our reaction to other humans, but is even more pronounced in regard to nonhuman organisms. Thus sheep ranchers see any and all coyotes as vicious, cruel beasts fit only to be destroyed. It is an unusual woolgrower indeed who can look at a coyote objectively and fully understand its point of view (even when he might think it necessary to kill it). As the sheep raiser views the coyote, so does the gardener view weeds, the farmer locusts, the apartment dweller roaches. Objectivity is equaly absent from our view of "friendly" animals and plants. We tend to have a distorted understanding of our pets, of our favorite wildflowers, of pretty birds singing on a spring morning. It often takes the intellectual detachment and emotional neutrality of scientific observation to overcome such tendencies. Certainly our acquiring scientific knowledge about certain kinds of animals and plants can help us enormously in the attempt to understand objectively the everyday existence of particular individuals of those kinds.

Besides adopting the detachment and neutrality of scientific inquiry, we can increase our objectivity by becoming aware of the particular distortions we are prone to, and then making deliberate efforts to free ourselves from them. Just as we are often able to raise our plane of consciousness above the biases and prejudices that our social community might have concerning certain human groups, so we can sometimes overcome by sheer self-discipline the partiality and warped outlook of our less thoughtful moments in re-acting to animals and plants around us. To the extent we are able to do this, we more closely approximate the ideal state of reality-awareness concerning individual living things.

Wholeness of vision is a second main feature of such reality-awareness. We achieve wholeness of vision in our under-standing of an animal or plant to the extent that we no longer look at it in terms of a role or function it might have in human life. Consider, for example, the way a typical hunter views a pheasant. He sees it always as a game bird, something to be shot during hunting season. What the life of the pheasant is like outside the hunting season is of no interest to him unless it has some relevance to its status as a game bird. Here there is lack of wholeness of vision. Sim-ilar absence of wholeness is found in the lumberman's con-sciousness of a tree (so many square feet of board), a fur trapper's view of a wild raccoon (skin worth so many dol-lars on the market), a research worker's consideration of a rat (suitable subject for his experiment). In all these cases the animal or plant is looked at only in terms of the interests and desires of the human viewer. Thus only a one-sided picture of the organism enters the viewer's consciousness.

To free ourselves from such one-sidedness is to gain an understanding of the whole character or "personality" of an individual based on our recognition of its concrete qual-ities in all their particularity. The animal or plant is not seen through a screen of abstract forms, categories, or stereo-types imposed by human interests and purposes. Insofar as we are able to achieve wholeness of vision in our grasp of an organism's uniqueness, we come to know the life of that individual as it is lived by it. We then conceive of it as a com-plete, many-faceted being carrying out its own mode of ex-istence, responding in its own way to the particular circum-stances confronting it.

When our consciousness of the life of an individual or-ganism is characterized by both objectivity and wholeness of vision, we have reached the most complete realization, cognitively and imaginatively, of *what it is to be that particular individual*. We have let the reality of another's life enter the world of our own consciousness. We know it as fully and intensely as it can be known.

This sets a relevant frame of reference for our conduct as moral agents. As a result of our heightened awareness of the reality of another living thing's existence, we gain the genuine *capacity* to take its standpoint and make judgments based on its good. Shifting out of the usual boundaries of anthropocentricity, the world-horizon of our moral imagination opens up to encompass all living things. Seeing them as we see ourselves, we are ready to place the same value on their existence as we do on our own. If we regard ourselves as possessing inherent worth, so will we be disposed to regard them.

A parallel with human ethics can easily be made here. If one does not have the capacity for imaginative awareness of another person's experienced world, one will not be able fully to conceive of what it means to be that other person living his or her own life. On the other hand, to the extent that we develop the imaginative power to envisage what it is like to experience the world as other people do, to that extent we are able to achieve in our own consciousness a clear grasp of the reality of others' lives. Our sense of another person's existence then becomes a recognition that the other is a subjective center of awareness, just like ourselves. In this way we acquire the cognitive understanding of another's individuality needed for making the moral commitment involved in having the attitude of respect toward that person, even though such cognitive understanding by itself does not logically entail the moral commitment.

So it is with the third element of the biocentric outlook. Our conceiving of each organism as a teleological center of life is our recognition of the reality of its existence as a unique individual, pursuing its own good in its own way. By developing the powers of heightened awareness of it as the particular individual it is, we achieve a full understanding of the point of view defined by its good. We then have the capacity needed to make the moral commitment involved in taking the attitude of respect toward it, even though having this capacity does not necessitate our making the moral commitment.

5. The Denial of Human Superiority

Of all the elements that make up the biocentric outlook, the fourth is the most important as far as taking the attitude of respect for nature is concerned. This fourth element consists in a total rejection of the idea that human beings are superior to other living things. Most people in our Western civilization are brought up within a belief-system according to which we humans possess a kind of value and dignity not present in "lower" forms of life. In virtue of our humanity we are held to be nobler beings than animals and plants. Our reason and free will, it is supposed, endow us with special worth because they enable us to live on a higher plane of existence than other living things are capable of. It is this belief, so deeply and pervasively ingrained in our cultural traditions, that is brought into question and finally denied outright in the fourth element of the biocentric outlook.

In what sense are human beings alleged to be superior to other animals? We are indeed different from them in having certain capacities that they lack. But why should these capacities be taken as signs of our superiority to them? From what point of view are they judged to be signs of superiority, and on what grounds? After all, many nonhuman species have capacities that humans lack. There is the flight of birds, the speed of a cheetah, the power of photosynthesis in the leaves of plants, the craftsmanship of spiders spinning their webs, the agility of a monkey in the tree tops. Why are not these to be taken as signs of their superiority over us?

One answer that comes immediately to mind is that these capacities of animals and plants are not as *valuable* as the human capacities that are claimed to make us superior. Such uniquely human characteristics as rationality, aesthetic creativity, individual autonomy, and free will, it might be held, are more valuable than any of the capacities of animals and plants. Yet we must ask: Valuable to whom and for what reason?

The human charcteristics mentioned are all valuable to humans. They are of basic importance to the preservation and enrichment of human civilization. Clearly it is from the human standpoint that they are being judged as desirable and good. It is not difficult to recognize here a begging of the question. Humans are claiming superiority over nonhumans from a strictly human point of view, that is, a point of view in which the good of humans is taken as the standard of judgment. All we need to do is to look at the capacities of animals and plants from the standpoint of *their* good to find a contrary judgment of superiority. The speed of the cheetah, for example, is a sign of its superiority to humans when considered from the standpoint of a cheetah's good. If it were as slow a runner as a human it would not be able to catch its prey. And so for all the other abilities of animals and plants that further their good but are lacking in humans. In each case the judgment of human superiority would be rejected from a nonhuman standpoint.

When superiority-claims are interpreted in this way, they are based on judgments of merit. As we saw in Chapter Two, to judge the merits of a person or an organism one must apply grading or ranking standards to it. Empirical investigation then determines whether it has the "good-making" properties (merits) in virtue of which it fulfills the standards being applied.

The question that naturally arises at this juncture is: Why should standards that are based on *human values* be the only valid criteria of merit and accordingly be considered the only true signs of superiority? This question is especially pressing when humans are being judged superior in merit to nonhumans. It is true that a human being may be a better mathematician than a monkey, but the monkey may be a better tree climber than a human being. If we humans value mathematics more than tree climbing, that is because our conception of civilized life makes the development of mathematical ability more desirable than the ability to climb trees. But is it not unreasonable to judge nonhumans by the values of human civilization, rather than by values connected with what it is for a member of *that* species to live a good life? If all living things have a good of their own, it at least makes sense to judge the merits of nonhumans by standards derived from *their* good. To use only standards based on the good of humans is already to commit oneself to holding that the good of humans counts more than, or is more worthy of consideration than, the good of nonhumans, which is the point in question.

A further logical flaw should be noted here. Many standards of merit do not apply to nonhuman organisms at all. Only humans can meaningfully be judged as good, excellent, fair, or poor research scientists, aeronautical engineers, drama critics, or Supreme Court justices. But this implies that a category mistake is made if the standards being applied in such judgments are used to judge that humans are superior to nonhumans. One kind of entity can significantly be judged to be superior in merit to another only if both kinds of entities properly fall within the range of application of the standards being used. Animals and plants cannot therefore be judged to be *poor* research scientists, aeronautical engineers, drama critics, or Supreme Court justices. With regard to these positions and activities they are neither good nor bad. More precisely, it is *nonsense* to speak of them as being good or bad scientists, engineers, critics, or justices.

Now consider one of the most frequently repeated assertions concerning the superiority of humans over nonhumans. This is the claim that we humans are *morally* superior beings because we possess, while animals and plants lack, the capacities that give us the status of moral agents. Such capacities as free will, accountability, deliberation, and practical reason, it is said, endow us with the special nobility and dignity that belong only to morally responsible beings. Because human existence has this moral dimension it exemplifies a higher grade of being than is to be found in the amoral, irresponsible existence of animals and plants. In traditional terms, it is freedom of the will and the moral responsibility that goes with it that together raise human life above the level of the beasts.

There is a serious confusion of thought in this line of reasoning if the conclusion drawn is understood as asserting that humans are morally superior to nonhumans. One cannot validly argue that humans are morally superior beings on the ground that they possess, while others lack, the capacities of a moral agent. The reason is that, as far as moral standards are concerned, only beings that have the capacities of a moral agent can meaningfully be said to be *either* morally good *or* morally bad. Only moral agents can be judged to be morally better or worse than others, and the others in question must be moral agents themselves. Judgments of moral superiority are based on the comparative merits or deficiencies of the entities being judged, and these merits and deficiencies are all moral ones, that is, ones determined by moral standards. One entity is correctly judged morally superior to another if it is the case that, when valid moral standards are applied to both entities, the first fulfills them to a greater degree than the second. Both entities, therefore, must fall within the range of application of moral standards. This would not be the case, however, if humans were being judged superior to animals and plants, since the latter are not moral agents. Just as animals and plants can be neither good nor bad scientists, engineers, critics, or Supreme Court justices, so they can be neither good nor bad moral agents. More precisely, it is meaningless to speak of them as morally good or bad. Hence it is meaningless to say either that they are morally inferior to humans or that humans are morally superior to them. I conclude that it is not false but simply confused to assert that humans are the moral superiors of animals and plants.

Up to this point I have been interpreting the claim that humans are superior to other living things as a judgment regarding the comparative merits of humans and nonhumans. There is, however, another way to understand the idea of human superiority. According to this interpretation, humans are superior to nonhumans not as regards their merits but as regards their *inherent worth*. Thus the claim of human superiority is to be understood as asserting that all human beings, simply in virtue of their humanity, have a greater inherent worth than animals and plants.

If we were to view animals and plants this way, we might not take a purely exploitative attitude toward them, since we might still grant that they have *some* degree of inherent worth and so are not to be used in any way humans wish. But to conceive of them as inherently inferior beings would mean that, whenever a conflict arose between their wellbeing and the interests of humans, human interests would automatically take priority. Although both humans and nonhumans would deserve moral consideration, they would not deserve equal consideration. A human's good, just because it is a human's, would always outweigh the good of an animal or plant.

The idea of human superiority over the so-called "lower" orders of living things pervades our Western culture and shapes our whole perspective on the natural world. If the doctrine of inherent human superiority were to be shown to be without rational foundation and if it could further be demonstrated that there are logically sound reasons for rejecting that doctrine, the whole structure would collapse. We would have to face the possibility that our true relation to other forms of life, even to those that might do us harm, is a relation among beings of *equal* inherent worth, and not a relation between superior, higher beings and inferior, lower ones. We could then no longer rightly look down on animals or plants, or think of a human individual as naturally having a greater claim-to-existence than any "mere" animal or plant. We would see ourselves and our place in the natural world in a new light. Our whole ethical orientation would undergo a deep and far-reaching transformation, entailing profound revisions in our treatment of the Earth and its biotic communities. A total reordering of our moral universe would take place. Our duties with respect to the "world" of nature would be seen as making claims upon us to be balanced against our duties with respect to the "world" of human culture and civilization. We would no longer simply assume the human point of view and consider the effects of our conduct regarding other living things exclusively or primarily from the perspective of what will promote our own good.

Now, this radical change in our view of the natural world and of our proper ethical relationship to other living things is just what is involved when we accept the biocentric outlook. The fourth component of that outlook is nothing else but the denial of the doctrine of inherent human superiority. This denial, we shall see, is the key to understanding why acceptance of the biocentric outlook underlies and supports a person's adopting the attitude of respect for nature.

The denial of human superiority is the logical outcome of two steps of reasoning, a negative one and a positive one. The negative step is a matter of showing that there are *no* good reasons for *accepting* the doctrine of human superiority, and the positive step is a matter of showing that there *are* good reasons for *rejecting* it. The conclusion of the first step is that the doctrine is totally groundless, that it lacks any rational foundation whatever. To establish this claim it must be shown that the arguments given to justify the doctrine are all seriously flawed. They fail to prove what they are intended to prove. The second step involves giving a sound argument to show that the doctrine is false or ration-

ally unacceptable and that we are therefore entirely justified in rejecting it. (My strategy in presenting this second
step of reasoning will be to argue that *if* the first three components of the biocentric outlook are accepted *then* the doctrine of human superiority must be denied, and to show
that there are indeed good reasons for accepting the first
three components.)

The first step, now, is to examine the main arguments
that have been given in support of the idea that humans are
inherently superior to, or have greater inherent worth than,
other living things, and to show that they (and any other arguments like them) are unsound. First I shall consider the
three arguments which, in the history of Western philosophy, have had the greatest influence. The central ideas contained in these three arguments are the historical roots of
the widespread acceptance of the doctrine as a fundamental
part of our culture's value system and world view. Then I
shall examine one contemporary argument.

The three historical arguments are based on: (a) the essentialist view of human nature found in classical Greek humanism; (b) the idea of the Great Chain of Being found in
the metaphysics of traditional Christian monotheism; and
(c) the dualistic theory of the philosophy of René Descartes,
according to which human beings possess minds as well as
bodies, but animals, lacking minds, are mere automata.

(a) The inherent superiority of humans over other species
was implicit in the classical Greek definition of a human
being as a rational animal. This definition was intended to
state the essence of human nature by specifying the general
kind of entity a human being is (an animal) and the characteristic that differentiates humans from all other animals
(being rational). The capacity of reason was seen not only as
defining what is essential and unique to human nature, but
also as a mark of special value or worth. Reason gives a kind
of nobility and dignity to humans that is lacking in crea-

tures without reason. Furthermore, within human nature it is our reason that must control and give order to the passions and desires of the animal side of us. Thus the very function of reason places it in a higher position as the proper master of our animal nature, enabling us to live on a more elevated plane than other animals. Beings that cannot live a rational life cannot develop greatness or nobility of character. They are unable to achieve the kind of virtue which humans can achieve.

The philosophical outlook of classical Greek humanism linked up the idea of the Human Good with the essentialist definition of humans as rational animals. It is in living a fully rational life that we realize our truly human potentialities and thereby achieve our true good. Human happiness or well-being is the life of reason, and to guide our conduct by reason, both in the choice of means and of ends, is to exist on the highest level possible for a living thing. It is in our nature to pursue this rational good. Hence our superiority over nonrational beings is inherent in our essence, that is, in the very thing that makes us human.

This way of comparing humans with other species will no doubt seem quite familiar to us; it is deeply ingrained in our Western philosophical outlook. The point to consider here is that this view does not provide an *argument* for human superiority. Rather, it simply articulates and makes explicit a certain way of conceiving of that superiority. It is not a reasoned *defense* of the truth of the assertion that humans have greater inherent worth than other living things, but instead is a systematic account of what that assertion means (or what it should be taken to mean). This becomes clear when we realize that the views presented above all *presuppose* that the essence of being human endows us with a kind of worth, dignity, or nobility that is not attributable to beings lacking that essence. If we ask *why* having the human essence gives us greater inherent worth, no answer is forthcoming. The claim is simply repeated that our nobility consists in a special value that attaches to us in virtue of our rationality, which is what makes us human beings. Let us examine this point more closely.

It is in the first place clear that, once we are disposed to look at human existence in the classical Greek way, we will indeed regard every entity governed by reason as possessing higher worth than entities not so governed. But this way of regarding rational beings does not constitute a justification of the claim that humans are superior to nonhumans. The reason it does not becomes evident when we consider the context in which the capacity of reason is held to properly rule over our "animal" nature. For the Greeks the great importance of reason lies in the fact that only by having it guide our lives is it possible for us to realize the Human Good. Unless our reason has supremacy over our animal nature, we cannot be fully human and so cannot achieve a state of well-being. But as rational beings we all seek that state. It is the true end or purpose of human life, that which makes our lives worth living. Human happiness, the kind of well-being suitable to our essential human nature, is the highest good (the *summum bonum*). This supreme value, however, applies only to the life of human beings. It is not a value in the context of the lives of creatures that lack the capacities of reason. Here is where the Greek view fails to establish the superiority of humans over nonhumans. That the realization of the Human Good requires a proper use of reason in the guidance of life tells us nothing about the worth of the lives of those living things whose end is not the Human Good.

I am not here questioning the Greek view that the Human Good consists in the life of reason, nor that this Good is to be thought of as the full actualization of those capacities and potentialities that are characteristically human and that set us off from other species. For even if we were to accept this essentialist conception of human nature and human well-being, nothing follows from it concerning other organisms. In particular, it does not provide any reason for claiming that the kind of life most fit for humans to live is of greater worth than the kind of life most fit for other animals to live. The Greeks, after all, did not deny that each living thing pursues its own good. Indeed, they thought of the good of each animal or plant to be a state or condition in which it fulfills its nature as a member of its species. The well-being of a lion is the kind of life a lion is best suited to live. Such a life does not require rationality (in the sense in which humans must be rational if they are to realize *their* good). That lions lack the kind of rationality exemplified by those humans who are fully realizing their human nature does not imply that those lions that are realizing their lion nature have less inherent worth than humans.

One further point should be noted in connection with this criticism. When we consider not only that animals and plants have no need of reason to realize the kind of good most suitable to their species, but also that they do need to make use of capacities that humans *lack*, the unjustifiability of the claim of human superiority over them becomes even more obvious. There is clearly no more reason why the intellectual and rational abilities of humans should be evidence for their inherent superiority to, say, eagles than eagles' powers of vision and flight should be evidence for their inherent superiority to humans. The one claim is as groundless as the other.

The upshot of these reflections is that, however inspiring or admirable we may find the ethical ideal of classical humanism to be as a standard for *human* living, that outlook gives no support to the judgment that humans have greater inherent worth than nonhumans. We must realize that rationality is but one capacity of a certain class of living things which depend on exercising it for their well-being. Other classes of living things achieve their good without the need of that capacity, although they often exercise capacities that are far beyond the range of human capabilities. If one of these classes of beings is to be shown to be inherently superior to the others, it cannot be on the basis of their unique capacities. The humanistic viewpoint of classical Greek thought does not give us an objective ground for the doctrine of human superiority.

(b) The second of the chief historical roots of the idea that humans are inherently superior to all other living things is found in the concept of the Great Chain of Being, a concept that shaped the whole metaphysical outlook of the Middle Ages and still lies at the foundation of many people's picture of the world. The Great Chain of Being is the view that every existent thing has a certain place in an infinite hierarchy of entities extending from the most real and perfect to the least real and most imperfect. Beginning with God at the top, this hierarchical order continues down through various levels of angels and archangels, then to humans, followed by animals and plants (which are themselves arranged hierarchically), and ends with mere matter at the bottom. This is a metaphysical or ontological order as well as a valuational one. All things fall into a continuum of degrees of inherent worth that reflects the very structure of reality. Within the created world God has made things of every possible grade of existence and value. The universe is a plenitude of beings, manifesting infinite variety in their attributes and value.[9]

For many centuries this way of looking at the realm of existence was at the core of Christian monotheism. It was elaborated upon and defended by theologians on the basis of reason and was accepted by the common believer on the basis of faith. The most fundamental idea in the whole pattern of belief is that the world and God together comprise the totality of existence and constitute one great hierarchy from the lowest form of being to the highest.

This ontological order is the metaphysical background against which humans must understand their own nature and purpose. They fit into the order between the angels and the beasts. The angels are spiritual (nonmaterial, bodi-

[9] This analysis of the idea of the Great Chain of Being is derived from Arthur O. Lovejoy, *The Great Chain of Being: A Study of the History of an Idea* (Cambridge, Mass.: Harvard University Press, 1936).

less) beings and are immortal. Being closest to God in the hierarchy, they are as perfect as finite and contingent entities can be. In Biblical theology they serve as messengers between God and humans. Humans themselves have a two-sided existence, partaking of the nature of both angels and beasts. Like the angels they have immortal souls; like the beasts they have animal bodies. They are thus both spiritual and material. It is as spiritual beings that they are "made in God's image" and are subject to God's moral law. Though inferior to the Divine both in respect of their being contingent and in respect of their limited virtue, they are nevertheless superior to all other creatures God placed on Earth. God Himself has given humans a special status on Earth as lords and masters of all other living creatures. Because humans are made in God's image they have been placed on the scale of existence in a position higher than other forms of life and have been given dominion over them. Their proper purpose is to further their good by "subduing" these other creatures, though they must also be good stewards of the Earth and make use of nature's bounty in a responsible way. They are not given free reign to destroy what is not needed for their own well-being.

Although many philosophers would hold that this whole hierarchical picture of reality is untenable on epistemological grounds, I shall not here attempt to criticize it in its entirety. I shall instead concentrate on the part of it that bears directly on the claim that humans have greater inherent worth than other living things. For the purposes of my argument the existence of God, at least in the form of the idea of a necessary being, need not be questioned. The specific belief I am concerned with is the proposition that different degrees of inherent worth are attributable to living things according to their positions along the Great Chain of Being, when this metaphysical idea is understood in the traditional way.

The main point to notice is that a being's superior or inferior worth is held to depend on the position that has been assigned to it by God, the source of all existence and value. If God places one kind of being in a higher position than another, the first kind of being has greater inherent worth than the second. This is so either because the first kind of being is more similar to the absolute perfection of God than the second, or because God Himself holds the first in higher esteem than the second. Whichever of these two views is taken, however, it presupposes the moral goodness (if not the absolute perfection) of the being that assigns the positions. For if that being were morally evil, greater similarity to its nature would certainly not be a ground for greater inherent worth. Nor would the fact that one thing was more highly esteemed than another by such an evil being constitute a reason for considering the first to have greater inherent worth than the second. Whatever may be its true basis, then, inherent worth cannot be something that depends on the action or valuation of a morally evil being. In order to establish the superiority of humans over nonhumans on the ground of the different positions assigned them by their Creator on the Great Chain, it is necessary to show that the Creator is morally good in assigning them those positions. How, then, can this be shown?

The moral goodness of the Creator of all things does not follow from the mere fact of His being a creator. However we may wish to conceive of the creative activity of God, the role of creator-of-the-universe does not entail goodness of character on the part of the being which has that role.

It is sometimes argued by theologians that the goodness of the Creator can be established by referring to some of His moral attributes, such as His being merciful, just, and loving. There is, however, a serious objection to this way of thinking. Even if the Creator exists and is known to have these attributes, we humans would not thereby know that the Creator is good unless we already knew that mercy, justice, and love are true virtues. And we could know this only if we knew that such attributes fulfill valid standards of good character. Now love, mercy, and justice may indeed be valid norms for a system of *human* ethics. As was argued in Chapter One, insofar as these norms embody the basic principle of respect for persons they are valid standards of human ethics. This means that their correct range of application is the relations among human persons. It does not mean that they apply correctly to the relations between human persons and other living things. Thus their validity for human ethics does not justify our using them for determining the superiority of humans over animals and plants. Even if it is the case that the Creator of humans, animals, and plants arranges them in a hierarchical order and in doing this shows love, mercy, and justice, this does not entitle us to draw any conclusion concerning the comparative inherent worth of the beings so arranged. Love, mercy, and justice are signs of goodness within the realm of human ethics, but not necessarily in a domain of relations that go beyond the human sphere.

Why not, then, hold that God's love, mercy, and justice also manifest His goodness in creating humans and other living things and assigning them their places along the Chain of Being? The basic problem here is this. If we were to take the standpoint of an animal or plant, God would *not* be considered to be loving, merciful, or just in making it an inferior being and giving humans dominion over it. On the contrary, He would show Himself to have a bias in favor of one form of life over another. To reply that no bias is being shown because an animal or plant does not have as much inherent worth as, and therefore does not deserve equal consideration with, humans is clearly to beg the very point in question. At the very least this down-grading of animals and plants by their Creator would cast doubt on the supposed absolute perfection of His love for all His creatures. And this doubt cannot be avoided by appeal to the Creator's goodness as seen from the human point of view without again begging the whole question. To give thanks to the Lord for giving us plants to eat and animals to work for us is to assume that those creatures were placed on Earth for

142

our benefit. From their standpoint this is not likely to establish the perfect love of God, nor His mercy, nor His justice. I conclude that the metaphysical picture of the Great Chain of Being is fundamentally anthropocentric and consequently cannot be used to justify the assertion that humans have greater inherent worth than other living things.

(c) The third major historical source of the idea of inherent human superiority is the metaphysical dualism of René Descartes. According to this view, human beings are superior to animals and plants because humans have souls or minds as well as bodies while animals and plants are only bodies. It is the human mind that gives us reason and free will, without which we would be nothing but automata, that is, mere physical mechanisms. Animals, indeed, are precisely that. Since they are only material substances they can have only the properties of matter: extension in space, motion and rest, size, shape, weight, and being composed of chemical compounds. Animals are therefore essentially no different from inanimate objects. The same holds for plants. Their being alive only means that certain complex processes (metabolism, reproduction, growth, and the like) take place in them. They remain physical things, incapable of conscious experiences. Descartes even thought that animals such as horses and dogs do not feel pain and that they accordingly do not suffer when operated on without anesthesia. They can be treated like machines.

Human beings belong to an entirely different category of entities. A person is a physical body plus a mind. The mind gives direction to the body whenever a person performs an intentional action. The mind also possesses the powers of thought, imagination, and moral judgment. In fact, the mind includes all the variety of conscious experiences we are immediately aware of: having ideas and images, feeling pleasures and pains, emotions and desires, perceiving colors, hearing sounds, remembering past events, and so on. It is our minds that differentiate us from all other living things. At the same time it is our minds that enable us to exist on the level of conscious awareness, a level distinctly more elevated than the unconscious, mechanical, merely physical existence of the brutes. Thus it is the fact that we have minds as well as bodies that accounts for our inherent superiority to animals and plants.

There are three major problems with this position, which I shall consider in turn. First and foremost is the problem concerning the two-substance view of a human being. Are the mind and body of a person two substances, that is, two distinct things having entirely different sorts of properties? According to Cartesian metaphysics the mind is a thinking substance that does not take up any space and hence cannot be located anywhere. We must not picture it as something that exists inside the body, nor is it to be found somewhere outside the body. It is simply nonspatial. The body, on the other hand, is a solid three-dimensional object that lacks the properties of thought and consciousness. If we think of a person's mind and body in these terms we are confronted with an unsolvable problem of how the two substances are connected with each other to form one individual person. When someone decides to do something and then does it, the Cartesian view is that the person's mind causes certain motions to take place in that same person's body. But how can a nonphysical, nonspatial entity produce changes in the physical state of something in space? Descartes thought that the place where the mind directly causes changes in the body is at a certain point in the brain. Not only does this seem to contradict the idea that the mind cannot be located in space, but it makes the connection between mind and body incomprehensible since it requires that chemical transformations in a person's brain occur as the direct effect of something that has no chemical properties. Yet a person's deciding to do something and then doing it is an everyday occurrence. Because the metaphysical dualism of mind and matter precludes any clear or coherent account of such an occurrence, as well as of other equally commonplace occurrences, most contemporary philosophers have rejected the Cartesian concept of a person as a nonphysical substance somehow connected with a physical substance.

A second problem has to do with the Cartesian way of distinguishing between human beings and other animals. Since humans are held to be both physical and mental beings while animals are only physical, there is an absolute metaphysical gulf between them. They are utterly distinct and completely different kinds of entities. Now this total separation of humans from animals seems to fly in the face of recent biological knowledge of humans and certain closely related mammals like the primates. Not only do such mammals give every evidence of the capacity to feel pleasure and pain, but both their external behavior and the internal structure of their brains and nervous systems indicate that they can experience many kinds of emotion, including fear, anger, excitement, anxiety, and even concern for others in their group. They appear to possess certain powers of intelligence and thought. Gorillas and chimpanzees have been found to have the ability to acquire a small vocabulary of terms when taught sign language and to communicate their intentions and wants to humans who live closely with them. They can even develop a sense of self-identity, which is supposed to be one of the sure signs of having a mind! When we bring into consideration the additional knowledge we have gained concerning our genetic makeup and the evolutionary origins of human life, as well as the findings of biochemistry concerning molecular changes in human and animal cells, the similarity between ourselves and other animals cannot be denied. Although there are differences, they appear to be a matter of degree, not of kind. At least those differences do not seem to support the Cartesian view that there is a deep and fundamental separation of ourselves from animals grounded on the absolute divergence of the two ontological categories we and they belong to. Cartesian dualism cannot accommodate the whole trend of recent scientific understanding of humans as biological beings.

The third problem arises in connection with the claim

that we humans have greater inherent worth than animals because we possess minds as well as bodies. Even if we do not question the metaphysical dualism of minds and bodies we must still face the question: Why does the addition of a mind to a body make a person superior in inherent worth to a body alone?

It is quite true that, assuming there is such a thing as a mind, a human being would not *be* human without a mind. Having a mind is necessary for having human characteristics and therefore necessary for possessing the kind of worth a human has. But a mind is not necessary for being a nonhuman animal. In the Cartesian view a bear, for example, can be a bear and have no mind. A bear does not *need* a mind. It can live and fully realize its potentialities as a bear and be a physical substance. Why, then, can it not have the same inherent worth as a human, who *does* need a mind to realize human potentialities?

An immaterial or nonphysical something that thinks adds value to a material something that does not think only if thinking itself is of value, either intrinsically or instrumentally. Now, it is intrinsically valuable only to humans, who value it as an end in itself, and it is instrumentally valuable only to those who benefit from having the capacity to use it, which again (in Descartes' view) are humans alone. For animals that neither enjoy thinking for its own sake nor need it for living the kind of life for which they are most suited, it has no value. Even if "thinking" is broadened to include all forms of conscious awareness, there are still many animal species, as well as all plant life, that can do without it and yet live what is for their species a good life.

We are again forced to the conclusion that it is only an anthropocentric bias that makes us claim superior worth on the basis of something we have and other organisms do not have, which in this case is a substance that thinks. It must be acknowledged that this extra thing would be of no benefit to those other organisms. The Cartesian dualism of mind and matter and its way of differentiating between humans and other forms of life give us no better reason for accepting the claim to human superiority than did classical Greek humanism and the idea of the Great Chain of Being.

(d) I shall now consider one contemporary defense of the idea of the superiority of humans over animals and plants. Professor Louis G. Lombardi has argued that, although animals and plants have *some* inherent worth, they have less worth than humans.[10] It is wrong, he holds, to use animals and plants as if they had nothing but instrumental value as means to human ends. This would overlook their inherent worth. Nevertheless, he claims, they do not deserve equal consideration with humans. Since they have a lower degree of inherent worth it is right to allow the good of humans to outweigh or override the good of nonhumans when there is a conflict between them. Humans, being a higher type of entity, are more worthy of having their good furthered.

The central argument of Lombardi's paper runs as follows. (1) Animals, plants, and humans are different types of living things. (2) These types are differentiated by the range of their capacities. (3) The greater the range of an entity's capacities, the higher the degree of its inherent worth. On the basis of these propositions and the further proposition that (4) humans have a greater range of capacities than animals and plants, it is concluded that humans are superior in inherent worth to animals and plants.

There is no doubt that the range of human capacities extends beyond that of animals and plants, if "range" refers to various kinds of capacities, such as those exercised in abstract reasoning, moral judgment, and aesthetic creativity. These may all be contrasted with biological capacities (reproduction, growth, adaptation to environment, and other functions common to all living things) and with mere physical capacities such as motion and rest. Humans have these biological and physical capacities and, in addition, the psychological, moral, cognitive, and cultural capacities that are

[10] Louis G. Lombardi, "Inherent Worth, Respect, and Rights," *Environmental Ethics* 5/3 (Fall 1983): 257-270.

special to them. Thus they have a wider range of capacities than other living things.

The crucial point at issue, however, is this: Why does having a wider range of capacities correlate with, or serve as the ground for, greater inherent worth? Unless this connection is made clear, no conclusion concerning human superiority follows from the mere fact that humans have additional capacities to those found in other species.

The general principle by which degrees of inherent worth are to be determined is stated by Lombardi thus: "a type of being that (1) has the capacities of other beings and (2) has additional capacities that differ in kind from the capacities of other beings, ought to have more inherent worth."[11] In support of the reasonableness of this principle, Lombardi asserts that ". . . it is simply an extension of the strategy used for determining grounds for ascribing any inherent worth."[12] Just as any inherent worth is ascribed to a living thing because it has certain capacities not found in nonliving objects, so differences in "levels" of inherent worth can be posited for different kinds of living things, where differences in kind are based on different ranges of capacities.

This reasoning overlooks what it is about all living things that serves as the ground of their inherent worth (if they do have any inherent worth). It is not their capacities taken by themselves. Rather, it is the fact that those capacities are organized in a certain way. They are interrelated functionally so that the organism as a whole can be said to have a good of its own, which it is seeking to realize. The concepts of benefit and harm, of what is good for it or bad for it, of faring well or poorly, and other connected ideas must be applicable to such an entity. For it is by virtue of its having a good of its own that we can meaningfully say that its good is deserving of moral concern and consideration, and that the realization of its good is to be promoted and protected *for the sake of* the being whose good it is. Insofar as all living

[11] Ibid., pp. 263-264.   [12] Ibid., p. 264.

things are ascribed some inherent worth, it is the simple truth that each one has a good of its own that counts as the sufficient ground for such worth. Lombardi himself takes this view of the sufficient ground for any living thing's inherent worth. For him as for me, this is what their having inherent worth *means*, as distinct from their being inherently valuable to—because they happen to be valued by— some person or group of persons.

There is no analogous line of thought that would entitle us to use differences in capacities among living things as grounds for ascribing different degrees of inherent worth to them. To say that some have greater worth than others is to say that the good of some is more deserving of realization than that of others. The fact that organisms can be categorized into various types according to their different ranges of capacities does not provide any reason for such a judgment of differential worth. Assuming, as Lombardi does, that the inherent worth of an entity is not something that is conditional upon its being valued by humans, but depends solely on the fact that it has a good it is seeking to realize, then unless differing ranges of capacities can be shown to make a difference in worth, the mere fact that some beings have a wider range of capacities than others has no bearing on the issue. Those with a relatively narrow range of capacities (plants and single-celled protozoa, for example) can, after all, realize their good at an optimum level by the actualization of those capacities under favorable environmental conditions. They don't need any additional capacities to have the kind of existence that, for those of their species, constitutes a good life. Why should their capacities be played down, or assigned a lower grade, simply because they are not as wide as the capacities of others (who need such capacities for the realization of *their* good)?

Lombardi cites Peter Singer's statement that ". . . concern for the well-being of a child growing up in America would require that we teach him to read; concern for the well-being of a pig may require no more than that we leave him alone with other pigs in a place where there is adequate food and room to run freely."[13] This is just what would be required if we have a moral duty to give the same consideration to the well-being of children and pigs alike. The variation in how they are to be treated is due to the fact that what furthers a child's good does not further a pig's, and vice versa. It has nothing to do with a difference in the worth of a child and a pig.

A second sort of consideration is raised by Lombardi in connection with what he takes to be the crucial relevant difference in kind between humans and other animals. This is the set of capacities that enable humans to be moral agents.[14] He grants that these capacities are not more *valuable* (in the instrumental sense) than those of animals, since animals can realize their good without them. But he claims that these capacities do provide the ground for a higher level of inherent worth.

Why do the capacities of moral agency endow greater inherent worth on an entity which has them, when compared to an entity lacking them? Lombardi's answer to this question makes reference to the idea that humans, being moral agents, have rights while animals and plants do not. Even if we agree with this (and in Chapter Five I shall give my reasons for agreeing with it), it does not follow that humans have greater worth than animals or plants. Here is why.

Lombardi reasons thus: To have moral rights is to have valid moral claims to certain things, such as life and liberty. These claims cannot justifiably be overridden by the interests of others or by the furthering of others' well-being. This status of having supreme priority is the role that rights perform in a moral system. Thus one would never be justified in violating a human being's rights simply in order to help an animal or plant realize its good. But, continues

[13] Ibid., p. 265. The quotation is from Peter Singer, *Animal Liberation: A New Ethics for Our Treatment of Animals* (New York: A New York Review Book, 1975), p. 6.
[14] Lombardi, "Inherent Worth," pp. 265-266.

Lombardi, if we accept this inference, aren't we granting that those who have moral rights are inherently superior to those who lack such rights, since we are giving greater weight to the interests of the former than to the interests of the latter?

The difficulty with this argument is that it illegitimately moves from the role of rights in a system of *human* ethics, where the claims of moral rights override all other moral considerations, to making rights play a similar role with reference to the relations between humans and nonhumans. That I have a valid moral claim which other moral agents have a duty to acknowledge and respect does not entail anything about how I should treat, or be treated by, animals and plants. Since they are not moral agents it is nonsense to talk about their respecting or not respecting my rights. Human rights simply have no role to play in relation to the actions of animals and plants. They don't place any constraints on such organisms, as they do place constraints on the actions of humans.

A human right to life, for example, is a valid moral claim which the right-holder has *against other humans*. It is a claim that entails the negative duty on the part of others not to deprive one of life and the positive duty to protect one if one's life is threatened. Those who have such duties must of course be moral agents, since only moral agents can be under the requirements of moral principles and rules. Animals and plants are not the sort of beings that have duties and therefore they cannot do wrong. It follows that if they should somehow be the cause of a person's death, they are not to be judged as having done a wrong in violating the person's right to life. Such cases are not similar in any morally relevant respect to the act of murder in human affairs, where causing another's death is seen as a violation of the victim's right to life.

Human rights, then, are not claims that validly hold against animals and plants. Even if animals and plants do not have rights themselves, they may yet possess a degree or amount of inherent worth equal to that of humans. To say that they possess a worth equal to ours means that we owe duties to them that are prima facie as stringent as those we owe to our fellow humans. It means that, other things being equal, their good is to be given as much weight in moral deliberation as our own good. This by itself tells us nothing about what ought to be done, all things considered, when there is an unavoidable conflict between furthering their good and respecting the rights of humans. (It is not clear to me, for example, that our liberty-right to use paper products always overrides the well-being of the trees that would have to be cut down for the paper.) When we have validly binding prima facie duties of equal stringency that are in conflict, some principle must be appealed to in order to find a fair way to resolve the conflict. Unless it can be shown that the fair way is always to fulfill the rights of humans at the expense of the good of animals and plants, the principle is not determined in advance by any consideration of which entities have rights and which do not. Now, a principle of always favoring human rights over the good of nonhumans *would* be entailed by the proposition that humans have greater inherent worth than nonhumans. But reference to the concept of rights has not enabled Lombardi to establish the truth of this proposition.

I have now examined three main historical sources and one contemporary defense of the idea that a human being has more inherent worth than any other kind of living thing. No doubt other sources and arguments could be found in Western intellectual history, but I hope to have shown that, as far as these four examples are concerned, conceptual confusion and unsound reasoning make them unacceptable. Assuming that other attempts would fare no better,[15]

[15] The doctrine of human superiority has been forcefully attacked in three contemporary studies, using arguments quite different from mine. A utilitarian case against "speciesism" is given in Singer, *Animal Liberation*. "Speciesism" is defined as "a prejudice or attitude of bias toward the in-

we are left with the conclusion that the claim to human superiority as regards inherent worth is a widely accepted but totally unfounded dogma of our culture. In the absence of any convincing reasons establishing the claim, it is arbitrary to pick out one genetic structure (defining but one species among millions of others) and, disregarding its merits or its relation to anything else, simply state that it is superior in worth to any other genetic structure.

To show that a claim is groundless, however, is not to show that it is false. That there are no good reasons for affirming a proposition does not mean there are good reasons for denying it. So our critical assessment of arguments given in support of the claim to human superiority does not itself justify the *denial* of that claim. It is the denial of human superiority, however, and not merely the assertion that it is groundless, which constitutes the fourth component of the biocentric outlook on nature. How, then, can this fourth component be established?

The thesis I shall defend here is that the transition from the groundlessness of the assertion of human superiority to its denial is made by way of accepting the first three elements of the biocentric outlook analyzed earlier in this chapter: the conception of humans as members of the Earth's Community of Life; the view of nature as a system of interdependence of which we along with all other living things are integral parts; and our awareness of the reality of the lives of individual organisms seen as teleological centers of life. Once we acknowledge the groundlessness of the claim to human superiority and also accept these three elements of the biocentric outlook, we then find that claim to

---

terests of members of one's own species and against those of members of other species" (*ibid.*, p. 7). In a different philosophical context, Val and Richard Routley have shown the many mistakes and confusions in arguments that have been offered in support of "human chauvinism." R. and V. Routley, "Against the Inevitability of Human Chauvinism," in K. E. Goodpaster and K. M. Sayre, eds., *Ethics and Problems of the 21st Century* (Notre Dame, Ind.: University of Notre Dame Press, 1979), pp. 36-59. A third criticism of the idea of human superiority over certain animals is set forth in Regan, *The Case for Animal Rights*, chapters 7 and 8.

be unjustified. If it can further be shown that there are good reasons for accepting the first three elements of the biocentric outlook, we can rightly conclude that the claim to human superiority must be rejected by any rational and informed person.

I am not arguing that a strict formal deduction can be made here. I do not believe it is possible to show that a logical entailment holds between the first three elements of the biocentric outlook and the fourth. It seems to me that the negative statement, "It is not the case that humans are superior to other forms of life," does not follow by logical necessity from the three premises: "Humans are members of the Earth's Community of life"; "All living things are related to one another in an order of interdependence"; "Each organism is a teleological center of life." The argument I offer is an informal one. I propose the reasonableness of denying human superiority on the ground that the whole notion of human superiority over other species does not fit coherently into the view of nature and life contained in the first three elements of the biocentric outlook. These elements taken together, I hold, would be found acceptable as a total world-perspective by any rational, informed person who has a developed capacity of reality-awareness regarding the lives of individual organisms. (This point will be fully defended in the next section of this chapter.)

My justification for the denial of human superiority, then, comes down to this. If we view the realm of nature and life from the perspective of the first three elements of the biocentric outlook, we will see ourselves as having a deep kinship with all other living things, sharing with them many common characteristics and being, like them, integral parts of one great whole encompassing the natural order of life on our planet. When we focus on the reality of their individual lives, we see each one to be in many ways like ourselves, responding in its particular manner to environmental circumstances and so pursuing the realization of its own good. It is within the framework of this conceptual system that the idea of human superiority is found to be unreasonable. If this conceptual framework became our own way of looking at the natural world and if the groundlessness of the notion of human superiority were brought clearly before us, we would not remain intellectually neutral toward that notion but would reject it as being fundamentally at variance with our total world outlook. In the absence of any good reasons for accepting it, the idea that humans are superior to all other living things would appear simply as an irrational bias in our own favor. And the same way of thinking would apply to any claim that one species is inherently superior to another. Such a claim would appear completely arbitrary and unreasonable from the viewpoint of the first three elements of the biocentric outlook.

The rejection of the idea of human superiority and, more broadly, of the idea that any species is inherently superior (or inferior) to any other, entails its positive counterpart: the principle of species-impartiality. This is the principle that every species counts as having the same value in the sense that, regardless of what species a living thing belongs to, it is deemed to be prima facie deserving of equal concern and consideration on the part of moral agents. Its good is judged to be worthy of being preserved and protected as an end in itself and for the sake of the entity whose good it is. Subscribing to the principle of species-impartiality, we now see, means regarding every entity that has a good of its own as possessing inherent worth—the *same* inherent worth, since none is superior to another.

In the last chapter it was shown that insofar as one thinks of an organism as possessing inherent worth, one conceives it to be the appropriate object of the moral attitude of respect, that attitude itself being considered to be the only fitting or suitable one for an agent to take toward the entity in question. Thus it is through the denial of human superiority (and of the superiority of any other species) along with the correlative affirmation of the principle of species-impartiality that the biocentric outlook is linked to the attitude of respect for nature.

A crucial factor in my overall argument for the rational

justifiability of the attitude of respect for nature has now been brought to light. We see that the attitude is not only made intelligible by the biocentric outlook but is also supported by it in a special way. If the outlook is accepted, the attitude is understood to be the only appropriate one to take toward all wild creatures of the Earth's Community of Life. Thus if it can be shown that there are good reasons for accepting the biocentric outlook, taking the attitude of respect for nature will thereby be shown to rest on rational grounds. It will be my aim in the following section to specify what sort of reasons there are for accepting the biocentric outlook and to make clear why they are good (sound, adequate) reasons.

6. *The Argument for the Biocentric Outlook*

The four elements that make up the biocentric outlook fit together in an internally coherent way to form a comprehensive view of the entire realm of life and nature on our planet. The whole biosphere of the Earth and the role that human life plays in it are encompassed in one unified vision. The biocentric outlook, we might say, provides a general "map" of the natural world, enabling us to see where we are and how we fit into the total scheme of things. It presents the realm of nature and life as a setting for human existence. Our history, our culture, our ways of living, our individual values are viewed against the wider background of the natural environment and evolutionary change. We come to see how all that gives meaning to human existence is made possible by the surrounding conditions of life and nature.

From the perspective of the biocentric outlook we see ourselves as biological creatures. Without denying our special abilities or our uniqueness, we nevertheless become fully aware that we are but one species of animal life. This biological aspect of our human existence places certain requirements and constraints on the manner in which we conduct ourselves in relation to the Earth's physical environment and its living inhabitants. Our oneness with all the other members of the great Community of Life is acknowledged and confirmed.

The perspective of the biocentric outlook also reveals to us the significance of our ecological situation. We understand that we are an integral part, along with every species that shares the Earth with us, of a world order that is structured in a certain way. Each individual organism, each species-population, each biotic community is one component in that whole, and all these living constituents of the natural world order are related to one another as functionally interdependent units. In this respect humans are no different from the others.

In addition, when we accept the biocentric outlook and when we view the realm of life and nature from its perspective, our awareness of the moment-to-moment existence of each living thing is sharpened and clarified. Concentrated attention upon a particular organism discloses certain features that we as individuals share with it. Like ourselves, other organisms are teleological centers of life. The constant tendency of their behavior and internal processes is patterned around the realization of their good. Although the content of our good and the means by which we pursue it may be vastly different from theirs, the teleological order exemplified both in our lives and in theirs signifies a fundamental reality common to all of us. What is more, the uniqueness of each organism, human or nonhuman, is made manifest in the particular way it carries on its daily existence in its given circumstances.

Finally, within the conceptual framework provided by all the foregoing beliefs about ourselves and other living things, we are disposed to view all species of animals and plants in an impartial light. None is then deemed more worthy of existence than another. And just as we humans place intrinsic value on the opportunity to pursue our own good in our own individual ways, so we consider the realization of the good of animals and plants to be something that should be valued as an end in itself. As moral agents we see ourselves under an ethical requirement to give equal consideration to the good of every entity, human and non-human alike, that has a good of its own. When the good of one conflicts with that of another, we recognize the duty to be initially unbiased in our approach to finding a way to resolve the conflict. Since all are viewed as having the same inherent worth, the moral attitude of respect is equally due to each.

This account sums up what it means to accept the biocentric outlook on nature. By what reasoning can it be shown to be rationally acceptable? On what grounds would any moral agent be justified in accepting it? To answer these questions I propose the following argument. First I will show that the biocentric outlook satisfies certain well-established criteria for the acceptability of a philosophical world view. Then I will argue that insofar as moral agents are rational, factually enlightened, and have a developed capacity of reality-awareness, they will adopt those criteria as the basis for deciding what outlook on nature to accept as their own. Thus the reasoning is in two distinct steps, the first being a matter of pointing out certain characteristics of the biocentric outlook that make it prima facie worthy of being accepted by moral agents, and the second a matter of showing why those characteristics do in fact justify the acceptance of that outlook by moral agents.

When considered as a whole the biocentric outlook exemplifies a set of properties that satisfy certain classical, well-established criteria for judging the acceptability of philosophical world views. These criteria are traditional ones, found throughout the history of philosophy. They are:

(a) Comprehensiveness and completeness.

(b) Systematic order, coherence, and internal consistency.

(c) Freedom from obscurity, conceptual confusion, and semantic vacuity.

(d) Consistency with all known empirical truths.

These criteria have served as tests for the overall adequacy and satisfactoriness of a world view. When we apply them to the biocentric outlook, I submit, we find them to be fully met.

(a) *Comprehensiveness and completeness.* With respect to the scope of the biocentric outlook, which is limited to the natural ecosystems on our planet, their communities of life, and the relation of human existence to those ecosystems and communities, the outlook provides a comprehensive view that leaves out nothing important or relevant. It gives us a total philosophical perspective on the whole realm of life and nature on Earth. From that perspective we gain a unified vision of all the salient features of that world. Further, the structure of that world is articulated in the pattern of relationships it describes as holding among organisms and between organisms and their environments. Thus we are able to grasp the total order of that world and locate our "place" in it. Finally, the picture of life and nature set forth in the biocentric outlook leaves no serious gaps in our understanding. It is a fully adequate world view regarding the domain of reality it is intended to cover.

(b) *Systematic order, coherence, and internal consistency.* The internal coherence of the biocentric outlook as a whole should be evident from the account contained in this chapter of its four components and their relations to each other. It became clear as we proceeded that all the elements fit together not only without any inconsistencies among them but also in a mutually reinforcing way. Although it is not a logically formal system, the outlook brings together and systematizes a set of ideas that make good sense when conjoined. For this reason I have often referred to the outlook as a belief-system. It constitutes a well-ordered set of concepts and propositions. Of special note is the manner in which the fourth (the denial of human superiority) is connected with and supported by the other three. But each of the elements has its proper "fit" in the total scheme so that the resulting structure of thought presents a cohesive, unified account of the whole domain of life and nature on our planet.

(c) *Freedom from obscurity, conceptual confusion, and semantic vacuity.* Although the belief-system of the biocentric outlook contains many abstract concepts and broad generalizations (which are found in any philosophical world view), these ideas and beliefs can be stated with a fair degree of clarity and precision. Because the entire outlook is firmly rooted in the findings of the physical and biological sciences, it is not flawed by obscure notions and vague abstractions. When value judgments and normative principles are introduced, as in the discussion of the idea of human superiority, they are given clear, unambiguous expression. As far as statements about reality and existence are concerned, the outlook makes no vacuous or tautological claims. We are not confronted with a wall of obscure terms, confused images, or unhelpful and misleading metaphors. On the contrary, the outlook enhances our understanding of and sharpens our focus on the natural world and our place in it.

(d) *Consistency with all known empirical truths.* The relation between the biocentric outlook and scientific knowledge has been frequently brought out in this chapter. There is both a negative and a positive aspect of this relation. Negatively, the belief-system of the outlook contains no empirically false propositions, as far as can be ascertained on the basis of present knowledge in the physical and biological sciences. Positively, the belief-system of the outlook may be said to be "informed by" scientific knowledge. By this I mean that the empirical or factual content of the belief-system is dependent upon and shaped by the ongoing discoveries of the physical and biological sciences. As these sciences advance, the biocentric outlook is modified accordingly. Its empirical content is constantly expanded to accommodate new observations, newly established hypotheses, new explanatory theories. If revolutions occur in those sciences, revolutions will also take place in the outlook. Thus it will always present a scientifically enlightened way of understanding the system of nature. In its description of the order and objects of the empirical world, the biocentric outlook will be acceptable not only to the scientific community itself but also to all those who are scientifically informed.

Assuming that the foregoing account of the biocentric outlook is accurate, do the characteristics pointed out justify our accepting it? Do they recommend the outlook to our rational assent? It might at first seem that they do. But all that actually has been shown is that the outlook meets the standard, established criteria for judging the acceptability of a philosophical world view. What must now be made clear is that those standard, established criteria are the very tests that moral agents, under ideal conditions for accepting a world view, would use in deciding whether to adopt one particular world view as their own. The ideal conditions for accepting a world view, in other words, are those which, when fulfilled by moral agents, would put them in the best possible position for choosing one world view rather than another to be their own way of understanding the domain of reality in which, as agents, they will be acting.

The ideal conditions in question are three: rationality of thought and judgment, factual enlightenment, and a developed capacity of reality awareness. I shall now briefly discuss each condition and then indicate why they are the traits that would make a moral agent an ideally competent evaluator of world views. The argument will conclude by showing the connection between the concept of an ideally competent evaluator and the four established criteria for the acceptability of a world-view given above.[16]

Rationality of thought and judgment covers a number of rather closely interrelated capacities and dispositions. There is, first, objectivity, the capacity and disposition to take into account only reasons that are relevant to the decision to be made, and only reasons that are open to all inquirers for consideration. Objectivity means being disposed to consider only the merits of an argument, regardless of who offers it and regardless of their motives. In examining the reasons for and against any world view, the objective evaluator avoids all *ad hominem* appeals. Closely allied to objectivity is detachment, or the disposition to be disinterested in one's judgment. One is not swayed by the fact that accepting a world view would be in one's personal interest or in the interests of one's family, friends, social group, race, sex, or any other particular class of persons.

Other traits of an ideally rational evaluator are logicality (the capacity and disposition to reason deductively in accordance with the rules of valid inference) and what might be called "belief-rationality" (the capacity and disposition to hold factual beliefs only when one has good evidence in support of them, and to hold them with a degree of conviction proportional to the level of probability warranted by the evidence). A rational evaluator will also have the powers of lucidity and preciseness in thinking, and will be dis-

[16] The answer to the question, Why should people who are not fully rational, enlightened, and aware be obligated to do what they *would* be committed to doing *if* they were ideally rational, enlightened, and aware?, lies in being able to show that people are actually committed to what they would accept under these ideal conditions. This point is well argued in David Zimmerman, "The Force of Hypothetical Commitment," *Ethics* 93/1 (April 1983): 467-483.

posed to insist on conceptual clarity in understanding the content of any world view being assessed.

In addition to these capacities and dispositions, rationality includes two others: critical reflection and independence of judgment. An ideally rational evaluator will be reflectively critical in judging the merits of a world view, constantly raising questions and doubts concerning its meaning and adequacy as an account of a domain of objects and events. Independence of judgment is the capacity and disposition to think for oneself and so exercise full autonomy as a reasoner. A rational evaluator will not simply accept the reasons offered by another, and will reject any appeal to authority (unless the authority appealed to is an expert who can give reasons open to all inquirers to examine and evaluate for themselves).

These various characteristics of rationality are all relevant to the question of how the acceptance of a philosophical world view is to be justified. A world view, we have seen, is a belief-system that provides a general conception of reality covering a wide domain or "world" of objects and events. (Some are intended to cover the whole of existence, the entire domain of what there is.) To accept a world view is to understand in a certain way the world in which one exists and acts. This understanding includes an overall picture or "map" of the structure and order of things and events, including the experiences and circumstances of human living. Now, in order to decide whether there are good grounds for accepting any such belief-system, it is necessary to be a competent evaluator. Being rational in the various senses given above is one aspect of competence in this area of decision making. For one must have a clear and complete grasp of all the concepts and propositions, reasons and principles that make up the content of the belief-systems being evaluated. To have such a grasp one must be able and disposed to think objectively, disinterestedly, logically, informedly, lucidly, critically, and autonomously. Being a *fully* competent evaluator of world views requires that these capacities and dispositions be raised to an ideal level of rational thought and judgment.

The second general condition for an ideally competent evaluator is simply the condition of having well-established empirical knowledge of all relevant matters of fact. A relevant matter of fact in the given context is any empirically confirmable truth included in or presupposed by the system of beliefs constituting a world view whose acceptability is being judged. Since having empirical knowledge is a matter of degree, we can think of an ideal condition of factual enlightenment in terms of being as fully informed as possible, on the basis of all available evidence, concerning the empirical content of every alternative world view among which a decision is to be made.

It is quite obvious why this condition is a qualification for being an ideally competent judge in respect of evaluating the acceptability of world views. One can only judge competently if one thoroughly knows what one is judging, and this includes knowing whatever empirical truths are part of, or presupposed by, the world views among which the decision is being made.

The third ideal condition refers to a moral agent's capacity for heightened awareness of the reality of individual organisms' lives. The organisms in question are all those about which a world view makes assertions. In addition, they are all the organisms whose conditions of life would be affected for better or for worse by an agent's accepting a world view. The moment a world view is accepted by an agent it comes to have a direct bearing on practical life. Its belief-system underlies and supports certain fundamental attitudes, which in turn are expressed in normative principles that guide the agent's choice and conduct. In this way a world view has consequences for the good of living things.

The kind of reality awareness of individual organisms that is an aspect of an ideally competent judge has been described earlier in connection with the third component of the biocentric outlook on nature. We saw how a state of heightened consciousness of the individuality of each living thing is developed through close observation of its behavior and environmental circumstances. One becomes more fully and more deeply cognizant of what it means to be that particular center of life. One is thus enabled to take its standpoint and imaginatively to view the world from its perspective. On the basis of this capacity one can then make accurate judgments concerning what is favorable or detrimental to the realization of its good.

Why would an ideally competent evaluator have the capacity for this kind of awareness? The answer is that this kind of reality awareness increases an evaluator's understanding of all that is involved in the acceptance of the world views which are being assessed. It yields a kind of knowledge that goes beyond the factual enlightenment of the second condition. Since the actual lives of organisms are either directly referred to in the belief-system of a world view or would be affected by its acceptance, to know *all* that is relevant to evaluating a world view requires having this special kind of knowledge concerning the reality of organisms' lives.

The second step of the argument is now in order. This is to show that moral agents who are fully rational, enlightened, and reality-aware, and hence who are competent evaluators of the acceptability of world views, will use as their basis of evaluation the standard criteria discussed earlier: (a) Comprehensiveness and completeness; (b) Systematic order, coherence, and internal consistency; (c) Freedom from obscurity, conceptual confusion, and semantic vacuity; and (d) Consistency with all known empirical truths.

To see why ideally competent evaluators would use these criteria as tests for the overall adequacy of a world view, let us ask ourselves: What would such evaluators look for in a world view to decide whether it is acceptable? They would certainly want to know whether it gives a complete description of all important aspects of the domain of reality it is intended to cover, or only presents a partial view. They would likewise want to know whether it provides an understanding of a world order with reference to which human existence can be seen to occupy a certain role or place in the total scheme. In these matters comprehensiveness and completeness will be among their chief criteria of acceptability.

Next, any belief-system that is internally inconsistent will immediately be rejected by rational judges on logical grounds. But if the various propositions and principles of a belief-system support each other in a coherent way, comprising a clearly delineated and unified outlook, this will be taken to be a reason for preferring it to one that lacks a cohesive and well-ordered structure. Consistency, systematization, and internal coherence are criteria that competent judges will apply.

The condition of freedom from obscurity, conceptual confusion, and semantic vacuity will naturally be a major factor in the judgment of those who have a firm disposition to think lucidly and to formulate their ideas with clarity and precision. The degree to which the concepts of a belief-system are clearly defined and carefully elucidated, and the extent to which they bring out useful distinctions and are applied in illuminating ways, to that extent the world view being presented will be assessed favorably by competent judges.

Finally, with regard to a world view's being not only consistent with all empirically known facts but also "informed" by scientific discoveries and advances, these characteristics will be considered relevant because competent evaluators themselves are factually enlightened and have a developed capacity for reality awareness. Any world view that is known by them to contain false beliefs or to give an inadequate account of the lives of individual organisms will be found unacceptable.

My conclusion is that ideally competent evaluators of world views would indeed use the established criteria enumerated. If this is granted, then we have a complete argument for the justifiability of accepting the biocentric outlook as one's world view of the domain of life and nature on our planet. For we saw that the biocentric outlook does satisfy to a high degree the criteria in question. Since these are the very conditions that would make any world view acceptable to ideally competent evaluators, the biocentric outlook will be judged acceptable by those who are in the best position to consider the matter. It therefore seems to me to be reasonable to affirm that the biocentric outlook on nature is, from the philosophical point of view, an acceptable world view in its domain.

It must be emphasized here that the biocentric outlook has not been *proven*. It cannot be. The only sort of reasoning it is possible to use in trying to establish its justifiability, I submit, is that given in this section. Since world views are neither formal deductive systems nor explanatory scientific theories, neither pure logic nor the procedures of empirical confirmation are appropriate methods. We have seen that deciding the overall adequacy of a world view does *include* applying the tests of deductive validity and inductive probability. But these are parts of a larger process of rational justification. It is this larger process which I have tried to explicate and apply in my argument. If that argument holds up, then we can have at least reasonable confidence in asserting that there are good reasons for any moral agent's accepting the biocentric outlook on nature.

Since the biocentric outlook underlies, supports, and makes intelligible the attitude of respect for nature, the foregoing argument also provides a justification for taking that attitude toward all the wild living things of the Earth's natural ecosystems. It was shown earlier that when the whole biosphere of our planet and the relation of humans to it are understood in terms of the four components of the biocentric outlook, the attitude of respect is seen to be the only appropriate attitude for moral agents to take toward the natural world and its living inhabitants. Thus if there are good grounds for a moral agent's accepting the world view contained in the biocentric outlook, there are likewise good grounds for a moral agent's taking the attitude of respect for nature. In this way the foundations of the whole system of environmental ethics I am defending are made explicit and shown to be philosophically sound.

FOUR

THE ETHICAL SYSTEM

1. *The Basic Rules of Conduct*

Two of the three parts of the theory of environmental ethics being defended here, the biocentric outlook and the attitude of respect for nature, have now been examined in detail. It remains for us to consider the third component, which is the system of standards and rules that moral agents would be guided by if they were to accept the biocentric outlook and take the attitude of respect for nature.

As we saw in Chapter Two, when moral agents have the attitude of respect for nature they subscribe to a set of normative principles and hold themselves accountable for adhering to them. The principles comprise both standards of good character and rules of right conduct. The attitude of respect is embodied or expressed in their character and conduct to the extent that their character fulfills the standards and their actions are in accordance with the rules. It is, indeed, a test of the sincerity and depth of one's moral commitment in taking that attitude whether one acknowledges the ethical requirements imposed by those standards and rules and holds oneself responsible for abiding by them.

The rules and standards constitute a system of ordered principles, the details of which I shall be making explicit in this chapter. For convenience of exposition I shall first discuss rules of conduct and the priority principles for ordering them. Then I shall consider standards of good character and the types of virtues associated with the various rules of conduct.

The first thing to notice is that the rules to be set forth are principles that specify different types of duty. These principles do not themselves always determine what a particular moral agent in a particular set of circumstances ought to do, all things considered. The rules of duty, in other words, tell us what general *kinds* of actions we are morally required to perform or refrain from performing. Such a rule prescribes that we are duty-bound to do or not do a particular act of a given kind *unless* there is a contrary duty that is more stringent than and hence overrides the given duty. However, in the absence of any contrary duty the rule does determine what we are morally required to do or not do in a particular set of circumstances.

In a situation where two or more contrary rules apply, we are confronted with a conflict of duties. If we follow one rule we violate others. We then do not know what we ought to do, all things considered. In order to decide what is the act that should be done in these circumstances we must find out which alternative open to our choice is the one that has the weightiest moral reasons behind it; that is to say, we must know which of the conflicting duties takes priority over all the others. This will be determined by an ordering of the rules according to a set of priority principles. On the basis of those principles we can make a well-grounded judgment as to which duty outweighs the others in the given circumstances. In this section I shall discuss only the basic rules of duty, putting aside until the following section consideration of priority principles.

A second level of conflict of duties occurs when the rules of a valid system of environmental ethics are in opposition to the rules of a valid system of human ethics. In these cases if we carry out our duties to animals and plants in natural ecosystems we fail in our duties toward our fellow humans, but if we fulfill the latter we do not do what is required of us regarding the good of nonhumans. So even when we have worked out an acceptable ordering among the rules of the ethics of respect for nature we still must decide on what priorities hold between that system and the rules that bind us in the domain of human ethics. I shall explore this problem at length in Chapter Six, where I make some suggestions about resolving conflicts between human ethics and environmental ethics. We must therefore keep in mind during the discussion that follows that any of the duties enumerated below might be outweighed in certain circumstances by duties that moral agents owe to humans. The fact that we have a duty not to destroy or harm animals and plants in natural ecosystems does not mean that, all things considered, we must never do such things under any circumstances whatever. It only means that we must not do them without a valid moral reason that justifies our overriding the duty to refrain. Such a reason might derive from priority principles within a system of environmental ethics, as well as from the more general priority principles that range over environmental and human ethics.

I shall now set out and examine four rules of duty in the domain of environmental ethics. This is not supposed to provide an exhaustive account of every valid duty of the ethics of respect for nature. It is doubtful whether a complete specification of duties is possible in this realm. But however that may be, the duties to be listed here are intended to cover only the more important ones that typically arise in everyday life. I suggest later on, in connection with the discussion of priority principles, that in all situations not explicitly or clearly covered by these rules we should rely on the attitude of respect for nature and the biocentric outlook that together underlie the system as a whole and give it point. Right actions are always actions that express the attitude of respect, whether they are covered by the four rules or not. They must also be actions which we can approve of in the light of the various components of the biocentric outlook. (These topics will be taken up in the next section of the chapter.)

The four rules will be named (a) the Rule of Nonmalefi-cence, (b) the Rule of Noninterference, (c) the Rule of Fidel-ity, and (d) the Rule of Restitutive Justice.

(a) *The Rule of Nonmaleficence*. This is the duty not to do harm to any entity in the natural environment that has a good of its own. It includes the duty not to kill an organism and not to destroy a species-population or biotic commu-nity, as well as the duty to refrain from any action that would be seriously detrimental to the good of an organism, species-population, or life community. Perhaps the most fundamental wrong in the ethics of respect for nature is to harm something that does not harm us. (The ethical treat-ment of organisms which are *harmful* to us will be consid-ered in Chapter Six, under the heading of the principle of self-defense.)

The concept of nonmaleficence is here understood to cover only nonperformances or intentional abstentions. The rule defines a negative duty, requiring that moral agents refrain from certain kinds of actions. It does not re-quire the doing of any actions, such as those that *prevent* harm from coming to an entity or those that help to *alleviate* its suffering. Actions of these sorts more properly fall under the heading of benefiting an entity by protecting or pro-moting its good. (They will be discussed in connection with the Rule of Restitutive Justice.)

The Rule of Nonmaleficence prohibits harmful and de-structive acts done by moral agents. It does not apply to the behavior of a nonhuman animal or the activity of a plant that might bring harm to another living thing or cause its death. Suppose, for example, that a Rough-legged Hawk pounces on a field mouse, killing it. Nothing morally wrong has occurred. Although the hawk's behavior can be thought of as something it does intentionally, it is not the action of a moral agent. Thus it does not fall within the range of the Rule of Nonmaleficence. The hawk does not violate any duty because it *has* no duties. Consider, next, a vine which over the years gradually covers a tree and finally kills it. The activity of the vine, which involves goal-oriented movements but not, of course, intentional actions, is not a moral wrongdoing. The vine's killing the tree has no moral properties at all, since it is not the conduct of a moral agent.

Let us now, by way of contrast, consider the following case. A Peregrine Falcon has been taken from the wild by a falconer, who then trains it to hunt, seize, and kill wild birds under his direction. Here there occurs human conduct aimed at controlling and manipulating an organism for the enjoyment of a sport that involves harm to other wild organisms. A wrong is being done but not by the falcon, even though it is the falcon which does the actual killing and even though the birds it kills are its natural prey. The wrong that is done to those birds is a wrong done by the falconer. It is not the action of the Peregrine that breaks the rule of duty but the actions of the one who originally captured it, trained it, and who now uses it for his own amusement. These actions, it might be added, are also violations of the Rule of Noninterference, since the falcon was removed from its wild state. Let us now turn our attention to this second rule of duty.

(b) *The Rule of Noninterference*. Under this rule fall two sorts of negative duties, one requiring us to refrain from placing restrictions on the freedom of individual organisms, the other requiring a general "hands off" policy with regard to whole ecosystems and biotic communities, as well as to individual organisms.

Concerning the first sort of duty, the idea of the freedom of individual organisms which is relevant here was analyzed in some detail in Chapter Three. According to that analysis, freedom is absence of constraint, where a constraint is any condition that prevents or hinders the normal activity and healthy development of an animal or plant. A being is free in this sense when any of four types of constraints that could weaken, impair, or destroy its ability to adapt successfully to its environment are absent from its existence and circumstances. To be free is to be free *from* these constraints and to be free *to* pursue the realization of one's good according to the laws of one's nature. The four types of constraints, with some examples of each, are:

(i) Positive external constraints (cages; traps).
(ii) Negative external constraints (no water or food available).
(iii) Positive internal constraints (diseases; ingested poison or absorbed toxic chemicals).
(iv) Negative internal constraints (weaknesses and incapacities due to injured organs or tissues).

We humans can restrict the freedom of animals and plants by either directly imposing some of these constraints upon them or by producing changes in their environments which then act as constraints upon them. Either way, if we do these things knowingly we are guilty of violating the Rule of Noninterference.

The second kind of duty that comes under this rule is the duty to let wild creatures live out their lives in freedom. Here freedom means not the absence of constraints but simply being allowed to carry on one's existence in a wild state. With regard to individual organisms, this duty requires us to refrain from capturing them and removing them from their natural habitats, *no matter how well we might then treat them*. We have violated the duty of noninterference even if we "save" them by taking them out of a natural danger or by restoring their health after they have become ill in the wild. (The duty is not violated, however, if we do such things with the intention of returning the creature to the wild as soon as possible, and we fully carry out this intention.) When we take young trees or wildflowers from a natural ecosystem, for example, and transplant them in landscaped grounds, we break the Rule of Noninterference *whether or not we then take good care of them and so enable them to live longer, healthier lives than they would have enjoyed in the wild*. We have done a wrong by not letting them live out their lives in freedom. In all situations like these we intrude into the domain of the natural world and terminate an organism's existence as a wild creature. It does not matter that our treatment of them may improve their strength, promote their growth, and increase their chances for a long, healthy life. By destroying their status as wild animals or plants, our interference in their lives amounts to an absolute negation of their natural freedom. Thus, however "benign" our actions may seem, we are doing what the Rule of Noninterference forbids us to do.

Of still deeper significance, perhaps, is the duty of noninterference as it applies to the freedom of whole species-populations and communities of life. The prohibition against interfering with these entities means that we must not try to manipulate, control, modify, or "manage" natural ecosystems or otherwise intervene in their normal functioning.[1] For any given species-population, freedom is the absence of human intervention of any kind in the natural lawlike processes by which the population preserves itself from generation to generation. Freedom for a whole biotic community is the absence of human intervention in the natural lawlike processes by which all its constituent species-

[1] Although no ethical system is presented by Tom Regan in his essay, "The Nature and Possibility of an Environmental Ethic," he does set forth the following rule, which is somewhat broader than my rule of noninterference but captures its essence. Regan calls this "the preservation principle" and explains it as follows: *"The admiring respect of what is inherently valuable in nature gives rise to the preservation principle.* By the 'preservation principle' I mean a principle of nondestruction, noninterference, and, generally, nonmeddling. By characterizing this in terms of a principle, moreover, I am emphasizing that preservation (letting be) be regarded as a moral imperative." See Regan, "The Nature and Possibility of an Environmental Ethic," *Environmental Ethics* 3:1 (Spring 1981): 31-32 (the italics are Regan's). As an example Regan gives this: "Thus, if I regard wild stretches of the Colorado River as inherently valuable and regard these sections with admiring respect, I also think it wrong to destroy these sections of the river; I think one ought not to meddle in the river's affairs, as it were" (p. 32). Regan goes on to say that the preservation principle would not be a principle of environmental ethics if it were overridable by considerations of human benefit. Regan thus takes an anti-anthropocentric stance in his account of what "an environmental ethic" must be.

populations undergo changing ecological relationships with one another over time. The duty not to interfere is the duty to respect the freedom of biologically and ecologically organized groups of wild organisms by refraining from those sorts of intervention. Again, this duty holds even if such intervention is motivated by a desire to "help" a species-population survive or a desire to "correct natural imbalances" in a biotic community. (Attempts to save endangered species which have almost been exterminated by past *human* intrusions into nature, and attempts to restore ecological stability and balance to an ecosystem that has been damaged by past *human* activity are cases that fall under the Rule of Restitutive Justice and may be ethically right. These cases will be considered in connection with that rule.)

The duty of noninterference, like that of nonmaleficence, is a purely negative duty. It does not require us to perform any actions regarding either individual organisms or groups of organisms. We are only required to respect their wild freedom by letting them alone. In this way we allow them, as it were, to fulfill their own destinies. Of course some of them will lose out in their struggle with natural competitors and others will suffer harm from natural causes. But as far as our proper role as moral agents is concerned, we must keep "hands off." By strictly adhering to the Rule of Noninterference, our conduct manifests a profound regard for the integrity of the system of nature. Even when a whole ecosystem has been seriously disturbed by a natural disaster (earthquake, lightning-caused fire, volcanic eruption, flood, prolonged drought, or the like) we are duty-bound not to intervene to try to repair the damage. After all, throughout the long history of life on our planet natural disasters ("disasters," that is, from the standpoint of some particular organism or group of organisms) have always taken their toll in the death of many creatures. Indeed, the very process of natural selection continually leads to the extinction of whole species. After such disasters a gradual readjustment always takes place so that a new set of relations among species-populations emerges. To abstain from intervening in this order of things is a way of expressing our attitude of respect for nature, for we thereby give due recognition to the process of evolutionary change that has been the "story" of life on Earth since its very beginnings.

This general policy of nonintervention is a matter of disinterested principle. We may want to help certain species-populations because we like them or because they are beneficial to us. But the Rule of Noninterference requires that we put aside our personal likes and our human interests with reference to how we treat them. Our respect for nature means that we acknowledge the sufficiency of the natural world to sustain its own proper order throughout the whole domain of life. This is diametrically opposed to the human-centered view of nature as a vast piece of property which we can use as we see fit.

In one sense to have the attitude of respect toward natural ecosystems, toward wild living things, and toward the whole process of evolution is to believe that nothing goes wrong in nature. Even the destruction of an entire biotic community or the extinction of a species is not evidence that something is amiss. If the causes for such events arose within the system of nature itself, nothing improper has happened. In particular, the fact that organisms suffer and die does not itself call for corrective action on the part of humans *when humans have had nothing to do with the cause of that suffering and death.* Suffering and death are integral aspects of the order of nature. So if it is ever the case in our contemporary world that the imminent extinction of a whole species is due to entirely natural causes, we should not try to stop the natural sequence of events from taking place in order to save the species. That sequence of events is governed by the operation of laws that have made the biotic Community of our planet what it is. To respect that Community is to respect the laws that gave rise to it.

In addition to this respect for the sufficiency and integrity of the natural order, a second ethical principle is implicit in the Rule of Noninterference. This is the principle of species-impartiality, which serves as a counterweight to the dispositions of people to favor certain species over others and to want to intervene in behalf of their favorites. These dispositions show themselves in a number of ways. First, consider the reactions of many people to predator-prey relations among wildlife. Watching the wild dogs of the African plains bring down the Wildebeest and begin devouring its underparts while it is still alive, they feel sympathy for the prey and antipathy for the predator. There is a tendency to make moral judgments, to think of the dogs as vicious and cruel, and to consider the Wildebeest an innocent victim. Or take the situation in which a snake is about to kill a baby bird in its nest. The snake is perceived as wicked and the nestling is seen as not deserving such a fate. Even plant life is looked at in this biased way. People get disturbed by a great tree being "strangled" by a vine. And when it comes to instances of bacteria-caused diseases, almost everyone has a tendency to be on the side of the organism which has the disease rather than viewing the situation from the standpoint of the living bacteria inside the organism. If we accept the biocentric outlook and have genuine respect for nature, however, we remain strictly neutral between predator and prey, parasite and host, the disease-causing and the diseased. To take sides in such struggles, to think of them in moral terms as cases of the maltreatment of innocent victims by evil animals and nasty plants, is to abandon the attitude of respect for all wild living things. It is to count the good of some as having greater value than that of others. This is inconsistent with the fundamental presupposition of the attitude of respect: that all living things in the natural world have the same inherent worth.

The principle of species-impartiality is logically connected with the Rule of Noninterference. It entails that we must not intervene in the natural course of events to further the good of certain organisms at the expense of others. Of special importance for practical considerations, we are duty-bound not to intervene in behalf of those creatures that happen to be beneficial to us. When we achieve the objective contemplation of the whole order of nature which our acceptance of the biocentric outlook involves, we renounce the point of view that makes human interests and human values the center of concern. To respect nature is to be willing to take the standpoint of each organism, no matter what its species, and view the world from the perspective of its good. None makes a greater claim on our sympathy than another. In this light the Rule of Noninterference can be seen to embody the moral attitude of respect for nature.

(c) *The Rule of Fidelity*. This rule applies only to human conduct in relation to individual animals that are in a wild state and are capable of being deceived or betrayed by moral agents. The duties imposed by the Rule of Fidelity, though of restricted range, are so frequently violated by so many people that this rule needs separate study as one of the basic principles of the ethics of respect for nature.

Under this rule fall the duties not to break a trust that a wild animal places in us (as shown by its behavior), not to deceive or mislead any animal capable of being deceived or misled, to uphold an animal's expectations, which it has formed on the basis of one's past actions with it, and to be true to one's intentions as made known to an animal when it has come to rely on one. Although we cannot make mutual agreements with wild animals, we can act in such a manner as to call forth their trust in us. The basic moral requirement imposed by the Rule of Fidelity is that we remain faithful to that trust.

The clearest and commonest examples of transgressions of the rule occur in hunting, trapping, and fishing. Indeed, the breaking of a trust is a key to good (that is, successful) hunting, trapping, and fishing. Deception with intent to harm is of the essence. Therefore, unless there is a weighty moral reason for engaging in these activities, they must be condemned by the ethics of respect for nature. The weighty moral reason in question must itself be grounded on disinterested principle, since the action remains wrong in itself in virtue of its constituting a violation of a valid moral rule. Like all such violations, it can be justified only by appeal to a higher, more stringent duty whose priority over the duty of fidelity is established by a morally valid priority principle.

When a man goes hunting for bear or deer he will walk through a woodland as quietly and unobtrusively as possible. If he is a duck hunter he will hide in a blind, set out decoys, use imitative calls. In either case the purpose, of course, is to get within shooting range of the mammal or bird. Much of the hunter's conduct is designed to deceive the wild creature. As an animal is approaching, the hunter remains quiet, then raises his rifle to take careful aim. Here is a clear situation in which, first, a wild animal acts as if there were no danger; second, the hunter by stealth is deliberately misleading the animal to expect no danger; and third, the hunter is doing this for the immediate purpose of killing the animal. The total performance is one of entrapment and betrayal. The animal is manipulated to be trusting and unsuspicious. It is deliberately kept unaware of something in its environment which is, from the standpoint of its good, of great importance to it. The entire pattern of the hunter's behavior is aimed at taking advantage of an animal's trust. Sometimes an animal is taken advantage of in situations where it may be aware of some danger but instinctively goes to the aid of an injured companion. The hunter uses his knowledge of this to betray the animal. Thus when the hunting of shorebirds used to be legally permitted, a hunter would injure a single bird and leave it out to attract hundreds of its fellows, which would fly in and gather around it. This way the hunter could easily "harvest" vast numbers of shorebirds. Even to this day a similar kind of trickery is used to deceive birds. Crow hunters play recordings of a crow's distress calls out in the field. The recording attracts crows, who are then easy targets to shoot. This aspect of hunting, it should be repeated, is not some peripheral aberration. Much of the excitement and enjoyment of hunting as a sport is the challenge to one's skills in getting animals to be trusting and unsuspecting. The cleverer the deception, the better the skill of the hunter.

Consider, next, the case of trapping. Traps are set in locations where the "target" animals are expected to pass by and the traps are concealed to take the animals by surprise. Most traps are also baited to lure the animals into them. The very terms "bait" and "lure" being used in this context entail the notion of betrayal of a trust. To set out bait in order to lure an animal into a trap is deliberately and purposefully to break faith with a creature (in-fidelity). A note might be added here to give some idea of the extent of destruction of wildlife currently taking place in the United States by legal trapping. (It is mostly done by the use of steel leghold traps, which hold an animal by one leg. Some animals, in their pain and terror, chew off their own leg to escape.) The following figures were released by one state's Fish and Game Department (Arizona, 1980-81) on the total numbers of fur-bearing species trapped in one season: 14,871 coyotes, 26,150 gray foxes, 2,897 kit foxes, 9,696 bobcats, 3,289 ringtails, 1,127 badgers, 839 raccoons, 4,063 skunks, 83 beavers, and 2,949 muskrats.[2] Although trapping is sometimes done to obtain food or to protect crops and livestock, in recent years it has been almost entirely a matter of making quick profits by selling skins to the fur trade.

Just as violations of the Rule of Fidelity are central to the activities of hunting and trapping, so they are equally central to fishing. The fisherman's use of lures, bait, "flies," and even the simple acts of wiggling and jerking a fishing line are all aimed at attracting the fish and getting it hooked. The skilled fisherman is the one who (aside from "fishermen's luck") can most effectively deceive the fish and so

[2] *Defenders* (magazine of Defenders of Wildlife) 56/5 (October 1981): 45.

succeed in betraying it. It should not be overlooked that *a fish is a wild animal*, just as much as a mammal on land or a bird in the air is a wild animal. Fishes are wild animals because they exist in natural ecosystems and because they are members of species that belong to the animal kingdom (along with birds, mammals, reptiles, amphibia, crustacea, insects, and other classes of organisms). That fishing is not usually viewed in the same way as hunting is mainly due to the fact that the fish's ecosystem is hidden from us by the surface of the water. But if we have ever gone scuba-diving or snorkeling, we have seen what the undersea environment is like. There all sorts of marine life, both animal and plant, live together in natural ecosystems just as do creatures on the Earth's land surface. Each species has its own ecological "niche" and its own particular habitat. Food chains, predator-prey relations, migratory patterns, and other aspects of a complex functioning ecosystem are all present beneath the surface. Perhaps if we land-based humans could keep before our minds a clear image of that underwater world as we gaze upon the surface of a lake, a stream, or an ocean, the ethical aspects of fishing would be seen in a truer light.

It is not a question here of whether the animal being hunted, trapped, or fished has a *right* to expect not to be deceived. The animal is being deceived in order to bring advantage to the deceiver and this itself is the sign that the deceiver considers the animal as either having no inherent worth or as having a lower degree of inherent worth than the deceiver himself. Either way of looking at it is incompatible with the attitude of respect for nature. Of course, hunters, trappers, and fishermen often say they have great respect for the animals. (Think of those who struggle for hours after hooking a big game fish from their yachts, "battling" the fish to hold it on the line and finally bring it in. They will express admiration for the "fighting spirit" of the fish and will claim to have great respect for it.) It should be clear, however, that in all such claims to respect the animal it is *appraisal* respect, not recognition respect, that is meant. Animals are being admired, are being held in high regard, for their various excellences or merits, those characteristics that make the hunting, trapping, or fishing of them an exciting challenge. Appraisal respect, however, is a matter of the degree to which something is esteemed because of its merits. But as we saw in Chapter Two, inherent worth and the recognition respect appropriate to it must be sharply contrasted with the idea of different degrees of merit and the varying attitudes of appraisal respect called forth by those degrees of merit.

Besides breaking the Rule of Fidelity, hunting, trapping, and fishing also, of course, involve gross violations of the Rules of Nonmaleficence and Noninterference. Whether such practices can ever be justified on moral grounds is an issue that will be considered in Chapter Six, where conflicts between the duties of environmental ethics and those of human ethics are analyzed and resolved. It may be the case that in circumstances where the only means for obtaining food or clothing essential to human survival is by hunting, trapping, or fishing, these actions are morally permissible. The ethical principles that justify them could stem from a system of human ethics based on respect for persons plus a priority principle that makes the duty to provide for human survival outweigh those duties of nonmaleficence, noninterference, and fidelity that are owed to nonhumans. But when hunting and fishing are done for sport or recreation, they cannot be justified on the same grounds. I shall take up this question, which involves separating subsistence hunting and fishing from sport hunting and fishing, in Chapter Six.

There are cases of deceiving and breaking faith with an animal, however, which can be justified *within* the system of environmental ethics. These cases occur when deception and betrayal must (reluctantly) be done as a necessary step in a wider action of furthering an animal's good, this wider action being the fulfillment of a duty of restitutive justice. If breaking faith is a temporary measure absolutely needed to alleviate great suffering or to prevent serious harm coming to an animal, such an act may be required as an instance of restitutive justice. Putting aside for the moment a consideration of the idea of restitutive justice as it applies to environmental ethics, it may be helpful to look at some examples.

Suppose a grizzly bear has wandered into an area close to human habitation. In order to prevent harm coming not only to people but also to the bear (when people demand that it be killed), the bear may be deceived so that it can be shot with harmless tranquilizer darts and then, while it is unconscious, removed to a remote wilderness area. Another example would be the live-trapping of a sick or injured animal so that it can be brought to an animal hospital, treated, and then returned to the wild when it is fully recovered. Still another kind of case occurs when a few birds of an endangered species are captured in order to have them raise young in captivity. The young would then be released in natural habitat areas in an effort to prevent the species from becoming extinct.

These human encroachments upon the wild state of mammals and birds violate both the Rule of Noninterference and the Rule of Fidelity. But the whole treatment of these creatures is consistent with the attitude of respect for them. They are not being taken advantage of but rather are being given the opportunity to maintain their existence as wild living things.

What the Rule of Fidelity absolutely forbids is the exploiting of a situation where an animal is deliberately led to be trusting, or is made unaware of any danger, as a way to further the nonmoral interests of humans to the detriment of the animal. Let it be repeated that there need not have been any agreement made between human and animal. The animal acts in a certain manner because it does not suspect that the situation is threatening or dangerous, and the human knows this. Indeed, the human may be doing his best to hide from the animal the threat or danger that his presence poses for it. When the animal is then taken advantage of by this deception, it is being treated as a mere means to human ends.

We can easily see here an outright negation of respect for nature. Hunters and fishermen often argue that they show true respect for nature because they advocate (and pay for) the preservation of natural areas which benefit wild species-populations and life communities. And it is quite true that the setting aside of many "wildlife refuges," both public and private, has resulted from their efforts. Wild animals and plants have benefited from this. What is being overlooked in this argument is the difference between doing something to benefit oneself which happens also to benefit others, and doing something with the purpose of benefiting others as one's ultimate end of action. Hunters and fishermen want only those areas of the natural environment protected that will provide for them a constant supply of fish, birds, and mammals as game. Indeed, sportsmen will often urge the killing of nongame animals that prey on "their" (the sportsmen's) animals. In Alaska, for example, hunters have persuaded state officials to "manage" wolves—the method used is to shoot them from helicopters—so as to ensure that a large population of moose is available for hunting. The argument that hunters and fishermen are true conservationists of wildlife will stand up only when we sharply distinguish conservation (saving in the present for future consumption) from preservation (protecting from both present and future consumption). And if the ultimate purpose of conservation programs is future exploitation of wildlife for the enjoyment of outdoor sports and recreation, such conservation activities are not consistent with respect for nature, whatever may be the benefits incidentally brought to some wild creatures. As I pointed out in Chapter Two, having the attitude of respect for nature involves not only actions but also reasons for actions. Actions that bring about good consequences for wildlife do not express the attitude of respect unless those actions are motivated in a certain way. It must be the case that the actions are done with the intention of promoting or protecting the good of wild creatures as an end in itself and for the sake of those creatures themselves. Such motivation is precisely what is absent from the conservation activities of sportsmen.

(d) *The Rule of Restitutive Justice*. In its most general terms this rule imposes the duty to restore the balance of justice between a moral agent and a moral subject when the subject has been wronged by the agent. Common to all instances in which a duty of restitutive justice arises, an agent has broken a valid moral rule and by doing so has upset the balance of justice between himself or herself and a moral subject. To hold oneself accountable for having done such an act is to acknowledge a special duty one has taken upon oneself by that wrongdoing. This special duty is the duty of restitutive justice. It requires that one make amends to the moral subject by some form of compensation or reparation. This is the way one restores the balance of justice that had held between oneself and the subject before a rule of duty was transgressed.

The set of rules that make up a valid system of ethics define the true moral relations that hold between agents and subjects. When every agent carries out the duties owed to each subject and each subject accordingly receives its proper treatment, no one is wronged or unjustly dealt with. As soon as a rule is willfully violated, the balance of justice is tilted against the agent and in favor of the subject; that is, the agent now has a special burden to bear and the victim is entitled to a special benefit, since the doing of the wrong act gave an undeserved benefit to the agent and placed an unfair burden on the subject. In order to bring the tilted scale of justice back into balance, the agent must make reparation or pay some form of compensation to the subject.

The three rules of duty so far discussed in this section can be understood as defining a moral relationship of justice between humans and wild living things in the Earth's natural ecosystems. This relationship is maintained as long as humans do not harm wild creatures, destroy their habitats, or degrade their environments; as long as humans do not interfere with an animal's or plant's freedom or with the overall workings of ecological interdependence; and as long as humans do not betray a wild animal's trust to take advantage of it. Since these are all ways in which humans can express in their conduct the attitude of respect for nature, they are at the same time ways in which each living thing is given due recognition as an entity possessing inherent worth. The principles of species-impartiality and of equal consideration are adhered to, so that every moral subject is treated as an end in itself, never as a means only.

Now, if moral agents violate any of the three rules, they do an injustice to something in the natural world. The act destroys the balance of justice between humanity and nature, and a special duty is incurred by the agents involved. This is the duty laid down by the fourth rule of environmental ethics, the Rule of Restitutive Justice.

What specific requirements make up the duty in particular cases? Although the detailed facts of each situation of an agent's wrongdoing would have to be known to make a final judgment about what sorts of restitutive acts are called for, we can nevertheless formulate some middle-range principles of justice that generally apply. These principles are to be understood as specifying requirements of restitution for transgressions of *any* of the three rules. In all cases the restitutive measures will take the form of promoting or protecting in one way or another the good of living things in natural ecosystems.

In working out these middle-range principles it will be convenient to distinguish cases according to what type of moral subject has been wronged. We have three possibilities. An action that broke the Rule of Nonmaleficence, of Noninterference or of Fidelity might have wronged an individual organism, a species-population as a whole, or an

187

entire community. Violations of the Rules in all cases are ultimately wrongs done to individuals, since we can do harm to a population or community only by harming the individual organisms in it (thereby lowering the median level of well-being for the population or community as a whole). The first possibility, however, focuses on the harmed individuals taken separately.

If the organisms have been harmed but have not been killed, then the principle of restitutive justice requires that the agent make reparation by returning those organisms to a condition in which they can pursue their good as well as they did before the injustice was done to them. If this cannot wholly be accomplished, then the agent must further the good of the organisms in some other way, perhaps by making their physical environment more favorable to their continued well-being. Suppose, on the other hand, that an organism has been killed. Then the principle of restitutive justice states that the agent owes some form of compensation to the species-population and/or the life community of which the organism was a member. This would be a natural extension of respect from the individual to its genetic relatives and ecological associates. The compensation would consist in promoting or protecting the good of the species-population or life community in question.

Consider as a second possibility that a whole species-population has been wrongly treated by a violation of either nonmaleficence or noninterference. A typical situation would be one where most of the animals of a "target" species have been killed by excessive hunting, fishing, or trapping in a limited area. As a way of making some effort to right the wrongs that have been committed, it would seem appropriate that the agents at fault be required to ensure that permanent protection be given to all the remaining numbers of the population. Perhaps the agents could contribute to a special fund for the acquisition of land and themselves take on the responsibility of patrolling the area to prevent further human intrusion.

Finally, let us consider those circumstances where an entire biotic community has been destroyed by humans. We have two sorts of cases here, both requiring some form of restitution. The first sort of case occurs when the destructive actions are not only wrong in themselves because they violate duties of nonmaleficence and noninterference but are wrong, all things considered. They are not justified by a rule of *either* environmental ethics *or* of human ethics. The second sort of case is one in which the actions are required by a valid rule of human ethics though they are contrary to valid rules of environmental ethics. Even when greater moral weight is given to the rule of human ethics, so that the actions are justified, all things considered, they still call for some form of restitution on grounds of justice to all beings having inherent worth. This idea holds also within the domain of human ethics.

A duty of restitutive justice (as a corollary of the Rule of Reciprocity) arises whenever one of the other valid rules of human ethics is broken. Even if the action was required by a more stringent duty, a human person has been unjustly treated and therefore some compensation is due her or him. That the action was morally justified, all things considered, does not license our overlooking the fact that someone has been wronged. Hence the propriety of demanding restitution. (We shall see in the next chapter how this principle also applies to all cases of the violation of people's rights.) So in our present concerns, even if the destruction of a biotic community is entailed by a duty of human ethics that overrides the rules of environmental ethics, an act of restitutive justice is called for in recognition of the inherent worth of what has been destroyed.

There are many instances in which human practices bring about the total obliteration of biotic communities in natural ecosystems. Whether or not these practices are justified by valid rules of human ethics, they all come under the Rule of Restitutive Justice. A northern conifer woodland is cut down to build a vacation resort on the shore of a lake. A housing development is constructed in what had been a pristine wilderness area of cactus desert. A marina and yacht club replace a tidal wetland which had served as a feeding and breeding ground for multitudes of mollusks, crustacea, insects, birds, fish, reptiles, and mammals. A meadow full of wildflowers, both common and rare, is bulldozed over for a shopping mall. Strip mining takes away one side of a mountain. A prairie is replaced by a wheat farm. In every one of these situations and in countless others of the same kind, wholesale destruction of entire natural ecosystems takes place. Unrestrained violence is done to whole communities of plants and animals. Communities that may have been in existence for tens of thousands of years are completely wiped out in a few weeks or a few days, in some cases in a few hours. What form of restitution can then be made that will restore the balance of justice between humanity and nature? No reparation for damages can possibly be given to the community itself, which exists no more. As is true of a single organism that has been killed, the impossibility of repairing the damage does not get rid of the requirement to make some kind of compensation for having destroyed something of inherent worth.

If restitutive justice is to be done in instances of the foregoing kind, what actions are called for and to whom are they due? Two possibilities suggest themselves here. One is that compensation should be made to another biotic community which occupies *an ecosystem of the same type* as the one destroyed. If it is a northern conifer woodland, then the organizations or individuals who were responsible for its destruction owe it to the life community of another conifer woodland to help it in some way to further or maintain its well-being. Perhaps a partially damaged area of woodland could be restored to ecological health (removing trash that had been put there, cleaning up a polluted stream flowing through the area, stopping any further contamination by acid rain or other atmospheric pollution, and so on).

The other possible recipient of compensation would be any wild region of nature that is being threatened by human exploitation or consumption. Compensatory action would be taken in behalf of a biotic community somewhere on Earth that might be damaged or destroyed unless special efforts are made to protect it. Acquiring the land and giving it legal status as a nature preserve would be suitable measures.

These suggested middle-range principles are all derived from the one broad Rule of Restitutive Justice: that any agent which has caused an evil to some natural entity that is a proper moral subject owes a duty to bring about a countervailing good, either to the moral subject in question or to some other moral subject. The perpetrating of a harm calls for the producing of a benefit. The greater the harm, the larger the benefit needed to fulfill the moral obligation.

It is worth adding here that all of us who live in modern industrialized societies owe a duty of restitutive justice to the natural world and its wild inhabitants. We have all benefited in countless ways from large-scale technology and advanced modes of economic production. As consumers we not only accept the benefits of industrialization willingly, but spend much of our lives trying to increase those benefits for ourselves and those we love. We are part of a civilization that can only exist by controlling nature and using its resources. Even those who go out to a natural area to enjoy "the wilderness experience" are recipients of the benefits of advanced technology. (What marvels of modern chemistry went into the creation of plastics and synthetic fabrics in their backpacks, tents, sleeping bags, and food containers!) None of us can evade the responsibility that comes with our high standard of living; we all take advantage of the amenities of civilized life in pursuing our individual values and interests. Since it is modern commerce, industry, and technology that make these amenities possible, each of us is a consumer and user of what the natural world can yield for us. Our well being is constantly being furthered at the expense of the good of the Earth's nonhuman inhabitants. Thus we all should share in the cost of preserving and restoring some areas of wild nature for the sake of the plant and animal communities that live there. Only then can we claim to have genuine respect for nature. (Further consideration of the relation between human civilization and the natural world will be given in Chapter Six.)

This completes my account of the four basic types of duty in the Ethics of Respect for Nature. In order to show how these constitute an orderly and consistent system of norms, their interrelations must be examined and their various degrees of stringency compared. What moral weight is to be assigned to the different types of duty? Reference to certain priority principles is necessary for answering this. This will be the focus of our concern in the next section.

2. *Priority Principles*

The rules of duty we have discussed lay down four sorts of moral requirements upon the choice and conduct of moral agents. By themselves they do not tell moral agents what they should do, all things considered, in any given set of circumstances. They specify only those properties of actions that are morally relevant considerations for agents to take into account when deciding what they ought or ought not to do. If a course of action open to their choice has one of these properties, they are duty-bound to choose or refrain from choosing that course unless some other more important countervailing consideration applies. Thus a rule of duty provides a good reason for (or against) performing an action, but not a morally sufficient reason. A morally sufficient reason would be given in an all-things-considered judgment that a certain action ought or ought not be done when all its morally relevant properties are recognized and duly weighed. To arrive at such a judgment, different comparative weights would have to be assigned to the properties according to the degree of their ethical importance. The question we must now confront is: How is the degree of ethical importance to be determined?

As before, it should be noted that we are here concerned solely with the internal order of a valid system of environmental ethics and are disregarding the norms of human ethics, which might be applicable to the same sets of circumstances. My procedure will be to locate sources of conflict among the four rules we have considered and to suggest priority principles for resolving those conflicts.

Starting with the Rule of Nonmaleficence, the first thing to note is that the duty not to harm cannot conflict with the duty of noninterference. Our refraining from intruding into the natural world can never itself bring about harm to wild creatures. To keep a "hands off" policy, however, may mean that we allow a natural cause of harm to take its course without our intervention. This is not to act contrary to the Rule of Nonmaleficence since it is not an action of ours that brings about the harm. The duty of nonmaleficence is only a negative one, prohibiting us from performing a harm-causing act. It does not obligate us to act to *prevent* harm from occurring. Thus our decision not to intervene in the workings of natural ecosystems never conflicts with the duty of nonmaleficence.

Since acts of fidelity and of restitutive justice *can* conflict with the duty of nonmaleficence, we must now determine the relative precedence of those duties. The priority principle that seems most in keeping with the attitude of respect for nature is that the duty of nonmaleficence outweighs those of fidelity and restitutive justice.

A situation of conflict between fidelity and nonmaleficence would *not* be the sort of circumstances where people led animals to trust them and then did harm to them. For in that case both duties, fidelity and nonmaleficence, would be violated. An example of conflict between the two would be the following. Suppose we have encouraged wild animals to come and live in a national park by making the park environment favorable to them and by laying down rules and regulations that prohibit hunting, disturbing natural habitat, or any molestation of the park's wildlife. If these human-produced conditions should lead to an overabundance of one species so that the whole ecosystem is profoundly disordered, we might then have to remove some members of that species from the park to restore the ecosystem. It may be necessary in that case to break faith with some in order not to do harm to others. This seems to be a justifiable solution to the dilemma because our respect for nature would seem to demand it rather than the alternative of letting the entire ecosystem be seriously damaged. So in that kind of situation nonmaleficence overrides fidelity.

The second sort of conflict is that between nonmaleficence and restitutive justice. We should first make every effort to avoid such conflicts by choosing methods of making restitution that do not involve harming any animals or plants. In fact, the usual ways of fulfilling the duty of restitutive justice do not bring harm to wildlife. Cleaning up a polluted river, saving an endangered species from extinction, and setting aside wilderness sanctuaries are cases in point. The direct intention and aim of such measures, of course, is to promote or protect the good of living things, although accidents might happen in carrying them out that cause some harm. But we can normally avoid conflicts between nonmaleficence and restitutive justice by taking care in our choice of ways to make reparation or give compensation for past wrongs. Nevertheless it is possible for situations to arise where conflicts are unavoidable. In such situations we should give priority to nonmaleficence, for otherwise we would be committing a further wrong in an attempt to make up for a past wrong. An example of a conflict of this sort would be the following. There is only one available habitat area to set aside as a protected sanctuary for a certain species-population which we have harmed in the past. To protect the species we would have to kill some of its natural predators in the area. If no other alternative is open to us, then we must not use this method of making restitution to the population in question. We may try to do what we can for other populations of the same species that exist elsewhere, but in any case we should not favor the given population at the expense of other wild creatures. This kind of wildlife "management" is not justifiable. Non-maleficence takes precedence over restitution.

Let us now consider possible conflicts between the duty of noninterference and that of fidelity. (As we saw above, there can be no conflict between noninterference and non-maleficence.) Here again our first moral requirement is to refrain from creating conditions where animals come to trust us if those conditions interfere with their freedom or impose constraints on other wild living things. The Rule of Noninterference must always guide us in deciding how, when, where, and under what circumstances a bond of trust should be *allowed* to develop on the part of animals toward humans. In some situations, however, we may be confronted with a choice of interfering in their lives in order to keep a trust that has *already* developed, or to break the trust and avoid the interference. Here it seems that the negative duty of noninterference can at least sometimes be overridden by the duty of fidelity. The following situation might be considered an instance of this. To prevent people from building fires, throwing out trash, and otherwise degrading a wooded area, the owners have put up a fence around their property, thus restricting the movement of certain small mammals that have come to use the woodland for feeding and breeding. If no serious harm is done to them, though they are being somewhat constrained, then the interference may be justified by fidelity to the animals' trust that the woodland is a safe and healthy place to obtain food and raise a family. It would depend finally on how great a benefit would result for the animals in question.

The general priority principle being appealed to in cases of this sort might be formulated thus. Where the duties of fidelity and noninterference conflict, fidelity takes precedence provided that (a) no serious harm is done by the interference; (b) a great good is brought about by sustaining the trust; (c) there is no way to sustain the trust without interfering; and (d) the interference is kept to the minimum consistent with these conditions. On the other hand, if any of these conditions are not satisfied by an act of interference, the act is not justified.

We turn now to the possibility of conflict between the duties of noninterference and restitutive justice. Here I must again emphasize that it is normally within our power to choose ways of making restitution that do not require interference in the lives of wild creatures. As a restitutive measure we might, for example, outlaw the dumping of toxic wastes in natural habitat areas. Although this places restrictions on the freedom of humans, it does not involve a lessening of the freedom of nonhumans. However, there could occur unusual circumstances where some constraints on wildlife are necessary to benefit those we have wronged in the past. If no permanent harm is caused by those constraints and a great benefit can thereby be produced, we might consider the duty of restitutive justice to outweigh that of noninterference. A case would be the saving of many lives of birds, mammals, reptiles, and other animals by setting up barriers to prevent them from entering a place where radioactive waste has been leaking into the ground. Protecting them in this way might compensate them for the destruction of their original habitat by the building of a nuclear power plant.

Finally there are cases of conflict between fidelity and restitutive justice. In circumstances where such conflicts are unavoidable, restitutive justice outweighs fidelity. For example, we may have to use deception and some element of surprise and betrayal in order to live-trap animals in the process of carrying out a form of restitution to an endangered species. Thus a few California condors may be caught in a captive-breeding program aimed at saving the entire species. It is currently a matter of dispute whether this program will succeed, but if it should, one might consider the instances where it was necessary to break faith with individual birds to be justified by the good that was brought about. Perhaps a clearer and less controversial instance of this type of conflict is given in the sometimes heroic efforts taken to help murres, cormorants, and other sea birds that have been caught in an oil spill. To clean the oil from their feathers the birds must be caught, and this often involves breaking a trust they place in us to leave them alone. As a direct way of making reparation to the creatures suffering from our own past acts, it would seem clear that this attempt to help them justifies the momentary acts of infidelity that cannot be avoided.

It will be helpful to summarize our findings by taking an overall look at the priority relations holding among the four rules of duty. The general picture we then get shows the Rule of Nonmaleficence to be at the top. Our most fundamental duty toward nature (putting aside possible conflicts with the duties of human ethics) is to do no harm to wild living things as far as this lies within our power. Our respect for nature primarily expresses itself in our adhering to this supreme rule.

With regard to the other three rules, we have found that it is usually possible to avoid violations of each of them by carefully choosing how we make restitution and when we set up the conditions that lead to the development of an animal's trust in us. But where conflicts cannot be avoided, the priority principles that generally hold are: (a) Fidelity and restitutive justice override noninterference when a great good is brought about and no creature is permanently harmed by the permitted interference. (b) Restitutive justice outweighs fidelity when a great good is brought about and no serious harm is done to a creature whose trust in us is broken.

It must be added that the two negative rules, to refrain from doing harm and to refrain from interfering in the natural world, are in ordinary circumstances almost always possible to comply with. We can usually find methods of making restitution that do not cause harm to or impose constraints upon living things. The same is true of developing in them the bonds of trust. The major modes of restitution are setting aside wilderness areas, protecting endangered and threatened species, restoring the quality of an environment that has been degraded, and aiding plants and animals to return to a healthy state when they have been weakened or injured by human causes. All of these measures can normally be taken without the necessity of breaking faith with or imposing restrictions upon the creatures of the wild.

Living the right kind of life in relation to the domain of nature and life on Earth is not simply a matter of having our choice and conduct conform to a set of rules and priority principles. The development or cultivation of certain character traits is equally essential. This part of the ethics of respect for nature will be our next subject of investigation.

3. The Basic Standards of Virtue[3]

In Chapter Two the concept of good character was briefly discussed in connection with explaining how the attitude of

[3] My views on virtue and character in this section are greatly influenced by Onora Nell's superb analysis of Kant's theory of moral virtue. See Onora Nell, *Acting on Principle: An Essay on Kantian Ethics* (New York: Columbia University Press, 1975). Kant's main work on character is *The Doctrine of Virtue: Part II of the Metaphysics of Morals,* trans. by Mary J. Gregor (Philadelphia: University of Pennsylvania Press, 1964). I have also gained from G. H. Von Wright's study, *The Varieties of Goodness,* Chapter 7. However, Von Wright connects all virtues with character traits that serve "the good of man" (human well-being, the Human Good). In this respect his views are close to Aristotle's. For Aristotle, virtues are human excellences that enable a person to live a good life (in the sense of realizing the Human Good in one's own life and in the lives of others).

For somewhat different conceptions of virtue, see Philippa Foot, *Virtues and Vices and Other Essays in Moral Philosophy* (Oxford: Basil Blackwell, 1978) and James D. Wallace, *Virtues and Vices* (Ithaca, N.Y.: Cornell University Press, 1978).

respect for nature can be expressed in a moral agent's character. It was stated that there are two aspects of a person's character, one deliberative and the other practical. The deliberative aspect consists in a steady disposition to think rationally and clearly when deliberating about what action would be the right thing for one to do in one's particular circumstances. The kind of situation calling for strength of character, that is, a situation in which one *needs* good character, is that in which one has a tendency to become confused, irrational, or biased in one's thinking. Having good character enables one to overcome that tendency when deliberating.

The practical aspect of good character is having the firm disposition, as well as the needed powers of will and resolve, to carry out one's decision by doing what one has concluded is the right thing in the given circumstances. Good character in its practical aspect is especially needed in situations where it is onerous or difficult to fulfill one's duty, or where doing so requires a real sacrifice of one's interests. We can therefore think of good character as a power of self-mastery and self-control that gives one the strength of will to meet one's responsibilities, particularly in the sorts of circumstances where failure due to weakness of will is common.

With reference to environmental ethics, the attitude of respect for nature is *expressed in one's character* when one has developed firm, steady, permanent dispositions that enable one to deliberate and act consistently with the four rules of duty: Nonmaleficence, Noninterference, Fidelity, and Restitutive Justice. Those dispositions are the virtues or good character traits that make it possible for a moral agent to regularly comply with the four rules and by doing so *express in its conduct* the attitude of respect for nature.

In analyzing the concept of good character in connection with the ethics of respect for nature, we must distinguish two types of character traits, which might be designated the general virtues and the special virtues. The general virtues are those traits of good character needed for deliberating and acting in the right way, no matter what particular moral rules and principles are being applied and followed. Thus a person of general virtue has those qualities of character that undergird and strengthen her or his ability to act morally in any circumstances. The special virtues, on the other hand, are the specific character traits associated with each of the four types of duty. A special virtue is a disposition or set of dispositions that enable moral agents to fulfill a particular kind of duty, such as fidelity. Possession of a special virtue gives one the capacity to deliberate clearly and accurately about what course of conduct a particular duty requires of one in a given situation, and also the capacity to carry out that duty by doing the right thing in the right way for the right reasons in that situation. Special virtues are needed in those circumstances when people are prone to become confused in their thinking about what a certain type of duty requires of them in the complexities of practical life, or when they are prone to shirk a certain type of duty when the time comes to fulfill it.

Putting aside consideration of the special virtues for the moment, let us look at the general virtues connected with the ethical system of respect for nature. There are two fundamental character traits that comprise the general virtues, which might be named "moral strength" and "moral concern." Moral strength covers the following elements of good character: conscientiousness, integrity, patience, courage, temperance or self-control, disinterestedness, perseverance, and steadfastness-in-duty. This cluster of character traits amounts to moral strength in that they are what we need to lead an ethically upright life no matter what particular kinds of duties and responsibilities might be imposed upon us in the varying circumstances of life. Women and men who have moral strength of character possess the developed capacity to give order to their thought and conduct, an order stemming from their firm commitment to moral principles. Whatever might be the particular requirements of duty facing them in a given set of circumstances, they have the inner strength to meet the demands of morality both in their deliberation and their action.

A brief definition of each of the constituent virtues that together comprise the general virtue of moral strength will serve to indicate the kind of character traits involved.

Conscientiousness: The firm desire to do what duty requires of one *because* it is one's duty. (This is not meant to exclude other reasons that may also be part of one's motivation to do the action but it must always be present and, in the absence of other reasons-for-action, must be sufficient to motivate the agent.)

Integrity: Perfect consistency between thought and conduct, so that one's judgments about right and wrong are made manifest in one's acting or refraining from acting on the basis of those judgments.

Patience: The powers of calm endurance and constancy in the pursuit of a troublesome, difficult, boring, or exasperating task required by a rule of duty.

Courage: The ability to think and act in the right way when one finds oneself in frightening, dangerous, or painful circumstances (physical courage), or when one's doing what is right goes against popular opinion and meets with the derision or disapproval of others (moral courage).

Temperance or self-control: The ability to place constraints on one's desires and interests when indulging in them would lead to violations of duty.

Disinterestedness: Objectivity of judgment when considering moral reasons for and against actions open to choice; freedom from undue influence of self-interest and from other distortions of thought (such as wishful thinking, personal prejudices, rationalization, and self-deception).

Perseverance: The capacity to keep at a specific task without giving up in the face of discouragement.

Steadfastness-in-duty: Consistency of right conduct over time as shown in unswerving devotion to duty regardless of obstacles and difficulties in the ever-changing circumstances of daily life.

Each of these constituents of the general virtue of moral strength is, of course, an ideal that no one's actual character ever fully exemplifies. They set standards of moral excellence that people fulfill or fail to fulfill in varying degrees. The duty of moral agents is to cultivate these traits in themselves as much as possible, knowing that each virtue defines an ideal of perfection that can never be completely realized. Such standards of character are nevertheless normative guides to practical life. In the first place they constitute for all moral agents a model of the kind of being each should endeavor to become. Secondly, they establish specific goals to aim at, setting ends that are truly worth striving for. Finally, insofar as they are valid criteria of moral merit, they serve as the proper grounds on which all agents should evaluate the strengths and weaknesses of their own character. In all these ways they are to be considered as important a part of a normative ethical system as rules of duty.

The various traits listed above form a network of interlocking dispositions and capacities which, to the extent that they are realized, endow a moral agent with the power of will needed to act in accordance with rules of duty, whatever content those rules might have. Thus they are elements of a general virtue, which I have referred to as "moral strength."

Turning now to the second of the general virtues, moral concern, we find a set of dispositions and capacities altogether different from, though perfectly compatible with, those that comprise moral strength. In the context of the ethics of respect for nature moral concern is the aspect of character most directly connected with a moral agent's re-

garding all wild living things in the natural world as possessing inherent worth. This, we recall, is presupposed by
the attitude of respect for nature.

Moral concern is the ability and disposition to take the
standpoint of animals or plants and look at the world from
the perspective of their good. Unless this ability and disposition are well developed in a moral agent there will be a
question of whether and to what extent the agent genuinely
has the attitude of respect for nature. For we have seen that
willingness to take the standpoint of an organism is part of
what it means to regard it as an entity possessing inherent
worth. And unless and until we so regard it we have not
taken an attitude of respect toward it. Here we must have
the moral capacity to overcome the all-pervasive tendency
to be dominated by our anthropocentricity, just as in human ethics we must have the power to overcome the ever
present tendency toward egocentricity. In particular, for a
life-centered system of environmental ethics it is necessary
to develop a certain kind of magnanimity. We must achieve
a breadth of concern that enables us to transcend the anthropocentric bias implicit in the assumption that the final
ground of all value is what furthers the good of humans.

Let us now analyze the structure of dispositions and capacities that make up the general virtue of moral concern.
We begin with four basic constituents: benevolence, compassion, sympathy, and caring. Although the terms "benevolence" and "compassion" are somewhat vague in
everyday usage, for our purposes we will consider them to
be the positive and negative aspects, respectively, of sympathy and caring. Benevolence is the capacity and disposition (a) to feel pleased at the realization of another's good,
whether due to one's own action or to some other cause; (b)
to place intrinsic value on the realization of another's good,
and (c) to act so as to promote or protect another's good as
an end in itself and for the sake of the being whose good it
is. The negative counterparts that define compassion are:
(a) the disposition to feel sad or disheartened at another's

pain, suffering, or incapacitation, whether due to one's own action or to some other cause; (b) the disposition to place intrinsic disvalue on or consider intrinsically bad any evil or harm that comes to another; and (c) the disposition to refrain from doing such evil or harm to another. Benevolence and compassion are each thus seen to be made up of a cluster of three dispositions: to have certain *feelings*, to *place value or disvalue on* certain things, and to *act* in ways appropriate to those feelings and valuations. The positive and negative valuations in each case, forming the positive and negative sides of sympathy and caring, are the dispositions to consider what is *good for* an entity as *good in itself* and to consider what is *bad for* an entity as *bad in itself*. It is these valuations that lie behind the benevolent person's disposition to further another's good and the compassionate person's disposition to avoid harming another. Thus to have developed the virtues of benevolence and compassion in one's own character is to have strengthened and deepened one's disposition to have sympathy for others and to care about their well-being. Sympathy and caring are found in the feelings and valuations that motivate one to act benevolently and compassionately toward others.

The relation between sympathy and caring is a very close one. The fellow-feeling that is the heart of sympathy is associated with the disposition to care about what happens to others. They go together. When one feels genuine concern for the well-being of others and so is disposed to help them and refrain from harming them, one also has the disposition of caring. One takes a special interest in the fate of another as to whether it fares well or ill in the circumstance of its life. With such caring goes a willingness to accept responsibility regarding the promotion or protection of its good. Thus sympathy and caring are two inseparable components of the general virtue of moral concern.

It is only when we have developed the character traits of benevolence, compassion, sympathy, and caring with regard to the living things of the natural world that we are disposed to take their standpoint in making ethical judgments concerning how they should be treated. And insofar as we have developed those traits we *will* be so disposed. We will then give equal consideration to all entities that have a good of their own and will place intrinsic value on the realization of their good. In other words, we will regard them as possessing inherent worth and so conceive of them as the appropriate objects of the attitude of respect. Given this attitude toward all wild creatures in the Earth's Community of Life, we will make a moral commitment to abide by the four rules of duty and the priority principles discussed earlier. In this manner, character and conduct together come to express the attitude of respect for nature.

I give the name "moral concern" to the whole structure of dispositions that constitute benevolence, compassion, sympathy, and caring for two reasons. First, this structure defines a general virtue quite different from that which I called "moral strength." Moral concern is a general virtue because it is the set of character traits which any moral agent will exemplify when he or she has sincerely taken the attitude of respect for nature. They are not traits particularized to any of the four rules of duty. Since they form the emotive and valuational background for *all* actions expressive of the attitude of respect, they comprise the motivational base for an agent's moral commitment to the ethical system as a whole.

The second reason for calling this general virtue "moral concern" is that the kind of concern for the well-being of wild animals and plants that respect for nature entails is found in moral agents to the extent that they have benevolence, compassion, sympathy, and caring as integral components of their character. The absence of concern would be an indifference toward the good of living things. Such indifference is incompatible with regarding living things as possessing inherent worth, and hence incompatible with the attitude of respect.

It should be noted that the feelings, valuations, and conative dispositions connected with benevolence, compassion, sympathy, and caring do not suddenly disappear when one of the four duties is overridden by a contrary and more weighty duty (whether of environmental ethics or of human ethics). We have seen that the Rules of Noninterference, Fidelity, and Restitutive Justice can sometimes be outweighed by higher or more stringent duties, and it will be shown in Chapter Six that even the Rule of Nonmaleficence can be overridden in certain circumstances by the system of human ethics based on respect for persons. In cases of this sort the action which a moral agent ought to do, all things considered, is one which violates a rule of duty. A deep sense of regret accompanies the performance of such an action since it does involve an interference in the lives of wild creatures, or an infidelity toward them, or a failure to make restitution, or brings about some harm to them. The feelings and dispositions of sympathy and caring, which extend to all creatures, are still present even though the actions in question are morally justified by priority principles. Benevolence and compassion for those who are treated wrongly by such actions give the moral agents who perform them a feeling of anguish based on their awareness of bringing some intrinsic disvalue into the existence of beings which have inherent worth. There is a sense of frustrated desire, a judgment that worthy ends are being unachieved. To acknowledge the overall rightness of the actions being performed does not diminish in the slightest the agents' sympathy toward and caring for the organisms whose good must be left unrealized. The general virtue of moral concern is exhibited by such conflicting emotions in cases like these. The sense of regret and anguish is in fact one of the chief psychological sources of the desire to make restitution to those who have been wronged.

I turn now to the special virtues. These are character traits needed for compliance with a single rule of duty or with some rules but not others. I shall consider each of the four rules in turn, discussing the special virtues connected with each one.

With reference to the duty of nonmaleficence, the one central virtue is that of *considerateness*. This is the disposition to have the kind of concern for others that shows itself in being attentive to and solicitous for their well-being. Compassion, of course, is one of the foundations of considerateness. But as I shall point out shortly, compassion is a broader, more general disposition than considerateness. To be considerate of another is to have that special concern for the other's good which makes one recoil from ever knowingly bringing harm to the other. In the sphere of action one who is considerate scrupulously adheres to the Rule of Nonmaleficence.

Compassion is a broader concept than considerateness, though a person who lacked compassion for others would tend to be inconsiderate of them. Compassion extends to all living things that suffer, whatever the cause of their suffering. One might feel compassion for creatures that were harmed by some distant natural cataclysm. Considerateness is focused on those particular beings which *we* could harm if we acted in a certain way. Thus being considerate is directly related to a disposition not to harm what we might harm if we are not especially attentive to the effects of our actions on others.

Considerateness is shown not only in the disposition not to harm but also in the disposition not to be negligent. One of the clearest signs of being inconsiderate is to be negligent in matters affecting another's well-being. Negligence is avoidable carelessness regarding the good of others. To be negligent is to take undue risks that might cause harm to others. The considerate person, in contrast, tends to refrain from any act that involves a risk of doing harm. The more probable the chance of doing harm to some entity, and/or the more serious the harm that might be brought about, the stronger the commitment to refrain from the act. Although any act *could* cause harm to some being, the considerate agent is one who does not do things that are judged to have a certain probability of causing harm. The greater the possible harm, the lower the probability needed for deciding against doing the act.

The deliberative aspect of the virtue of considerateness stems from the importance of not being negligent about the welfare of others. To the extent that an agent is considerate of others he or she will take pains to find out, on the best available evidence, whether an alternative of choice will be likely to lead to harm for others *before* making a decision to act. Calculation of probabilities based on good empirical grounds is a major factor in the deliberation of the considerate agent.

Like all other virtues considerateness is an ideal of good character. It sets a standard of excellence which actual moral agents can only approximate in varying degrees. But to the degree that they do fulfill the standard, they will in fact refrain from knowingly bringing harm to living things.

We now examine the special virtues associated with the Rule of Noninterference. There are two character traits in particular which are worth considering here: *regard* and *impartiality*. I use the term "regard" in a rather special way. It is intended to signify that kind of respect for living things which one has when one condemns the placing of constraints upon them, whether or not they are thereby harmed. To have regard for the wildness of individual organisms, species-populations, or whole communities of life in natural ecosystems is to feel antipathy toward any actions that either directly interfere with their freedom or bring about environmental conditions that impose artificial constraints on their ways of living. To have regard for the processes of nature as a whole is to be disposed to feel displeasure at humans' intruding upon the order of things as that order has worked itself out since the beginnings of life on our planet. It is also, of course, to be disposed to refrain from making such intrusions oneself.

Having regard for the natural world in this sense arises from a consideration for the wholeness and integrity of the system of nature as an independent realm of reality existing in its own right. Regard is the due recognition we give to that realm of reality as something worthy of our respect. It is seen to be sufficient in itself, not dependent on human agency for making possible the good of life. The kind of value that belongs to it is acknowledged to be wholly external to and independent of the kind of value which humans can create through their culture and civilization. To have regard for nature is also to have regard for wild living things, for they are part of nature. Hence the disposition to refrain from interfering in their lives, even with the well-meaning intention of saving them from a naturally caused harm.

The virtue of impartiality associated with the Rule of Noninterference is the disposition to be free of bias with reference to different species. It includes the disposition to remain neutral when, under conditions not controlled by humans, the good of one living thing or group of living things is in conflict with the good of another. In order to achieve such impartiality one's personal feelings for or against any particular species must not be allowed to influence one's judgment or conduct. One keeps one's distance from the course of events in nature, regardless of what species are faring well or ill according to the fortunate or unfortunate circumstances of their daily existence.

The idea of impartiality was introduced in Chapter Three in connection with the fourth component of the biocentric outlook (the denial of human superiority). It has also appeared in the present chapter in connection with the duties of nonmaleficence and noninterference, and it will be discussed further at various places in subsequent chapters. Here impartiality is being considered as a character trait. In this context it is seen to be a special virtue in relation to the Rule of Noninterference. A moral agent who has this character trait is firmly committed to a "hands off" policy with regard to natural events and processes as well as to the lives of individual organisms in the wild. To take one example of this kind of impartiality, consider the competition for sunlight, moisture, and soil nutrients among the various plants of a forest. Trees, ferns, vines, and other forms of vegetation struggle to realize their good in conflict with the adjacent flora of their biotic community. Some of the trees and wildflowers of this community may be the "favorites" of a moral agent who could, if he or she wished to do so, intervene in the ecosystem and help these particular plants to grow at the expense of others in competition with them. If such a moral agent possesses the virtue of impartiality, however, he or she will refrain from any actions of that sort, and will so refrain for the reason that treating some plants by favoring them over others is being partial to them. This partiality is seen to be a vice or moral defect insofar as it makes one disposed to act contrary to the duty of noninterference.

Directly related to the Rule of Fidelity is the character trait of *trustworthiness*. This connection is so clear that we will be brief in considering it. With regard to those animals in a wild state which can be deceived, tricked, or betrayed, a trustworthy agent will have a steady, firm disposition never to take advantage of animals in any of those ways. The dominant desire is to conduct oneself consistently with an animal's expectations, especially when those expectations have formed as a result of the actions of humans. A trustworthy person aims always to be open and honest in the presence of sentient creatures. Such a person feels nothing but contempt and disgust at any human behavior intended to break faith with an animal's trust. Similar revulsion is felt toward those who know that an animal is relying on them to do something and they take advantage of this fact to further their own ends at the animal's expense. To develop the virtue of trustworthiness as part of one's character is to enhance one's ability to comply with the Rule of Fidelity and to deepen one's commitment to that rule as a matter of principle.

Associated with the Rule of Restitutive Justice are two distinguishable but closely related virtues: *fairness* and *equity*. These may be distinguished as follows. Fairness is the general disposition to want to restore the balance of justice one has upset by one's own wrong-doing. It is the disposition to "make amends" by paying some form of compensation or making some kind of reparation to those whom one has treated badly. One's sense of fairness comes into play in the recognition that another has a legitimate claim to restitution, a claim against oneself based on one's past actions. A fair person never ignores such a claim. Although being fair does not itself tell a person how to satisfy the claim, it does dispose a person to want to extend some benefit to the claimant in a restitutive act.

The virtue of equity consists in having a sense of the proportionate weighting that corresponds to relevantly different claims of justice. It also consists in the disposition to make restitution in accordance with those relevant claims. It is our sense of equity that leads us to think that treating organisms in the same way is not just when there are morally relevant differences among them. Our sense of equity must be exercised in determining the kind and amount of reparation or compensation which should be made to those who have been unjustly treated in the past. The virtue of equity is the disposition to be scrupulously fair (equitable) in arriving at a balance between harm wrongly done by an agent and an appropriate measure of restitution required of that agent. Although it is often extremely difficult to decide exactly what kind and amount of restitution would be right in a particular case, there are certain modes of treatment that would be clearly wrong because grossly inequitable. By

211

developing the virtue of equity we can understand what it is that makes such conduct inequitable and so, by way of contrast, judge what would at least be a more equitable thing to do. To have a developed sense of what is equitable with respect to human treatment of living things in the natural world is a needed virtue in those circumstances.

When equity is combined with fairness there is a firm foundation in character for achieving the goal of finding the proper restitutive measures to restore the balance of justice between agents and subjects. We can then say that the most reliable judgment concerning what restitution in a given case is most just is that judgment which all who have genuine respect for nature would agree on when they exercised a fully developed capacity of fairness and equity.

These, then, are the general and special virtues that constitute good character on the part of all moral agents bound by the four rules of the ethics of respect for nature. A summary of the relations between rules of conduct and standards of character in that system of ethics may be presented as follows.

RULES OF CONDUCT	STANDARDS OF CHARACTER
I. *The system of rules as a whole*	*General virtues*

Moral Strength
{
Conscientiousness
Integrity
Patience
Courage
Temperance or self-control
Disinterestedness
Perseverance
Steadfastness-in-duty
}

Moral Concern	$\Big\{$ Benevolence Compassion Sympathy Caring

II. *Particular rules* — *Special virtues*

The Rule of Nonmaleficence — Considerateness

The Rule of Noninterference $\big\{$ Regard Impartiality

The Rule of Fidelity — Trustworthiness

The Rule of Restitutive Justice $\big\{$ Fairness Equity

As a concluding note to this examination of the concept of good character in environmental ethics, I wish to consider the question: Are virtues morally obligatory? The answer I shall defend is yes, not only because the virtues are needed for right conduct (doing the right thing for the right reasons) but also because they are obligatory in themselves. There are, in other words, two grounds on which the *duty* to develop and cultivate good character rests. The first is that both general and special virtues are necessary to enable agents to act morally. The second is that there is a duty to strive to become a fully moral being by making one's inner (private) motivational and affective life congruent with the outer (public) life of action and reasons for action. These two points hold for both human ethics and environmental ethics, but I shall here only be concerned with the latter.

Whether the obligatoriness of virtue rests on the first ground or the second, in every case the moral requirement involved is not to *be* virtuous (or to *have* good character) but to *develop and cultivate* virtue or goodness of character. To develop a virtue is to discipline oneself with the aim of acquiring a certain character trait which is lacking or relatively undeveloped in one. To cultivate virtues that one already has is to make the effort to strengthen one's character in those respects in which it is already essentially good. Developing and cultivating virtue means striving for self-improvement in moral matters. When an agent realizes that he or she has certain vices (undesirable character traits as judged from the moral point of view), the duty is to change one's character through the development of those virtues that are lacking and through the cultivation of those that are only weakly present.

Concerning the first ground of the obligatoriness of virtue, I emphasized in my opening account of the general nature of good character that virtues are needed for a person regularly and consistently to do the right thing for the right reason in the right circumstances. Having the feelings, desires, motives, and ends that make up a virtuous character trait helps persons gain the capacities necessary for deliberating clearly and accurately about what course of action they ought to take and for carrying out the decisions they arrive at on the basis of such deliberation. Especially when one is confronted by situations where it is difficult to fulfill one's duty and where there is a tendency to allow self-interest to distort one's thinking, the general virtues are indispensable for acting rightly. I have also pointed out with reference to each of the special virtues how the character traits in question contribute to a person's ability and disposition to abide by the various rules with which those virtues are associated.

In the light of these considerations, we see that the obligatoriness of virtue stems from the conjunction of our duty to comply with valid rules of conduct and the need for virtue in having such compliance become an invariable part of our practical life. Since certain acts are obligatory upon us, and certain virtues are necessary for the constant performance of those acts whenever morally demanded of us, it follows that our development and cultivation of those virtues is morally obligatory. As far as this first ground is concerned, the duty to acquire and strengthen good character traits is a derivative duty. A moral agent has that duty only because and to the extent that fulfilling it is a necessary means to the regular performance of the agent's primary duties. With respect to this ground, if an agent could always think and act in accordance with valid moral rules without having the virtues, then the development and cultivation of virtue would not be obligatory upon that agent.

A different picture emerges when we turn to the second ground of the obligatoriness of virtue. Here there is a direct, primary duty to develop and cultivate good character. The duty is not based on the contingent psychological fact that an agent has need of the virtues to act rightly. Rather, we are morally required to achieve as close an approximation as we can to fulfilling the standards of virtue because we are not fully moral beings until our inner character and our external practice are in perfect congruence. The duty to develop and cultivate all the virtues, general and special, is the duty to become fully moral both inwardly and outwardly. Just as we must adopt valid rules of conduct as our own normative principles, so we must adopt valid standards of character in the same way. These standards, just like the rules, are binding upon us and apply to us disinterestedly. Each standard sets an ideal for every moral agent to strive for. The pursuit of excellence in matters of good character is an obligatory end. All moral agents have a duty to set that end as their goal and to take steps to achieve it. It is a duty of self-improvement, of moral growth. We must create our moral selves by our own efforts, for only then are our inner and outer lives fully attuned to one another. We then conduct ourselves not only according to the letter of the moral law, but in accordance with its spirit as well.

The congruence between character and conduct, which constitutes the second ground of the duty to acquire virtue, is a state of being in which the emotive and conative aspect of a moral agent's inner life support the commitment to abide by valid moral rules. Right conduct, with its aims, intentions, and reasons for acting, is the public counterpart to the inner structure of feeling, desire, and purposiveness which make up the agent's character. When congruence between conduct and character is achieved, the agent chooses and acts as a whole being, a complete and integrated self. Perhaps no human person can become a whole moral being in this ideal sense, but this does not take away from the duty to make as close an approach to it as one can by one's own efforts.

With regard to others, the duty to develop and cultivate virtue is a duty to help others pursue this end in their own lives. This aspect of the duty is most applicable in situations where moral agents have considerable influence on other people, as is the case with one's own children and to some extent with one's personal friends. Teachers of children and adolescents are also in a position to contribute effectively to the character development of their students. At bottom, however, the acquisition of virtue can only come through an act of self-determination, an exercise of one's autonomy. Even when we have an influence on others, they cannot develop true excellence of character except by their own efforts. We can help them decide to make the effort by inspiring them through our own example, but ultimately they alone have the power to create their moral selves.

Here again we see the central role the autonomy of the will plays in ethics. In some respects, indeed, the creation of our moral selves by the development and cultivation of good character is the noblest exercise of our distinctively human powers of self-direction and self-governance. We have seen that there can be no genuine moral commitment to rules of conduct unless the agent to whom the rules apply prescribes them to himself or herself. This is the great truth in Immanuel Kant's doctrine of the autonomy of the will. One must autonomously place one's will and one's practical reason under the normative demands of rules of conduct if one is to regard such rules as laying down moral requirements on one's choice and conduct. The only moral duties we can conceive of ourselves as having are those we freely and willingly impose upon ourselves as matters of disinterested principle. Otherwise we merely see ourselves being coerced to obey rules laid down by others. We may outwardly conform to such socially sanctioned rules, but we have no sense of being morally obligated to adhere to them when we can escape the sanctions of disapproval or punishment that support them.

By the same reasoning, standards of good character can set morally obligatory ends for us only if we autonomously place ourselves under the governance of those standards by making them our own normative principles. We can understand ourselves as having a duty to develop virtue only insofar as we subscribe to the general principle that we should, as far as it lies within our power, become fully moral beings. The *validity* of this general principle depends on the justifiability of all moral agents autonomously subscribing to it. In the context of environmental ethics, this is a matter of showing that the principle embodies the moral attitude of respect for nature. Now it is clear that this is in fact the case. Since the various standards of character, both for the general virtues and the special virtues, are standards that would be adopted by anyone who had respect for nature, so the principle that we are morally required to fulfill those standards and so become whole beings in our moral life would also be adopted by anyone having that attitude. The dispositions of feeling and desire that make up the character traits of the virtues are all ways in which a moral agent embodies in its inner life the attitude of respect for nature (assuming that the four rules of conduct also embody that attitude). Thus the moral validity of the general principle that we have a duty to acquire virtue as far as we can by our own efforts is established in exactly the same way as the moral validity of the four rules of conduct.

We now see how both conduct and character can express, in a moral agent's whole life and being, the attitude of respect for nature. We might say that the various rules of duty and standards of virtue that make up the ethical system described in this chapter give practical, concrete meaning to the attitude. They define what it means to have respect for nature in all dimensions of human life.

FIVE

DO ANIMALS AND PLANTS
HAVE RIGHTS?

1. *Legal Rights and Moral Rights*

In setting out a theory of environmental ethics in the preceding chapters I did not claim that animals or plants have rights. This omission was deliberate. For reasons I am going to give in this chapter, I wanted to construct and defend a theory of environmental ethics that does not rely on the idea of rights.

The problem of whether animals and/or plants have rights involves two principal questions. The first is whether animals and plants are the sorts of things that *can* have rights. The second is how we might establish the truth of the proposition that they do (or do not) have rights, under the assumption that it is conceivable for them to have rights. Neither of these questions can be adequately dealt with until we have clarified what we mean when we talk about rights.

Generally speaking, to have a right is to have a legitimate claim or entitlement to something, the recognition of the legitimacy of that claim or entitlement being (morally or legally) required of others. For a moral right, the requirement of recognition is imposed by valid moral principles on all moral agents. For a legal right, it is imposed by a given system of law on all members of the legal community in question. Let us begin with the less controversial matter of legal rights.

Legal rights are claims or entitlements that persons can make on their own behalf under an established system of law. One can justifiably demand that others recognize (give due recognition to) the legitimacy of one's claims or entitlements, and that demand is backed up by legal sanctions. To have a legal claim to something (such as the repayment of a debt owed to one) or to be legally entitled to act in certain ways without restriction (such as being allowed to practice the religion of one's choice) is to have a claim or entitlement that is enforceable by law. Those who refuse to grant what one has a legal claim to, or who interfere with one in the exercise of one's legal freedom-rights, are liable to some form of punishment. Moreover, in a fully developed legal system that embodies the idea of rights, when one's legal rights are infringed, denied, or violated one has a further claim to redress of grievance and to some form of reparation or compensation. This further claim is required to be recognized as legitimate by all under the given legal system and is enforceable by punishment.

Whether it consists in a specific claim to something or an entitlement to exercise one's freedom of choice in some sphere of action, a legal right endows a person with a certain status in the community. This status is that of bearer-of-rights. As a result of having that status, not only are one's basic interests protected but one is given final authority over a certain domain of choice and action. This protection and authority are what one gains by being a bearer of legal rights. One is then in a position to make legally binding claims against others not to be deprived of what the law specifies to be one's due and not to be interfered with the areas of legally granted liberty. Legal constraints (backed by the threat of punishment) are placed on the conduct of others so that these claims and entitlements are made secure. To be recognized as a bearer of rights is to have security regarding one's most fundamental interests and values (such as life and liberty). One can then not only *expect* to be granted what one is entitled to by law but one can *rightfully insist on* being granted what one is entitled to.

Now, it is possible (and it actually happens) that a system of law confers rights on beings who are not capable of understanding themselves to be bearers of rights. Examples are small children, the severely retarded, and the insane. These human beings can correctly be described as having legal claims to certain things and as being entitled by law to be treated in certain ways. As is the case with all bearers of rights, others are legally required to respect their rights by acknowledging the legitimacy of their claims and by treating them in the way they are entitled to. But these rights-holders are not capable of *making* claims against others. Not understanding their own rights, they cannot demand or insist on being granted what they are entitled to. Proxies and guardians, friends and relatives must do this for them. Nevertheless, it is correct to say that they *have* rights because the law specifies what they are entitled to and places constraints on how everyone in the community is to treat them.

It is of the very nature of legal rights that they are entirely dependent on and relative to the particular system of law that happens at a given time to be established and accepted in a society. Some societies may have legal systems that grant rights to one class of citizens only, or may confer different rights on different classes. There could be systems of law that did not recognize anyone as a bearer of rights. In those societies no one would *have* any legal rights. Thus who has legal rights and what their legal rights are vary from time to time and place to place. (Before 1920 women in the United States did not have the right to vote; now they do. In one state young people of a certain age cannot buy alcoholic drinks in a bar; in another state they can.)

What any given person has a legal right to, then, depends on what the law says. Since laws are created by humans, it follows that legal rights are the products of human convention. It is humans who confer on people their legal rights. Such rights belong to the citizens of a state only by virtue of a decision made by those having the authority to enact rights-defining laws or by judicial decisions in courts. By enacting those laws and making those decisions, the authorities create rights. By terminating or rescinding the laws and by making new decisions, they change or abolish rights.

This conception of legal rights can quite easily be applied to animals and plants, especially if we keep in mind that children, the insane, and the severely retarded can correctly be said to have legal rights even though they do not understand what it means to be a rights-holder, are unaware of their rights, and cannot claim what they have a right to against others who may wish to deprive them of their rights. As long as we consider animals and plants to be entities that have a good of their own which can be furthered or damaged by the actions of human agents, it is logically conceivable for them to have the legal status of bearer-of-rights in a given society. Thus we can speak meaningfully of protecting their good by laws that entitle them to be treated in certain ways. Just as is the case with humans, their life and well-being can be made secure by laws that confer on them certain rights.[1]

When animals and/or plants are given legal rights their good makes a legally valid claim upon humans, who are required by law to recognize the legitimacy of that claim. Respect for an animal's or plant's rights in such a society has the same significance as respect for the rights of humans. To accord to an animal or plant what the law says it is entitled to is required of everyone who is in the position of being able to accord the right or to violate it. In such a system the laws give public recognition to animals and plants

[1] The case for conferring legal rights on animals and plants, as well as on wilderness areas and natural ecosystems, is made in Christopher D. Stone, *Should Trees Have Standing? Toward Legal Rights for Natural Objects* (Los Altos, Calif.: William Kaufmann, Inc., 1974).

as *having* legitimate claims against humans. The fact that those who have the claims cannot assert them, insist on them, or even understand them does not take away their legitimacy.

To take an example from our own legal system, the Endangered Species Act of 1973 gives legal protection to certain species-populations of animals and plants which, through a legally defined procedure, have been designated "endangered" according to a set of legally defined criteria. Members of those species must not be killed, harmed, or molested; anyone who commits such acts is subject to fines or imprisonment. On the basis of that law certain species-populations acquire the legal right to exist. Their preservation makes a valid, legally binding claim upon all American citizens.

Similarly, laws setting aside wilderness areas for preservation may be thought of as conferring legal rights on the communities of plants and animals which inhabit those areas. The good of a biotic community as a whole can thereby be endowed with a right to be given recognition by moral agents, who are under a legal requirement to do no harm to that community by acting contrary to its good. Laws that prohibit hunting, fishing, or trapping in designated areas likewise grant rights to the animals so protected. Each animal has the legal right not to be hunted, trapped, or caught by fishermen.

It is now clear that the theory of environmental ethics presented in the foregoing chapters entails that, under certain conditions at least, species-populations and communities of life in natural ecosystems *should* be granted legal protection and accorded the corresponding legal rights. Once the people of a nation come to regard all wild living things as possessing inherent worth, they will enact such laws as are needed to protect the good of those wild creatures as far as that is compatible with the rights of humans.

The question, Do animals and plants have *legal* rights? can now be answered quite simply. Yes, they do in those societies whose legal systems contain laws that protect their good in various ways. Animals and plants do not have legal rights in the absence of such laws. In light of the ethics of respect for nature, however, we can add that a society that gives recognition to wild creatures as bearers of legal rights is one which more completely fulfills valid moral principles concerning the relation between humans and the natural world than a society which does not.

In this way it is possible to argue for making animals and plants bearers of legal rights without claiming that they have *moral* rights (in a sense I will explain shortly). So even if it is the case that animals and plants do not have moral rights, they might still have legal rights or, if they do not, it might still be the case that they ought to be granted such rights. For the attitude of respect for nature, which involves looking at wild animals and plants as entities possessing in-herent worth, is a sufficient basis to justify our conferring legal rights on them. Laws that give protection to species-populations and life communities in natural ecosystems are laws which conform to the principle that nonhuman forms of life in the natural world are deserving of our moral con-cern and consideration. Such laws can be said to express or embody the attitude of respect for nature, just as our char-acter and conduct can be said to express or embody that at-titude.

Let us turn now to the idea of moral rights. The main point at issue among those who disagree about whether animals and plants can correctly be said to have rights has to do with moral rights, not legal ones. Perhaps the argument most frequently given to prove that animals and plants do not have moral rights is that they *cannot* have them because the claim that they do is strictly inconceivable. According to this position, to speak of their having moral rights is con-ceptually confused or, more strongly, logically absurd. It is held that the very meaning of the term ''moral rights'' makes it logically impossible for animals and plants to be bearers of such rights.[2]

Now, this argument is sound only if a certain way of understanding what it means for an entity to have moral rights is assumed. Specifically, it must assume the conception of moral rights that is used in discourse about fundamental human rights or the rights of persons, originally called "the rights of man." If we think of moral rights in this traditional way, it is true that animals and plants are not the sorts of beings that can be bearers of moral rights. (I will show just why this is so later on.) However, there is another conception of moral rights which can, without absurdity or confusion, be applied to animals and plants. This conception has certain similarities with that which we use in referring to the moral rights of the insane and the severely retarded. I shall later discuss this modified or extended sense of moral rights and show how it can be applied to animals and plants. We will then be confronted with the following choice. Should we limit the meaning of moral rights to its original and primary sense, where it strictly applies only to persons, or should we extend its meaning so that it can be applied to all members of the human species, and still further to all living things?

My final position in this chapter will be the following. I hold that, although it is not conceptually confused or logically absurd to ascribe moral rights in an extended sense to animals and plants, there are good reasons for not doing so.

[2] A careful argument in support of this position is found in H. J. McCloskey, "Moral Rights and Animals," *Inquiry* 22/1-2 (Summer 1979): 23-54. In a later work McCloskey admits "two serious errors" in that essay, but these do not affect his main argument; see H. J. McCloskey, *Ecological Ethics and Politics* (Totowa, N.J.: Rowman and Littlefield, 1983), pp. 65-66. An opposing position is held by Joel Feinberg; see J. Feinberg. "The Rights of Animals and Unborn Generations" and "Human Duties and Animal Rights," both in J. Feinberg, *Rights, Justice, and the Bounds of Liberty: Essays in Social Philosophy* (Princeton, N.J.: Princeton University Press, 1980). McCloskey criticizes Feinberg's views in "Moral Rights and Animals," pp. 38-39. The most fully detailed argument for the rights of sentient animals is presented in Regan, *The Case for Animal Rights*.

Everything which people hope to achieve by such an extension of the concept of rights can equally be accomplished by means of the ideas of respect for nature and the inherent worth of living things, along with the structure of thought that supports and makes intelligible a person's taking the attitude of respect and regarding living things as possessing inherent worth. This structure of thought is the belief-system that constitutes the biocentric outlook on nature. In other words, we can defend the proper treatment of animals and plants in the natural world by making clear the underlying beliefs and attitudes that validate the very same duties (not to harm, not to interfere, not to break faith, and to make restitution) which assertions of animal and plant rights are supposed to entail. By avoiding talk of the moral rights of animals and plants we do not lend aid to those who have no respect for them. On the contrary, by explaining the grounds on which we commit ourselves to the ethics of respect for nature, we give a solid basis for rejecting any human-centered viewpoint that would justify an exploitative attitude toward the Earth's wild creatures. Since we can in this way establish the four duties that embody respect for all wild living things without using an extended conception of moral rights, it is best that the original idea of moral rights be accepted in its full, uncompromised meaning as applicable to humans alone. The consequence would be that assertions of moral rights would be made and understood within the domain of human ethics and would be excluded from the domain of environmental ethics.

2. Analysis of the Assertion of Moral Rights

In order to clarify the idea of moral rights as it applies (in its original, primary sense) to persons, we must carefully examine what we are asserting when we say that a person has a moral right to something. The statement that someone has a moral right to something is parallel to the assertion of someone's legal right to something. It is to say that the person has a legitimate claim or entitlement to have, enjoy, or do something, the legitimacy of the claim or entitlement being grounded in this case not on law but on *a valid moral principle*. By the same token, others are morally, not legally, required to acknowledge and give recognition to the legitimacy of the claim or entitlement. They are under a moral duty, correlative with the individual's right, not to deprive the person of what he or she has a claim to and not to interfere with the person's liberty in the sphere in which he or she is entitled to have freedom of choice and action. And just as is the case with a legal right, when others threaten to violate or infringe upon one's moral rights one can justifiably demand that one's rights be respected and can expect others to acknowledge the justifiability of that demand.

Two normative features of an assertion of a moral right are worth noticing in the foregoing analysis. First, there is the normative idea of the *moral legitimacy* of a claim (along with the *moral justifiability* of one's demand that the claim be respected) and, second, the idea of a *moral duty or requirement* on the part of others to acknowledge the legitimacy of the claim (and the justifiability of the duty or requirement). These two ideas presuppose a set of moral norms which validly apply to both the right-holder and to those who have a duty to acknowledge the right in question. In order for any assertion of a moral right, whether referring to our own right or to another's, to be meaningful, there must be a valid normative ethical system whose rules specify the asserted right and the duties of others, correlative with that right, to acknowledge and respect it. The assertion that someone has a right to something, in short, is a normative statement, not a statement of fact.[3]

[3] This analysis of the concept of moral rights is derived mainly from studies by Joel Feinberg, "The Nature and Value of Rights," "Duties, Rights, and Claims," and "Voluntary Euthanasia and the Inalienable Right to Life," all in Feinberg, *Rights, Justice, and the Bounds of Liberty: Essays in Social Philosophy* (Princeton: Princeton University Press, 1980), and J. Feinberg, *Social Philosophy* (Englewood Cliffs, N.J.: Prentice-Hall, 1973), chapters 4, 5, and 6. Although Feinberg, as mentioned in note 2 above, holds

This normative element in any rights-assertion can be made clearer if we consider the differences between interests and rights. To say that one has an interest in something—that one desires it, needs it, or values it either as a means or as an end—is to assert a matter of empirical fact. We can determine whether such a statement is true or false by observing people's behavior, listening to what they say, noticing whether they make any effort to obtain the thing in question, and so on. But no such empirical evidence *by itself* can tell us what people's moral rights are. It may be that no one would claim to have a right to something unless he or she had an interest in it or valued it in some way. So interests may be said to be a necessary condition for having rights, or at least for asserting one's rights in one's own behalf. To have an interest in something, however, does not entail that one has a right to it. Even if people need a certain thing because it is necessary for their health or survival, it cannot be inferred that they have a right to it unless we assume the moral principle that people have a right to life. The having of the need is not a sufficient condition for having the right. To get from the need to the right reference to a valid moral principle must be made.

Interests, needs, and values, then, are not to be confused with rights. Nor do desires, needs, and values confer on a person the right to the thing desired, needed, or valued. Without the *legitimacy* of the person's claim to what she or he desires, needs, or values, there is simply a factual, contingent relation between the person and the desired, needed, or valued thing. This relation can be known empirically, through the evidence of our sense perceptions. Our sense perceptions can never provide evidence for people's rights unless we already presuppose a moral principle. This principle must specify what those rights are and state the

---

that animals can have moral rights as he analyzes such rights, for reasons I shall give in this chapter I do not believe this view can be held unless it is qualified in certain ways.

ground for the *legitimacy of a claim* that any person can make to those rights.

The language in which we make assertions about people's needs, interests, and (subjective) values is factual. The language of moral rights is normative. We don't always notice this difference because statements about rights are not usually expressed in terms of "ought," but rather in terms of "is" or "have." We talk about what a person's rights *are*, or whether a person *has* a right to something. But these grammatical points should not make us think that statements about rights assert matters of empirical fact. The statement that someone "has" a right to something is a hidden or implicit ought-statement. It asserts that the person *ought* to be allowed freedom of choice in a certain sphere of action or *ought* to be accorded the opportunity to obtain something or maintain possession of something. It asserts at the same time that all other moral agents have a *duty*, and hence *ought*, to allow the person that freedom or accord the person that opportunity. If we are asked *why* the person ought to be treated in that way we must appeal to a moral norm or principle, and if asked *why* that principle should be followed, we must show that it is a valid principle and morally binding on all agents.

Using the language of rights, then, presupposes a system of norms. (The language is normative.) Furthermore, those who assert their own or others' rights implicitly accept the norms as validly binding on all moral agents. Every agent is morally required to acknowledge the legitimacy of the claims being made. Thus to assert one's moral right to something is in effect to apply a moral principle to oneself and others, a principle one understands as *grounding one's entitlement* to the thing and as *imposing a moral requirement upon others* to respect one's entitlement to it. Since the principle one applies is a moral one, the right one asserts belongs to the category of moral rights.

When is a rights-assertion true? The answer is: when the principle on which it rests is a valid moral principle. We recall from Chapter One that in order to be valid a moral principle of human ethics must satisfy five formal conditions and a material one. The principle must be general in form, not referring to any particular person or set of circumstances. Second, it must be intended to apply to all moral agents as such. Third, it must be a categorical principle, applying impartially and disinterestedly to everyone without exception. Fourth, any individual who adopts it as his or her own normative guide must advocate that it be publicly acknowledged and recognized by everyone else as a universally applicable and categorical norm. The fifth formal condition is that it must be considered as correctly overriding any nonmoral norms, such as class-interest, custom, law, and the personal values of particular individuals. Finally, with regard to the material condition, a principle is valid in the domain of human ethics only if it embodies the concept of respect for persons as persons, and when it does embody that concept it *is* valid.

When the assertion of a right (in the domain of human ethics) presupposes a moral principle that satisfies all these conditions, the right being asserted is a *true* moral right, or in other words, the assertion is true. It follows that, for every true moral right, the legitimacy of the claim or entitlement that constitutes the right holds universally throughout the moral community (the community of moral agents). All members of that community must give due recognition to the right by acknowledging the duty to respect it. The very same principle that confers the right also lays down the duty. The truth of the statement "Person P has a right to X" entails the truth of the statement "Everyone (that is, every moral agent) in the universe other than P has a duty to P to recognize the legitimacy of P's claim to X." The rights of one impose duties on all others.

We can see that this is so if we imagine a situation where one person makes a claim to something but no one else is required to respect that claim as a legitimate one. Since others would have no duty to respect the claim, it would be permissible for them to deprive the person of the thing in question or to interfere with the person's freedom to choose it. Clearly we would not then say the person has a moral right to the thing claimed. If it is *true* that others can, if they wish, take away from the person what he or she makes claim to, then it cannot be *true* that he or she has a moral right to it.

A rights-assertion can be true even in a society whose established moral code does not recognize the rights being asserted. Thus a society which practices slavery may deny freedom-rights to slaves and believe such denial to be correct on the basis of its moral code. If the slaves themselves have been thoroughly indoctrinated in that code, they might also believe that they have no freedom-rights. Nevertheless it might still be true that they *do* have such rights. The truth of the statement, "The slaves have a right to be free," is not contradicted by the truth of the statement, "No one in that society believes or recognizes that the slaves have a right to be free." This again brings out the normative-descriptive distinction with regard to rights. What rights are *accepted* in a given moral code is a question of fact, the truth of which a historian or an anthropologist can discover by studying the society that has adopted that code. But this has nothing to do with the normative question whether everyone or anyone in that society has moral rights.

This is of great practical significance. The rise of modern egalitarian democracies was accompanied by the assertion on the part of social radicals and reformers that all humans have certain fundamental and inalienable rights. Such assertions were held to be true—even "self-evident" truths—in the face of authoritarian political regimes and conventional moral codes which gave little or no recognition to those rights. It is precisely because assertions of such rights, being normative assertions, do not depend for their truth on any political system or accepted moral code that far-reaching social changes could be demanded in the name of universal human rights.

Concerning those to whom such rights-assertions are addressed, two points should be noted. The first has to do with conditions under which those addressed came to accept the *truth* of the assertions being made. The second has to do with those who are addressed being able to understand the *meaning* of the assertions being made. We have seen that if a given rights-assertion is true, there must be a valid moral rule imposing a duty on all moral agents to respect the right being asserted. Now, unless that rule is *considered* to be a morally valid principle by a community of agents who see themselves bound by the rule, they will not *accept* the rights-assertion as being true. On the other hand, if they do accept its truth they thereby acknowledge the moral validity of the rule and accordingly conceive of themselves as being under a requirement to respect the rights being asserted as a matter of principle.

With regard to their comprehending the meaning of any rights-assertion addressed to them, unless they understand what it means for an agent's conduct to fall within the range of a moral rule and what it means to be bound by a duty as a matter of principle, they will not comprehend what is being asserted. They will lack the concept of moral rights. For they will not grasp what it means to recognize the moral legitimacy of a person's claim to something when such a claim is made against them.

We may infer from these considerations that the idea of a community of moral agents, bound together under a set of rules applicable to all alike, is conceptually integral to understanding both the truth and meaning of assertions of moral rights. Insofar as the rules on which rights-assertions are grounded belong to a valid system of human ethics based on respect for persons, all members of the moral community see themselves as being required to respect (recognize the legitimacy of) the rights which each member claims for itself. That is, each knows itself to be a person and, in the light of the general principle of respect for persons as persons, each claims against the others the supreme value of being allowed to exist as a person. Since each acknowledges the others to be persons like itself and so deserving the same consideration, each recognizes a moral duty to accord to others the same rights it believes should be accorded to itself. The duty to recognize the legitimacy of others' claims is seen to be the very same duty for others to recognize one's own claims to be legitimate.

Under a system of moral rules establishing rights enjoyed by all persons simply in virtue of their being persons, the moral relations holding between those who have rights and those who have duties (namely, all those to whom anyone's rights-assertions are addressed) have certain significant properties. Each bearer of rights is understood by all as being justified in demanding acceptance by others as an equal among equals, whose rights deserve the same recognition as others expect for their own rights. Acting justly toward rights-holders is viewed as a matter of responding to them in ways they are entitled to be treated. Moral constraints arising from the rights of others are understood to be valid duties owed to others out of respect for their personhood.

From the standpoint of a rights-holder, the actions of others are not merely benefits bestowed on one out of their feelings of kindness. Rather, one's rights place strict requirements on others, requirements that they must meet regardless of their feelings and inclinations. At the same time, each rights-holder conceives of other rights-holders in a similar way as entities who *must* be accorded respect. Thus a fundamental commitment to the general principle of reciprocity holds throughout the community. Each agent says to itself, "I have a duty to abide by the rules out of respect for the rights of others because, like them, I have rights that they must respect by complying with the same rules." In this kind of ethical system a violation of someone's rights involves more than a failure to be benevolent toward that person. It means that one has given an affront to the other by denying the other's equal status as a rights-holder. Thus the offender is *answerable to* the person offended, who can rightfully demand some form of restitution from the offender.

I have so far discussed what the concept of moral rights means in general and how that concept applies to a system of human ethics based on respect for persons. Our next question, still within the framework of human ethics, is: What does a person have a moral right to? As a first step in answering this, let us consider those things which a rational, enlightened, and autonomous person would claim for itself as a matter of moral right, when a moral right is understood in the manner analyzed above. Basically they would be things the person placed the greatest value on, things without which it could not exist as an autonomous and rational being pursuing its own values according to its own plan of life. What it would claim as its moral rights would be the fulfillment of conditions necessary for personhood itself, that is, conditions that must obtain if it is to preserve its life, its autonomy, and its rationality as a person. Seen in this light our moral rights are the claims we make to being entitled to protection from incursions by others into our lives, or from their depriving us of certain things, in ways destructive of our personhood. The things to which rational, enlightened, and autonomous beings would claim entitlement as a matter of moral right define a sphere of action, thought, and valuing over which they think they alone should have absolute authority. Those things would include whatever is essential to the realization of personhood itself. Thus the moral rights of persons in a system of human ethics based on respect for persons are the rights each would demand for itself to guarantee conditions needed for its developing into a person and preserving its existence as a person. These rights fall into three general categories or classes. I designate them as follows:

(a) Subsistence and security rights ("the right to life").
(b) Liberty rights.
(c) Autonomy rights.

Each set of rights includes both negative and positive rights. This means that the rights belonging to each category entail both negative and positive duties on the part of others. Negative duties, we have seen, are duties not to perform actions of certain kinds. Such duties are determined by valid moral rules that prohibit actions of the kinds in question. They require all moral agents to refrain from those actions. Positive duties are duties to perform certain kinds of actions in certain circumstances. They are laid down according to rules that require all moral agents to do actions of those kinds in the appropriate circumstances. I shall now briefly consider the three classes of moral rights in turn, bringing out their dual nature by giving a few examples of both negative and positive duties correlative with each set of rights.

(a) *Subsistence and security rights*. The right to subsistence is is the right to the physical necessities of biological survival. One's subsistence rights include the right to sufficient food, shelter, and clothing for the preservation of one's life and to a certain level of basic health care. Since it is the case in many countries that these things are not provided for one but can be obtained only by one's own efforts, then the right to subsistence must include in those countries the right to a level of education sufficient to enable a person to acquire what is needed for biological survival. It should be noted that people do not have a *subsistence* right to an income or to employment beyond what is required for the necessities of life. However, they do have a *liberty* right to choose their own vocation and to earn an income beyond the subsistence level under social conditions in which fair equality of opportunity is extended to everyone.

The right to subsistence is a negative right when understood as including the right *not* to be killed and the right not to be deprived of basic necessities for the preservation of one's life. The duties correlative with these negative rights are the duty to refrain from killing and the duty not to take away from others what they need to live.

The right to subsistence is a positive right insofar as it includes the right to be given assistance when in dire need through no fault of one's own. A condition of dire need is here understood to be one in which a person will not be able to stay alive unless aided by others. The positive duty correlative with this right is for each moral agent to do his or her fair share in making available to those in dire need what is required to sustain life. This could be accomplished through a cooperative effort, each agent contributing a fair share to the effort.[4]

Even within a system of human ethics, the right to subsistence has important implications regarding how humans should treat the Earth's natural environment. Correlative with the right is the duty to refrain from polluting or degrading the environment to such an extent that serious danger to human life results. There is also the positive duty to clean up pollution when that is necessary for protecting public health. One might say that the right to subsistence includes the right to an environment that is physically safe for people, and this could be spelled out in terms of a right to clean air, a right to have a water supply free of toxic chemicals, a right to be protected from dangerous levels of radiation, and so on.[5]

Let us now consider the other element in the right to life,

---

[4] A strong case for positive rights to subsistence and security is made in Henry Shue, *Basic Rights: Subsistence, Affluence, and U.S. Foreign Policy* (Princeton, N.J.: Princeton University Press, 1980).

[5] This relation between human rights on the one hand and duties regarding the natural environment on the other has been advanced by William T. Blackstone, "Ethics and Ecology," in W. T. Blackstone, ed., *Philosophy and Environmental Crisis* (Athens, Ga.: University of Georgia Press, 1974), pp. 16-42.

which I have referred to as "security rights." Security rights are the right not to be assaulted, raped, tortured, or otherwise violently harmed and the right to be protected from those who might do such harm. (Statements about violations of human rights in the contemporary world, especially violations by governments, usually refer to security rights.) Security rights are negative insofar as the correlative duty is to refrain from performing acts of violence against persons. There is also the negative duty not to be negligent with regard to the health and safety of others. Reckless automobile driving, for example, can be a violation of this duty even if no accident occurs. The duty requires that we take due care when our actions can affect the lives of others. We must avoid imposing unacceptable risks on the physical well-being of others, where an "unacceptable risk" is one which would not be accepted by those whose physical well-being is at stake.

As a positive right, the right to security is a right *to be protected* from those who intend to harm us. The correlative duty is for all moral agents to do their fair share in providing such protection. This will include the establishment and enforcement of a system of law which makes those who do violence to persons liable to punishment. The duty on the part of each individual to uphold and obey those laws is a fundamental aspect of respect for the security rights of others. Obedience to such laws is a moral duty, not simply a legal requirement.

(b) *Liberty rights*. For present purposes I understand "liberty" to mean freedom from positive external constraints upon the pursuit of one's permissible interests. A permissible interest is any interest the pursuit of which involves no breaking of a valid moral rule, including no violation of others' rights. Each person has the right to carry out those practices which he or she values as ends in themselves and to take effective means to achieve his or her goals in life without interference from others, as long as doing these things is not prohibited by a valid rule of duty. This means that the pursuit of one's interests, or more generally, the living of one's own way of life, must be compatible with the equal freedom of others to pursue their interests and live their ways of life. No one has the right to deprive another of liberty or life.

It might at first appear that the right to liberty is exclusively a negative right, entailing only a negative duty on the part of others to refrain from interfering with or placing restrictions upon the right-holder's freedom to do as he or she wishes (assuming no violation of others' rights). This, however, would be to overlook two important positive aspects of the right to liberty. We might call these aspects the right to protection and the right to assistance.[6]

If we are to have a right to liberty that *makes secure* our freedom from constraints imposed on us by others, we must be given adequate protection from those who would deprive us of our freedom, especially those who have power over us. Thus our right to the continuous assurance of our liberty in all circumstances of life entails a positive duty on the part of others to create and support those social institutions, policies, and practices that make secure our freedom on a permanent basis. These will include the establishment and enforcement of laws guaranteeing freedom of choice and action in all spheres of life where individual liberty is most valued by people. Thus there will be laws ensuring freedom of speech and other forms of public communication, freedom of religion and conscience, freedom of assembly, and the like. By obeying and upholding these laws we protect everyone's liberty. We create the social atmosphere of freedom that makes it possible for all of us to enjoy our liberty.

With regard to the positive right to *assistance* in matters of liberty, our right to liberty entails that others have a positive duty to come to our aid when our freedom has been taken away (for example, when we have been kidnapped, en-

[6] The distinction between the right to protection and the right to assistance is Henry Shue's; see Shue, *Basic Rights*, pp. 51-55.

slaved, or placed in a concentration camp). Duties of assistance in matters of liberty also apply in circumstances where
those in power are using various forms of coercion against
us or are threatening us in such a way that we are in imminent danger of losing our liberty.

The right to liberty, it should be emphasized, does *not* include a right to obtain whatever we happen to value or a
right to have our desires and interests fulfilled. We do not
have a right to the satisfaction of our interests but rather to
the opportunity to pursue our interests without interference from others. Our right to liberty is the right to take effective steps to realize the goals we have set for ourselves,
without hindrances or obstacles placed in our way by
others. Thus we are at liberty *to pursue our good* as we see fit
(under the assumption, as always, that we do not thereby
deprive others of what they have a right to). But we are not
entitled as a matter of moral right *to have our good realized*.
This is because our moral rights have to do with the basic
conditions essential for the preservation of our personhood, that is, for our existence as persons. One cannot be a
person—*any* kind of person, happy or unhappy, fulfilled or
unfulfilled—if one is systematically deprived of the necessities of life, of freedom, or of autonomy. But one can exist
as a person and preserve one's personhood even if one is
not able fully to realize one's good, satisfy one's desires, or
achieve one's valued ends.

(c) *Autonomy rights.* Autonomy, as we saw in earlier chapters, is the capacity for self-determination. Autonomous individuals lead lives of their own based on goals they set for
themselves and values they have chosen for themselves.
They have their own reasons-for-acting and reasons-for-
choosing. They are accordingly self-directed and self-gov-
erned beings. Each autonomous person's daily existence
may be thought of as the unfolding of a "plan of life" con-
tinuously being created by the individual. Such a life takes
on a certain internal coherence and unity, reflecting an ordering of means and ends which results from the individu-

239

al's own judgments concerning the relative importance or unimportance of things. As far as it lies within their power, autonomous people are masters of their own destiny.

Autonomy rights are rights to what is necessary for the development and preservation of an individual's autonomy. These are the essential conditions that make it possible for one to acquire the capacity to lead a self-directed life, ordered in accordance with one's own value system. They include the right not to be deprived of sanity, the right not to be subjected to manipulation by psychological techniques that destroy or impair one's powers of critical reflection and independence of judgment, and the right to a level and kind of education conducive to the development of autonomy. Without the capacity for self-determination which enables an individual to be and remain an autonomous being, directing and planning its life according to its own beliefs and values, it cannot achieve genuine personhood. The right to autonomy, like the right to life and the right to liberty, is the right to exist as a person.

Like other moral rights, autonomy rights are both negative and positive. Negatively, the duties correlative with autonomy rights are the duty not to destroy or impair anyone's capacity for self-determination and the duty not to prevent or hinder the development of that capacity, especially during another's childhood and adolescence when the capacity is just beginning to be acquired. Positive duties correlative with autonomy rights include doing what will help others develop their autonomy and what will strengthen and preserve their autonomy when developed. Connected with the latter is the duty to protect everyone's autonomy by abolishing or changing those social institutions and practices that tend to weaken or block the development of autonomy in people's lives. Finally, there is the positive duty to give assistance to those whose powers of autonomous choice and decision making are being threatened by the actions of others.

I do not claim that this account of moral rights is a full study of all the rights of individuals under a system of human ethics based on respect for persons. It is intended only to indicate some of the major types of rights as a way of clarifying the general idea of a moral right in human ethics.

3. The Defeasibility of Rights

One further aspect of what it means for a person to be a bearer of moral rights should now be considered. This has to do with the sense in which moral rights are "absolute." We can say that such rights are absolute insofar as they are natural rights, that is, rights belonging to individuals simply because they are persons and not because their status as rights-bearers has been conferred on them by society. Moral rights belong to a person by nature, not by convention. In this respect they are to be contrasted with legal rights, as we saw earlier.

Any being who is a person qualifies as a rights-holder just in virtue of her or his personhood. It follows that our moral rights are absolute in another sense, directly connected with the idea that they are natural rights. This is the sense in which moral rights are said to be "inalienable." The moral rights we have as persons cannot be taken away from us. No government, however powerful it may be, can cause us to lose our rights, though it may systematically violate them and deprive us of any chance to exercise or enjoy them. A totalitarian power can deny us what we are entitled to, but it cannot take away our entitlement; we still have a legitimate claim to what we are being deprived of. The legitimacy of our claim is a moral legitimacy, grounded on valid ethical principles. No human power can transform a valid principle of ethics into an invalid one, hence the absoluteness of our moral rights.

241

Our moral rights are also inalienable, and thus absolute, in another sense. We cannot transfer or sell our moral rights to another, nor surrender them voluntarily in return for something else we want. We can do these things with our legal property-rights, for example. But our moral rights are permanently attached to our personhood. Consider our right to life. We may indeed voluntarily take our own lives by committing suicide, but this does not destroy the right to remain alive (if we wish) while we are still persons. We can deprive ourselves of life, but not of the right to life; that remains inalienable. Perhaps a closer analogy with surrendering our property-rights to something (by giving away something we own) or transferring those rights to someone else (selling our car to someone) is the voluntary giving up of our life for the sake of someone we love or out of patriotic duty to our country. Even in these cases, however, our right to life remains inalienable. The analogy with property-rights breaks down. By sacrificing our life for another we give up that to which we have a moral right, but we do not give up the right itself. Until the final moment of death, when (presumably) we cease to be persons, we retain the right to life. Others still have a duty not to kill us or deprive us of the means to life. They must respect our right to remain alive, even though we have decided not to exercise or enjoy that right ourselves.

Whether we can *waive* our right to life by giving another permission to kill us is a matter of dispute in current discussions of moral rights. The waiving of one's right to life has practical importance in the matter of voluntary euthanasia. Many thoughtful people believe we have "the right to die" as one of our inalienable moral rights. If we have a fatal illness which is incurable and confront a future of, say, six months of unremitting pain or a condition of total brain deterioration, it is held that the person has a right to ask that he or she be painlessly put to death. To respect that right means complying with the person's request. Even if we grant that people do have such a moral right, however, this does not mean that they can take away their own right to life. To give permission to another to terminate one's life is not really to give up one's *right* to life. One can still demand that, as long as one *wishes* to remain alive, others must respect one's life. This is what the right to life means. One may come to the point where one no longer values having that right because one no longer wants to stay alive, but one still has that right. It remains inalienable.[7]

Now, in addition to the two senses of "absolute" we have considered, namely that moral rights are natural rights and inalienable rights, there is another sense sometimes given to the assertion that our moral rights are absolute. It is sometimes said that it is never morally justifiable to infringe upon anyone's rights or to fail to meet another's demand that his or her rights be respected in particular circumstances. This view, however, is not well grounded. Our moral rights are not absolute in this sense, since all rights are *defeasible*. There are situations, either actual or hypothetical, in which it is morally right to deny another what he or she has a right to. Let us see how this can be so.

When we assert that someone has a right to something, our assertion (if true) entails a *strong presumption* against any action of others that involves an infringement or denial of that right. But it does not entail an *absolute prohibition* that holds under any and all conditions. "Absolute" here means exceptionless, and it is in this sense that moral rights are not correctly viewed as being absolute.

The defeasibility of moral rights lies in the fact that there can occur exceptional circumstances in which it is morally justifiable to infringe upon them. To put the point another way, the wrongness of infringing upon anyone's moral rights is conditional. Such an action is to be judged wrong

---

[7] The concept of inalienability of rights used here is derived from Feinberg, "Voluntary Euthanasia and the Inalienable Right to Life." A somewhat different analysis of inalienability of rights is presented by A. John Simmons in "Inalienable Rights and Locke's *Treatises.*" *Philosophy and Public Affairs* 12/3 (Summer 1983): 175-204.

"other things being equal." It is sometimes necessary to deny what one person has a right to in order to meet the legitimate claims being put forward by others, claims which they hold as a matter of *their* moral rights. One might have to silence a person, for example, in order to prevent a riot.

When the rights of one person conflict with the rights of another so that it is impossible fully to accord to each what each is entitled to, neither's rights are nullified or canceled. But an additional right is created the moment the conflict is resolved in favor of one of the parties. This is the right of restitutive justice that belongs to the one whose rights are being infringed or denied. Our moral rights always stay with us. They remain in full force even when others are morally justified in not granting to us what is our rightful due. The recognition that our rights are being infringed or denied gives rise to a special right to restitution which we can claim against those who infringe or deny our rights.

It might be noted at this juncture that, in addition to an infringement or denial of someone's rights, there is another ground for a duty of restitutive justice. It is the ground that respect for any being which possesses inherent worth must be given restitution when a duty toward it is unfulfilled or violated. If we must do some harm to a being whom we regard as possessing inherent worth in order to meet a more pressing obligation to other beings whom we regard similarly, then the respect due each being requires us to make compensation to the one we harm. Since having inherent worth means that each being's good must be given *equal* consideration, we cannot let the imbalance of helping some but hurting others go uncorrected. The attitude of respect which is extended to every being in the conflict entails a special concern to make up for the wrong done to some, even when our actions in the given circumstances are morally justified.

In the next chapter we will find this ground for duties of restitutive justice to have a central place in the fair resolution of conflicts between human ethics and environmental ethics. For even if nonhuman animals and plants are said not to have any moral rights, as long as we regard them as beings which possess inherent worth we will see ourselves as owing them some form of reparation or compensation when their good is overridden by consideration of our own good.

4. Is It Logically Conceivable for Animals and/or Plants to Have Moral Rights?

If we look at moral rights as they have been analyzed in the foregoing sections of this chapter, it becomes highly questionable whether nonhuman animals and/or plants can be bearers of moral rights. The problem is a logical or conceptual one, not a normative one. That is, the problem has to do with *the possibility of conceiving* of animals or plants as having moral rights, not whether they *should* (or should not) be considered as having such rights. Does it make sense to talk about the moral rights of animals and plants at all?

The thesis I shall defend is that, if we think of moral rights in the ways indicated in our foregoing discussions, neither animals nor plants can logically be conceived as bearers of moral rights. (We saw earlier that they *can* be conceived as bearers of legal rights.) However, in the next section I shall consider a modified concept of moral rights which would make it possible for nonhumans to be conceived as bearers of moral rights. This will open the normative question whether they should be thought of as bearers of such rights, and I will discuss this further issue at that juncture. It should be remarked that the term "animal" in this chapter shall always be taken to refer to nonhuman animals, and it is being assumed that nonhuman animals are not persons in the sense given in our earlier analysis of personhood. (If there actually are nonhuman animals which have the characteristics of personhood, then it is not only conceivable for them to have moral rights but, given the argument presented above, they do have such rights just as much as human persons do.)

There are four aspects of moral rights that make it conceptually impossible for either animals or plants to be bearers of moral rights. (a) A bearer of moral rights is assumed to be a member of the community of moral agents. (b) There is a connection between being a bearer of moral rights and having self-respect such that, if it is inconceivable for something to have self-respect it is inconceivable for it to be a bearer of moral rights. (c) It must make sense to say that a being is able to choose to exercise or to enjoy a right if it makes sense to say it has that right. (d) A bearer of moral rights has certain second-order entitlements in virtue of its moral rights. I shall now take up each of these points in turn and show their implications concerning the inconceivability of animals or plants having moral rights.

(a) The first point pertains to the relation between being a bearer of moral rights and being a member of the community of moral agents. To assert that an entity has a right to something, we have seen, is to assert that the entity has a legitimate claim to the thing in question, a claim whose legitimacy all moral agents are obligated to acknowledge. The language in which rights are asserted is normative language, not descriptive language. To assert a right is not to describe a fact but to apply a moral principle (under the implicit assumption of its validity) that imposes a requirement on moral agents. Such a use of language, and the thoughts that must go with it if its statements are to have meaning, presupposes that the holder of the right, the one who asserts or ascribes the right to the holder (which may or may not be the holder itself), and the audience to whom the assertion is addressed are all members of a community of agents under a system of validly binding moral rules. The right-holders are assumed to be members of the community because they are understood to have claims that can rightfully be pressed against others, whether or not they do choose to press them against others. Since rights-holders are by definition entitled to respect, they are in a position of equality with regard to moral agents, who are duty-bound to acknowledge their rights and so treat them with the respect due them.

Now, if it is to make sense to say that bearers of moral rights are entitled to press their rights against moral agents and to demand that all such agents respect their rights, it must be *theoretically possible* for them to do what they are entitled to do. That is, it must be *conceivable* for them to press their claims against others if they choose to. It is quite clear, however, that this theoretical possibility does not hold in the case of animals and plants. It is not merely that such creatures are unable *physically* to press their legitimate claims against others, or that the laws of nature make it *empirically* impossible for them to do this (in the way such laws make it impossible for herbivores to eat other animals or for a plant to reproduce by copulation with another plant). It is a matter of logical conceivability. *What it means* to press claims against others and demand that the legitimacy of those claims be acknowledged is simply incompatible with *what it means* to be an animal or a plant. An animal or plant would not be the kind of thing it is if it were possible *for us* to conceive of it as choosing to press its legitimate claims against moral agents and to demand that they acknowledge the legitimacy of its claims. Therefore, as far as this aspect of what it means to be a bearer of moral rights is concerned, it is inconceivable for animals and plants to be bearers of moral rights.

(b) Consider, next, the connection between moral rights and self-respect.[8] A being has self-respect when it conceives of itself as a person and regards itself as possessing inherent worth in virtue of its personhood. It consequently

[8] Some aspects of the connection between self-respect and moral rights are examined in Thomas E. Hill, Jr., "Servility and Self-Respect," *The Monist* 57/1 (January 1973): 87-104.

believes that it deserves equal consideration with every other person and that all moral agents have a duty to respect its personhood. Now, if any entity did not conceive of itself in this way it would never assert its own moral rights, and if it did conceive of itself in this way it would assert its rights, particularly when others were treating it without the respect due it.

Thus the idea of self-respect is part of our understanding of what it means to be a bearer of moral rights. Again, the relation is a conceptual one, not a factual one. Having moral rights does not entail actually having self-respect. Others can assert our rights in our behalf when we do not assert them for ourselves because we lack self-respect. But it must be *conceivable* for us to come to have self-respect and so to make first-person assertions of our rights ("I have a right to X"). Unless it were conceivable for a being to make such first-person assertions, we would not understand what third-person assertions ("He, she, they have a right to X") mean. In other words, what is meant when moral rights are ascribed to a being does not change when the ascription is made by the being itself (a first-person ascription) and when it is made by others (a third-person ascription). "Having a moral right to X" has the same meaning whether predicated of ourselves or others. We predicate it of ourselves when we have self-respect. So if it were inconceivable for a being to have self-respect, neither first-person nor third-person ascriptions of rights to it would make sense.

Animals and plants, of course, are not the sort of beings one can conceive of as gaining self-respect, since they cannot regard themselves as possessing inherent worth. It is not just that animals and plants are (psychologically) incapable of ever coming to have self-respect: the point is that it makes no sense to say either that they have or that they lack self-respect, if we understand what it means to have or to lack self-respect when such things are said of people.

(c) In the third place, whenever we say that a being has a

moral right to something, we assume that the holder of the right may choose either to exercise or not to exercise the powers it has title to under the right, including the choice of whether or not to enjoy the possession of what it has a right to possess, as it sees fit. This holds for all three categories of rights. In the case of subsistence and security rights, the holders of these rights are in the position of deciding for themselves whether to enjoy what they are entitled to, namely, having their lives and basic health preserved and protected. It is understood that they need not take advantage of this status if they do not wish to. We tend to overlook this aspect of "the right to life" because it is almost invariably the case that holders of the right do want to enjoy the advantages they are entitled to under it. But as far as having the right to the preservation and protection of one's life and physical health is concerned, there is no requirement to stay alive or to enjoy health. One does not abrogate, deny, or violate one's rights by abusing one's body (by taking drugs, for example) or by committing suicide. One's subsistence and security rights give one the chance to stay alive if one wishes. For the rights-holder the right is not a necessity, but a guaranteed permission. It is permissible to enjoy it or not to enjoy it according to one's choice. The necessity lies with others, namely, to ensure one's preservation and protection and thus make it possible for one to choose either alternative. This permissibility presupposes that the rights-holder has the *capacity* to make such a choice.

Consider, next, liberty-rights. To say that certain beings have the right of religious freedom, for example, is to assume that it is a matter for the individuals in question to decide for themselves whether to practice one religion rather than another, or not to practice any. Similarly, the right to freedom of speech, of the press, or of any expression of opinion is a right to decide for oneself whether to make public one's views or to keep them to oneself, to speak one's mind or to remain silent. Freedom of speech does not mean we are required to speak but only that we may if we wish. To have a liberty-right is to be given the prerogative of choosing whether or not to use the freedom guaranteed to us by the right.

The same consideration holds for autonomy-rights. It is again an essential aspect of what it means to have a right to something that it is up to the rights-holder whether he or she shall exercise the right or enjoy what he or she has a right to. Insofar as our autonomy-rights are respected we are able to exercise and develop our autonomy if we so choose. The great value of such rights is that they give us the continuous opportunity to be and remain autonomous over our own existence, enabling us to shape our futures and give direction to our daily lives. The right to develop the capacities for autonomous choice and to exercise those capacities when developed is a right to endeavor to become full persons through our own efforts. And this presupposes our ability to choose whether or not to make the effort.

Thus the idea of having moral rights is conceptually linked to the idea of having a choice. An entity can be thought of as a rights-holder only if it has the capacity to make choices among alternatives that confront it. Such a capacity logically rules out animals and plants as bearers of moral rights. There is a conceptual incoherence involved in ascribing moral rights to them because, if they had the choice-making powers of rights-holders, they would be persons and not plants or animals.

(d) Finally, the assertion that an entity is a bearer of moral rights has certain further implications which it could not have if the assertion were made of an animal or plant. These further implications have to do with the second-order entitlements any rights-holder has in virtue of its first-order rights. One such entitlement, for instance, is that when others violate or fail to respect one's first-order rights (subsistence and security rights, liberty rights, and autonomy rights) one has a justified grievance or "right to complain" and accordingly is entitled to redress of grievance. Closely associated with this is the second-order entitlement to hold others to account and to demand restitution from them for infringements on one's rights. Finally, there is the second-order entitlement to have one's first-order rights publicly supported and upheld through the imposition of social sanctions on violations of one's rights. The ordinary way this entitlement is fulfilled in modern societies is by means of a legal system. One's second-order entitlement is not only to have one's moral rights enforced by law, but to make claim to the equal protection of the law.

All of these second-order entitlements assume certain capacities in those who have first-order rights, capacities which are not to be found in animals or plants. These creatures cannot—*logically* cannot—register complaints, demand redress, or call for the legal enforcement of their rights under an "equal protection" clause. Society cannot—logically cannot—give recognition to such entitlements even if animals and plants were somehow to be considered bearers of first-order rights. Thus what are normally taken as implications of having rights, indeed, part of the very significance (meaning and importance) of being a rights-holder, would become nonsense if moral rights were ascribed to animals or plants.

5. *A Modified Concept of Moral Rights*

As I mentioned at the outset of this argument for the inconceivability of animals and plants having moral rights, the concept of moral rights being used here is that analyzed earlier in this chapter. There is another, modified concept of moral rights, however, which makes it conceivable for animals and plants to have such rights. As a way of approaching this modified concept, let us consider the argument of Chapter Three. If that argument is sound, rational persons will accept the belief-system that constitutes the biocentric outlook on nature. They will accordingly take the attitude of respect for nature and regard wild living things as possessing inherent worth. Conceiving of animals and plants in this way, rational persons will judge them to be deserving of moral concern and consideration on the part of everyone. Rational persons will also commit themselves to the moral principle that the good of wild living things is to be preserved and protected as an end in itself and for their sake. This principle, as we saw in the last chapter, is the foundation for a whole ethical system of rules of conduct and standards of character. By living in accordance with these norms moral agents express the attitude of respect for nature in their conduct and character.

When those who have respect for nature make the moral commitment to abide by these norms, the rules of the system are adopted as matters of principle. They are seen as laying down duties that are *owed to* the living things in question. To carry out such duties is not only understood as fulfilling moral requirements binding upon agents. It is also thought of as the appropriate or suitable way for agents to respond to the moral subjects to which duties are owed. The rules of duty define a moral relationship between the agent and the subject. The subject is not conceived simply as an entity that happens to benefit by the agent's doing her or his duty. The agent believes the duty is obligatory. It is a requirement that must be fulfilled by actions which are properly owed to the subject. The subject, in turn, is seen to deserve the treatment extended to it because it has inherent worth.

When animals and plants are regarded as entities possessing inherent worth their good accordingly is understood to make a claim-to-be-respected upon all moral agents, and duties are seen to be imposed upon agents as ways of meeting that claim. The animals and plants themselves, of course, do not make claims against moral agents, nor do they conceive of themselves as beings whose good makes a claim-to-be-respected. But neither of these conditions is necessary for moral agents to consider their good as making such a claim. When their good is considered in this way its realization is seen to place constraints upon the choice and conduct of agents. Agents are not free to act as they please when their actions affect the lives and well-being of wild animals and plants.

In the light of these considerations it is easy to see how animals and plants could come to be thought of as bearers of rights. When moral agents believe duties are owed to such creatures as their due, those duties are seen as ways of embodying the attitude of respect in practical life. It is then but a short step to thinking of those duties as being correlated with a general moral right on the part of animals and plants to have their good preserved and protected. To acknowledge this general moral right is to consider their good as making a claim-to-be-respected, a claim whose legitimacy must be recognized and given great moral weight by all moral agents as a matter of principle.

Here, then, we have a whole conceptual structure which seems to provide a justification for asserting that animals and plants have at least one general moral right.[9] Since this right is the right to the preservation and protection of their good, it can be used as a basis for ascribing a number of specific moral rights to animals and plants. These are the rights that correspond to the four rules of duty which we saw in the last chapter to make up a valid ethical system grounded on respect for nature. The four rights in question would be: the right not to be harmed, the right not to be interfered with, the right not to have one's trust broken, and the right to restitution when one has been wronged. To carry out the duties correlative with each of these rights is to treat animals and plants in the way they are *entitled* to be treated. They are deserving of such treatment *in their own right*.

So we may conclude that there is a sense in which, within

[9] It is this concept of having a moral right that is set forth and defended by Tom Regan in *The Case for Animal Rights*, chapters 8 and 9. A full account of my objections to Regan's views on the relations between moral rights and inherent value (equivalent to my "inherent worth") is to be published in 1987 in an issue of *The Monist* devoted to critical studies of Regan's important work.

the conceptual framework of the ethics of respect for nature, wild animals and plants can meaningfully be said to have moral rights.

However, we must realize that to ascribe rights to animals and plants in this manner should never lead us to think of them as having rights in the same way *we* have rights, that is, in what might be called the primary sense of being a rights-holder. Because we have a tendency to do this, however, it is less confusing to consider wild plants and animals simply as beings having inherent worth and not to use the language of rights regarding them at all. We do not really add anything new to the consideration of them as possessors of inherent worth by ascribing rights to them. For as we have just seen, ascribing rights to them simply gets us to perceive their good as imposing on moral agents a claim-to-be-respected, which is fully met by moral agents' carrying out the four types of duties. But we look at their good in the same way if we have the attitude of respect for nature and regard them as possessing inherent worth. The use of the *language* of rights introduces no new *concepts*. If wild animals and plants have inherent worth, the duties we have toward them are owed to them as their due. We may, if we like, put this point in the language of rights by saying that they are "entitled" to be treated in certain ways. But no additional meaning is involved when we use such language.

It would be less misleading if we simply dropped the language of moral rights concerning them. (Legal rights, of course, could still be ascribed to them.) It would be less misleading because the language of moral rights has come to be well-established in assertions about the rights of persons, especially in first-person assertions of our own rights. Using such language, indeed, is the only adequate way to express certain truths that have a central place in the moral outlook of the system of human ethics grounded on the principle of respect for persons. If moral rights are ascribed to animals and plants a different moral outlook, based on different foundations, is being expressed.

We can say all we need to say about the principles of a valid system of environmental ethics without using the language of rights. The concepts of the good of a living thing, of the inherent worth of a living thing, of the attitude of respect for nature, and the traditional idea of moral principles as validity binding upon all moral agents, are fully adequate. To add the notion of moral rights to this conceptual structure is not to add anything ethically significant. And since people will naturally tend to think of moral rights according to the paradigm provided by the rights of persons, confusion is likely to be engendered by the use of the language of rights in the domain of environmental ethics.

COMPETING CLAIMS AND PRIORITY
PRINCIPLES

1. *The General Problem of Competing Claims*

In this final chapter I consider the moral dilemmas that arise when human rights and values conflict with the good of nonhumans. Such conflicts occur whenever actions and policies that further human interests or fulfill human rights are detrimental to the well-being of organisms, species-populations, and life communities in the Earth's natural ecosystems. To put it another way, such conflicts occur whenever preserving and protecting the good of wild living things involves some cost in terms of human benefit. Clear examples are given in the following situations:

> Cutting down a woodland to build a medical center.
> Destroying a fresh water ecosystem in establishing a resort by the shore of a lake.
> Replacing a stretch of cactus desert with a suburban housing development.
> Filling and dredging a tidal wetland to construct a marina and yacht club.
> Bulldozing a meadow full of wildflowers to make place for a shopping mall.
> Removing the side of a mountain in a stripmining operation.
> Plowing up a prairie to plant fields of wheat and corn.

Taken in and of themselves, the various human activities and projects involved in these situations do not violate any rules of *human* ethics. All the interests motivating the activities are legitimate interests, and within the frame of reference set by the ethics of respect for persons, the liberty-rights of people entitle them to pursue those interests if they so wish. Assuming a just social system, the actions are morally permissible from the human perspective.

In each case, however, a price has to be paid by nature for the exercise of human rights. Direct and irreversible harm is being done to the Earth's wild living things. If we have adopted the attitude of respect for nature, these activities present fundamental moral dilemmas for us. To further human values in these situations is to bring about severe, permanent adverse effects on the good of beings that have the same inherent worth as humans. Why should their good be sacrificed? On the other hand, to preserve and protect their good means preventing humans from achieving their valued ends. From the moral point of view, which alternative should be chosen?

Such conflicts between humans and nonhumans cannot be avoided. Not only must humans make use of the natural environment and thereby compete with animals and plants that might also need that environment as their habitat and food source, but humans must also directly consume some nonhumans in order to survive. (Perhaps only cultivated plants could be used as food, but some wildlife would have to be destroyed in making way for the required farms and greenhouses.) Furthermore, from the human standpoint those species of animal and plant life that are harmful to our survival and health must be controlled or gotten rid of. Every society that has an established culture interferes with and makes use of some parts of the natural world.

The clash between nature and civilization reaches its most extreme form in the total transformation of the natural world that takes place in modern industrialized nations. Here human manipulation, exploitation, and out-and-out destruction of what is given by nature is on so huge a scale that the entire physical and biological composition of our planet is profoundly affected. Given the rise of advanced technology, an economy dependent on and geared for high-level consumption, and the human population explosion, what is left of the natural world is quickly disappearing. The more we take for ourselves, the less there is for other species.

When we look at this conflict between human civilization and the natural world from an ethical standpoint, we do not see it as a brute, uncontrolled and uncontrollable struggle for survival. We view the competition between human cultures and the natural ways of nonhuman species as something that can exemplify a moral order. By imposing constraints on our own lifestyles and cultural practices, we who are moral agents have the capacity to replace the chaos of a world torn to pieces by human greed and voraciousness with a well-ordered moral universe in which both respect for wild creatures and respect for persons are given a place. There is no reason why, together with humans, a great variety of animal and plant life cannot exist side by side on our planet. In order to share the Earth with other species, however, we humans must impose limits on our population, our habits of consumption, and our technology. We will do this to the extent that we have genuine respect for the natural world and the living things in it.[1]

It is when we have adopted the attitude of respect for nature that there arise serious moral dilemmas posed by the competing interests of humans and nonhumans. The problems of choice take on an ethical dimension. Having respect for nature does not, after all, entail giving up or ignoring our human values. We may regard all wild animals and

---

[1] The need for limits to economic growth, justified on the basis of environmental considerations, has been advocated by a number of writers. Of special note are William Ophuls, *Economics and the Politics of Scarcity: A Prologue to a Political Theory of the Steady State* (San Francisco: W. H. Freeman, 1977), and Herman E. Daly, *Steady-State Economics: The Economics of Biophysical Equilibrium and Moral Growth* (San Francisco: W. H. Freeman, 1977). See also Joel Kassiola, "The Limits to Economic Growth: Politicizing Advanced Industrialized Society," *Philosophy and Social Criticism* 8/1 (Spring 1981): 87-113.

plants as possessing inherent worth, yet still believe that we are entitled to pursue our interests in the advancement of knowledge, the creation and appreciation of the arts, and many other aspects of civilized life. We may also think it is a basic moral right of every human person to choose her or his own plan of life and have the opportunity to live in accordance with it. Since we can retain the attitude of respect for persons even when we have also adopted the attitude of respect for nature, we may consider it our duty to allow people to exercise their moral rights, despite the fact that doing so inevitably involves using the resources of the natural world, including animals and plants themselves, for human benefit.

Suppose we do have both the attitude of respect for nature and that of respect for persons. The conflict between the good of other species and the realization of human values (including the opportunity to exercise human rights) then appears to us as a situation of *competing moral claims*. From the standpoint of respect for nature we recognize the duty not to harm or interfere with a viable life community of wild animals and plants. At the same time we acknowledge and accept the duty to provide for the freedom, autonomy, and well-being of ourselves and our fellow humans. When we are committed to both systems of ethics, the good of other species and the good of humans make claims that must equally be taken into consideration. Yet in many circumstances our meeting the demands of one claim precludes our meeting the demands of others.

If the argument against the idea of human superiority presented in Chapter Three is sound, it is not open to us to resolve such dilemmas by automatically giving greater moral weight to human claims and thereby letting them always override the competing claims of nonhumans. Nor can we avoid the issue by arguing that in the long run the interests of humans and the good of wild animals and plants coincide. Large numbers of organisms, species-populations, and communities of life can be destroyed for the sake of benefiting humans, and if care and foresight are taken, the future of human life on Earth could still be assured. The conflicts between humans and nonhumans are real.

The problem of competing claims that confronts us here, then, is the problem of finding a set of priority principles that cut across both the domain of environmental ethics and of human ethics. These priority principles must satisfy the five formal conditions of morality, since they are themselves moral principles. They must therefore be general in form, universally applicable, disinterested, advocated for all agents, and considered as properly overriding any nonmoral norms. As far as their material condition is concerned, they must embody the concept of *fairness*. Their content must be such that, when decisions are made on their basis, all parties to the conflict are treated fairly. Thus our search for valid priority principles is a search for an answer to the question: How can situations of competing moral claims arising from conflicts between human ethics and environmental ethics be fairly resolved?

2. *Human Rights and the Inherent Worth of Nonhumans*

One difficulty implicit in situations of competing claims between humans and nonhumans has to do with the view (which I defended in Chapter Five) that humans have moral rights while animals and plants do not. One might think that this entails the priority of human claims over those of animals and plants. We may see that this in fact is not so if we review to what beliefs and values we are committed when we have adopted the attitude of respect for nature on the basis of the biocentric outlook. The key point to remember is that we have rejected the whole idea of human superiority over other forms of life. This was made clear in the analysis of the fourth component of the biocentric outlook, where the notion of human superiority was shown to be nothing but an irrational and arbitrary bias in favor of our own species. Now, the reasoning leading to this conclusion is not affected in any way by the argument that shows that human persons alone are full-fledged bearers of moral rights. For that argument does not support the view that among those rights is the right to dominate and exploit nonhumans for the benefit of humans, nor does it support the view that other living things have less inherent worth than human rights-holders.

Human persons ascribe to themselves moral rights because they place supreme value on their personhood. Having self-respect, they address the community of moral agents and demand that the necessary conditions for their very existence as persons be secured. The same claim they make against others they also acknowledge as rightfully made by others against them. Thus the concept of moral rights sets a firm relationship of equality among all bearers of rights.

This equality among rights-holders, however, does not imply any *inequality* between rights-holders and other living things.[2] It is true that the latter cannot demand that they be respected as beings possessing inherent worth by addressing their claim-to-be-respected to the moral community. For this reason they are not the sort of beings to which (primary) moral rights can meaningfully be ascribed. But their claim-to-be-respected can still be acknowledged by moral agents, who can see themselves as being under constraints with regard to that claim. They will in fact see themselves this way when they consider nonhuman living things to have inherent worth, the *same* inherent worth they themselves possess as bearers of moral rights. And just as they believe that other moral agents must respect their good for their sake, so they believe that they must respect the good of animals and plants who, because they possess inherent worth, deserve equal concern and consideration with humans. To put it another way, to adopt the

[2] This point was also made in Chapter Three, where I examined Louis G. Lombardi's arguments for the superiority of humans over animals and plants.

attitude of respect for nature is to consider morally irrelevant the fact that wild animals and plants, unlike human persons, are not bearers of moral rights.

What, then, is the source of the special importance we all place on our rights? Doesn't the status of being a bearer of moral rights give us a claim that goes beyond that entailed by our inherent worth? The answer is no. What we *do* gain by having that status is the public recognition by the moral community of the inviolability or "sanctity" of our personhood. We are understood by everyone to have the same entitlement to our existence as persons as anyone else in that community.

The importance attached to our rights, therefore, is an importance connected with our membership in the moral community. It does not signify that our personhood endows us with greater inherent worth than the inherent worth of those who are not members of that community. Since all living things have a good of their own, the realization of which is the central goal of their lives (even if that goal is not an end consciously aimed at), their having the opportunity to pursue their good is as important to them as our having the opportunity to pursue our autonomously chosen values is to us. This sameness of importance is not undercut by the conceptual point that we have the *right* to pursue our values but they do not have the right to pursue their good (since they are not the sort of beings who can have rights in the primary sense in which persons have rights).

We are left, then, with the problem of competing claims set out in the earlier part of this chapter. We must still try to find priority principles for resolving conflicts between humans and nonhumans which do not assign greater inherent worth to humans, but consider all parties as having the same worth. The principles, in other words, must be consistent with the fundamental requirement of *species-impartiality*. For only then can there be genuine fairness in the resolution of such conflicts.

3. Five Priority Principles for the Fair Resolution of Conflicting Claims

I shall now consider in depth five such principles, to be designated as follows:

a. The principle of self-defense.
b. The principle of proportionality.
c. The principle of minimum wrong.
d. The principle of distributive justice.
e. The principle of restitutive justice.

Although I believe these five principles cover all the major ways of adjudicating fairly among competing claims arising from clashes between the duties of human ethics and those of environmental ethics, I must emphasize at the outset that they do not yield a neat solution to every possible conflict situation. Each principle represents one cluster of morally relevant considerations one must take into account, and these considerations can serve as rough guides in reaching decisions about what duties outweigh others. But the principles do not function as premises in a deductive argument. We cannot deduce from them, along with the facts of the case, a true conclusion expressible in a normative statement about what ought to be done, all things considered. We should strive to make our decisions on the basis of relevant considerations, and the relevance of a consideration is determined by the application of the principles. To the extent we are successful in this case we can have some confidence in the fairness of our judgment. Nevertheless, there will always be a degree of uncertainty, and our minds should accordingly be open to the possibility that we have made a mistake. We must remain ready to revise our judgment, not only in the light of new factual information but also on the basis of further critical reflection concerning the precise meaning of a principle and the conditions of its proper application.

Using these five principles as normative guides in our decision making will not enable us to avoid the "hard cases." (The same holds true for conflicts of duties *within* human ethics or environmental ethics.) These are the cases where the competing claims are so complex and so powerful on both sides that no solution by reference to the principles alone can be reached. These inevitable gaps in our decision-making procedure, however, need not mean that we must then become arbitrary in our choice of what to do. We must take another step in seeking a fair resolution of the conflict. This step involves appealing to *the ethical ideal* that underlies and inspires (defines the "spirit" of) the whole structure of priority relations contained in the five principles and their conditions of applicability. I shall analyze and explain what this ethical ideal is after discussing the five principles. It provides a comprehensive vision of the place of human values in the larger world of the natural order of living things. We might designate it "an ideal harmony between nature and human civilization." It is this vision of a "best possible world" that expresses the spirit behind the letter of the five principles, that unifies them and interrelates them in a coherent manner, and that gives them their overall point and purpose. It is in the light of this ethical ideal that all the hard cases must finally be resolved. Thus a fair resolution to a problem of competing claims, even when not wholly determined by one of the principles, is a decision that fits coherently into the overall vision of human civilization and nature that underlies and unifies the five principles.

Putting aside consideration of this ethical ideal until later, I shall now consider the five priority principles in the order given in the foregoing list.

a. The Principle of Self-Defense

The principle of self-defense states that it is permissible for moral agents to protect themselves against dangerous or harmful organisms by destroying them. This holds, how-ever, only when moral agents, using reasonable care, can-not avoid being exposed to such organisms and cannot pre-vent them from doing serious damage to the environmental conditions that make it possible for moral agents to exist and function as moral agents. Furthermore, the principle does not allow the use of just any means of self-protection, but only those means that will do the least possible harm to the organisms consistent with the purpose of preserving the existence and functioning of moral agents. There must be no available alternative that is known to be equally effec-tive but to cause less harm to the "attacking" organisms.

The principle of self-defense permits actions that are ab-solutely required for maintaining the very existence of moral agents and for enabling them to exercise the capaci-ties of moral agency. It does not permit actions that involve the destruction of organisms when those actions simply promote the interests or values which moral agents may have as persons. Self-defense is defense against *harmful* and *dangerous* organisms, and a harmful or dangerous organism in this context is understood to be one whose activities threaten the life or basic health of those entities which need normally functioning bodies to exist as moral agents.

There is a close parallel here with the principle of self-de-fense as it is found in the domain of human ethics. If we have a moral right to life it follows that we also have a moral right to protect ourselves, by forceful means if necessary, when our lives are threatened by others. But this does not mean we are permitted to use force against others merely to further our own ends and values. It should be noted that even when the attacker is an innocent human being, as would be the case where an insane man is going berserk and will harm us unless we use force to stop him, our right of self-defense makes it permissible to protect ourselves against him to the point of killing him if there is no other way to avoid being killed ourselves. Thus the parallel with self-defense in environmental ethics against nonhuman animals and plants holds. The fact that the "attackers" are morally innocent does not invalidate the principle.

The full meaning of this priority principle and the grounds on which it rests can be brought out by considering the following three points.

(i) The principle of self-defense does not justify harming creatures that do not harm us unless doing so is a practical necessity arising from a situation where we cannot separate harmless organisms from the harmful ones against which we are defending ourselves. In this respect we shall see that the principle of self-defense differs from the second, third, and fourth principles to be considered. In certain situations to which these other principles apply, harm may have to be done to at least some harmless creatures even when this is not a matter of protecting ourselves from harm.

(ii) Despite what might at first appear to be a bias in favor of humans over other species, the principle of self-defense is actually consistent with the requirement of species-impartiality. It does not allow moral agents to further the interests of any organism because it belongs to one species rather than another. In particular, humans are not given an advantage simply on the basis of their humanity.

There are two considerations that support this claim to species neutrality. In the first place the principle of self-defense is formulated in such a way as to be species-blind. The statement of the principle refers only to moral agents and organisms (of whatever species) that are not moral agents. No mention is made of humans and nonhumans. Of course, in discussing various aspects and implications of the principle, one ordinarily refers to humans defending themselves against nonhumans as typical of situations in which the principle applies to the practical circumstances of life. Strictly speaking, however, no reference to any species need be made. The fact that (most) humans are moral agents and (most) nonhumans are not is a contingent truth which the principle does not take to be morally relevant. Moral agents are permitted to defend themselves against harmful or dangerous organisms that are not moral agents. This is all the principle of self-defense allows. If there happen to be nonhuman moral agents whose existence as moral agents is endangered by the actions of humans who are not moral agents (such as the insane and the severely retarded), then the principle states that it is permissible for the nonhumans in question to kill those humans who endanger them, if this is required for the preservation of the nonhumans' status as moral agents and there is no alternative way to protect themselves.

The second consideration that supports the species-impartiality of the principle is that the principle is fully consistent with the idea that all living things, human and nonhuman alike, have the same inherent worth. It is helpful here to refer once again to the principle of self-defense in the domain of human ethics. Our right to use force against another human being who assaults us does not imply that we have greater inherent worth than the attacker. It only means that we can rightfully use a "least evil" means to preserve our own existence. Indeed, out of respect for the personhood of the other we are duty-bound to do him or her no greater harm than is absolutely needed for our defense.

Equality of worth between aggressor and defender in human ethics is shown in our willingness to make the principle of self-defense universal. From a moral point of view we would judge it right for another to defend herself or himself against ourselves if *we* were the aggressor. This idea of reversibility (if it is right for A to do X to B it is right for B to do X to A) entails the equal worth of agent and subject. For any person may be in the role of subject and any may be in the role of agent, without change in the justifiability of acts of self-defense.

In the case of self-defense against animals and plants, however, the universalizability and reversibility tests are inapplicable, since animals and plants cannot take the role of moral agents, though they can be in the position of moral subjects. What they do to us is neither right nor wrong, because their activities are not within the range of moral standards or rules. Still, the permissibility of our defense against them does not imply they are inferior in worth to us, as we can see from the following considerations. When we have a firm sense of our own worth we place intrinsic value on our existence as persons. Out of self-respect we judge our personhood to be something worthy of being preserved. At the same time we believe that we are not inferior in worth to animals or plants. Now if we were to refrain from defending ourselves against them and so allow them to kill us, we would be sacrificing our very existence to them. To *require* such a sacrifice as a moral duty could only be justified on the ground that they have greater inherent worth than we do. Assuming that we have no good reasons for accepting that ground, we may conclude that there is no validly binding duty on our part to sacrifice ourselves to them. It is therefore morally permissible for us to defend ourselves against them, even though they are equal to us in inherent worth.

(iii) The third point has to do with the unavoidability of actions taken under the principle. With regard to the parallel case in the domain of human ethics, we are permitted to use force against another in defense of our life only when we cannot avoid the other's attack or escape from the situation. If someone threatens us and we can safely get out of the way, we should do so. For the analogous case of resolving competing claims by reference to the principle of self-defense, we should make every reasonable effort to avoid situations where nonhuman organisms will be likely to harm us, and we should keep ourselves strong and healthy so that there is less need to destroy other creatures whose activities would endanger us in a weak condition. Finally, before the harming of nonhuman organisms can be permitted on grounds of self-defense, it must be the case that reasonable precautions have been taken by moral agents to guard against known circumstances where disease, poisoning, or other biologically caused dangers are apt to be present.

The reason for these restrictions and qualifications is that all living things, whether harmful or harmless to humans, possess inherent worth and so are the appropriate objects of the attitude of respect. To kill or otherwise harm such creatures is always something morally bad in itself and can only be justified if we have no feasible alternative. At the same time we must have a valid moral reason for doing so, and a moral reason sufficiently weighty to override the prima facie reason against doing so. Self-defense, when understood as an act absolutely required to preserve the very existence of a moral agent, can be such an overriding reason. It is only under these conditions that the principle of self-defense applies.[3]

b. The Principle of Proportionality

Before considering in detail each of the four remaining priority principles, it is well to look at the way they are interrelated. First, all four principles apply to situations where the nonhuman organisms involved are *harmless*. If left alone their activities would not endanger or threaten human life and health. Thus all four principles apply to cases of conflict between humans and nonhumans that are not covered by the principle of self-defense.

Next we must make a distinction between basic and nonbasic interests.[4] Using this distinction, the arrangement of

[3] For this account of self-defense as a moral principle, I am indebted to Charles Fried, *Right and Wrong* (Cambridge, Mass.: Harvard University Press, 1978), pp. 42-53.

[4] In one of the few systematic studies of priority principles holding between humans and nonhumans, Donald VanDeVeer argues that the distinction between basic and "peripheral" (nonbasic) interests, which applies to all species that can be said to have interests, is a morally relevant difference; see VanDeVeer, "Interspecific Justice," *Inquiry* 22/1-2 (Summer 1979): 55-79. VanDeVeer would not, however, be likely to accept any of the priority principles I set out since he considers the psychological capacity to live a satisfying life a ground for counting the interests of beings possessing that capacity to be of greater weight than the equally basic interests of beings lacking it. His main reason for opposing pure egalitarianism among species seems to be that such a view is counterintuitive, being incompatible with "our deepest and strongest pre-theoretical convictions about specific cases" (p. 58; see also pp. 66 and 76). For reasons given in Chapter

the four principles can be set out as follows. The principles of proportionality and minimum wrong apply to cases in which there is a conflict between the *basic* interests of animals or plants and the *nonbasic* interests of humans. The principle of distributive justice, on the other hand, covers conflicts where the interests of all parties involved are *basic*. Finally, the principle of restitutive justice applies only where, in the past, either the principle of minimum wrong or that of distributive justice has been used. Each of those principles creates situations where some form of compensation or reparation must be made to nonhuman organisms, and thus the idea of restitution becomes applicable.

What differentiates basic from nonbasic interests? To answer this it is necessary first to define what is meant by the term "interests" and then specify criteria for determining whether interests are basic or nonbasic. In our present context it will be convenient if we speak of those events and conditions in the lives of organisms that are conducive to the realization of their good as furthering, promoting, or advancing their interests. Events and conditions detrimental to the realization of their good will be described as being adverse to, opposed to, or unfavorable to their interests. I shall also use the term "interests" to refer to whatever objects or events serve to preserve or protect to some degree

One, I do not consider any appeal to pre-theoretical convictions, however deeply held, to be philosophically relevant.

VanDeVeer's position has recently been defended, with certain qualifications, by Robin Attfield in *The Ethics of Environmental Concern* (New York: Columbia University Press, 1983), chapter 9. Attfield holds that ". . . varying degrees of *intrinsic* value attach to lives in which different capacities are realized" (Attfield's italics, p. 176). This is a view similar to that of Louis G. Lombardi, which I critically examined in Chapter Three. Attfield's arguments, unlike Lombardi's, are marred by a failure to distinguish the concept of intrinsic value from that of inherent worth. The utilitarianism Attfield espouses is not seen to be logically incompatible with the principle that each organism has inherent worth as an individual, a principle he also appears to hold. The incompatibility of these two ideas has been clearly explained by Tom Regan in *The Case for Animal Rights*, chapters 7 and 8. See also note 6, below.

or other the good of a living thing. Whether or not an organism likes or dislikes anything, feels pleasure or pain, has any conscious desires, aims, or goals, cares about or is concerned with what happens to it, and whether or not it is even conscious at all, I shall here speak of its interests in this way.

In considering how interests can be classified as basic and nonbasic, we must take into account the fact that the interests of an organism can be of different degrees of comparative importance to it. One of its interests is of greater importance to it than another, either if the occurrence of the first makes a more substantial contribution to the realization of its good than the second, or if the occurrence of the first is a necessary condition for the preservation of its existence while the occurrence of the second is not. We might say that one interest is of greater importance than another to the extent that the nonfulfillment of the first will constitute a more serious deprivation or loss than the non-fulfillment of the second. The most important interests are those whose fulfillment is needed by an organism if it is to remain alive.

It is possible for us to make judgments of the comparative importance of interests of nonhuman animals and plants because, once we become factually enlightened about what protects or promotes their good, we can *take their standpoint* and judge what is, from their point of view, an important or unimportant event in their lives as far as their overall well-being is concerned. Thus we are able to make a reasonable estimate of how seriously they would be harmed or deprived of something good if a certain condition were absent from their lives.

What counts as a serious harm or deprivation will, of course, depend on the kind of organism concerned. If each organism has a good of its own, so that it makes sense to speak of its faring well or poorly to the extent that it is able or unable to live a life fitted for its species-specific nature, then we may consider a serious harm or deprivation as being whatever severely impairs its ability to live such a life or makes it totally unable to do so.

In the case of humans a serious harm or deprivation will be whatever takes away or greatly reduces their powers of rationality and autonomy, including conditions of mental or physical incapacity that make it impossible for them to live a meaningful life. Since properly functioning organs and the soundness and health of other components of one's body are essential to human well-being, whatever injures these parts of one's body is a harm. The seriousness of the harm depends on the extent and permanence of damage done to those parts and on their contribution to the ability of the organism as a whole to function in a healthy way. With regard to the psychological aspects of a human being, a serious harm will include anything that causes insanity, severe emotional disorder, or mental retardation of a kind that prevents the development or exercise of the basic powers of rationality and autonomy.

I might note that with reference to humans, basic interests are what rational and factually enlightened people would value as an essential part of their very existence as *persons*. They are what people need if they are going to be able to pursue those goals and purposes that make life meaningful and worthwhile. Thus for human persons their basic interests are those interests which, when morally legitimate, they have a *right* to have fulfilled. As we saw in the preceding chapter, we do not have a right to whatever will make us happy or contribute to the realization of our value system; we do have a right to the necessary conditions for the maintenance and development of our personhood. These conditions include subsistence and security ("the right to life"), autonomy, and liberty. A violation of people's moral rights is the worst thing that can happen to them, since it deprives them of what is essential to their being able to live a meaningful and worthwhile life. And since the fundamental, necessary conditions for such a life are the same for everyone, our human rights have to do with universal values or primary goods. They are the entitlement we all have as persons to what makes us persons and preserves our existence as persons.

In contrast with these universal values or primary goods that constitute our basic interests, our non-basic interests are the particular ends we consider worth seeking and the means we consider best for achieving them that make up our individual value systems. The nonbasic interests of humans thus vary from person to person, while their basic interests are common to all.

This discussion of basic and non-basic interests has been presented to introduce the second and third priority principles on our list, proportionality and minimum wrong. Both principles employ the distinction between basic and nonbasic interests, so it was necessary to clarify this distinction before examining them.

The principles apply to two different kinds of conflicts among competing claims. In both cases we are dealing with situations in which the *basic* interests of animals and plants conflict with the *nonbasic* interests of humans. But each principle applies to a different type of nonbasic human interests. In order to differentiate between these types we must consider various ways in which the nonbasic interests of humans are related to the attitude of respect for nature.

First, there are nonbasic human interests which are *intrinsically incompatible with* the attitude of respect for nature. The pursuit of these interests would be given up by anyone who had respect for nature since the kind of actions and intentions involved in satisfying them directly embody or express an exploitative attitude toward nature. Such an attitude is incompatible with that of respect because it means that one considers wild creatures to have merely instrumental value for human ends. To satisfy nonbasic interests of this first kind is to deny the inherent worth of animals and plants in natural ecosystems. Examples of such interests and of actions performed to satisfy them are the following (all actually occur in the contemporary world):

Slaughtering elephants so the ivory of their tusks can be used to carve items for the tourist trade.

Killing rhinoceros so that their horns can be used as dagger handles.

Picking rare wildflowers, such as orchids and cactuses, for one's private collection.

Capturing tropical birds, for sale as caged pets.

Trapping and killing reptiles, such as snakes, crocodiles, alligators, and turtles, for their skins and shells to be used in making expensive shoes, handbags, and other "fashion" products.

Hunting and killing rare wild mammals, such as leopards and jaguars, for the luxury fur trade.

All hunting and fishing which is done as an enjoyable pastime (whether or not the animals killed are eaten), when such activities are not necessary to meet the basic interests of humans. This includes all sport hunting and recreational fishing.

The ends and purposes of these practices and the human interests that motivate them are inherently incompatible with the attitude of respect for nature in the following sense. If we consider the various practices along with their central purposes as representing a certain human attitude toward nature, this attitude can only be described as exploitative. Those who participate in such activities with the aim of accomplishing the various purposes that motivate and direct them, as well as those who enjoy or consume the products while knowing the methods by which they were obtained, cannot be said to have genuine respect for nature. For all such practices treat wild creatures as mere instruments to human ends, thus denying their inherent worth. Wild animals and plants are being valued only as a source of human pleasure or as things that can be manipulated and used to bring about human pleasure.

It is important to realize that the human interests that underlie these practices are nonbasic. Even when hunters and fishermen eat what they have killed, this is incidental to the central purpose and governing aim of their sport. (I am not at this point considering the very different case of subsistence hunting and fishing, where such activities are not done as enjoyable pastimes but out of necessity.) That eating what they kill is a matter of pleasure and hence serves only a nonbasic interest is shown by the fact that they would continue to hunt or fish even if, for some reason of health or convenience, they did not eat the mammal, bird, or fish they killed. They are not hunting or fishing in order to have enough food to live.

With reference to this and to all the other examples given, it should be noted that none of the actions violate human rights. Indeed, if we stay within the boundaries of human ethics alone, people have a moral right to do such things, since they have a freedom-right to pursue without interference their legitimate interests and, within those boundaries, an interest is "legitimate" if its pursuit does not involve doing any wrong *to another human being*.

It is only when the principles of environmental ethics are applied to such actions that the exercise of freedom-rights in these cases must be weighed against the demands of the ethics of respect for nature. We then find that the practices in question are wrong, *all things considered*. For if they were judged permissible, the basic interests of animals and plants would be assigned a lower value or importance than the nonbasic interests of humans, which no one who had the attitude of respect for nature (as well as the attitude of respect for persons) would find acceptable. After all, a human being can still live a good life even if he or she does not own caged wild birds, wear apparel made from furs and reptile skins, collect rare wildflowers, engage in hunting and fishing as recreational pastimes, buy ivory carvings, or use horn dagger handles. But every one of these practices treats wild animals and plants as if their very existence is something having no value at all, other than as means to the satisfaction of human preferences.

Let us now consider another type of nonbasic human interest that can come into conflict with the basic interests of wild animals and plants. These are human interests which, in contrast with those just considered, are not *in themselves* incompatible with respect for nature. Nevertheless, the pursuit of these interests has *consequences* that are undesirable from the perspective of respect for nature and should therefore be avoided if possible. Sometimes the nonbasic human interests concerned will not be valued highly enough to outweigh the bad consequences of fulfilling them. In that case a person who has respect for nature would willingly forgo the pursuit of those interests. Other times the interests will be so highly valued that even those who genuinely respect nature will not be willing to forgo the pursuit of the interests. In the latter case, although having and pursuing the interests do not embody or express the attitude of respect for nature, neither do they embody or express a purely exploitative attitude toward nature. Wild animals and plants are not being used or consumed as mere means to human ends, though the consequences of actions in which the interests are pursued are such that wild creatures suffer harm. Examples of nonbasic interests of this type are:

Building an art museum or library where natural habitat must be destroyed.

Constructing an airport, railroad, harbor, or highway involving the serious disturbance of a natural ecosystem.

Replacing a native forest with a timber plantation.

Damming a free-flowing river for a hydroelectric power project.

Landscaping a natural woodland in making a public park.

Whether people who have true respect for nature would give up the activities involved in these situations depends on the value they place on the various interests being furthered. This in turn would depend on people's total systems of value and on what alternatives were available—in particular, whether substitutes less damaging to the environment could be found and whether some or all of the interests could be satisfied in other ways.

Let us recapitulate this classification of nonbasic human interests, since it is crucial to the examination of the priority principles I will consider below. First there are interests that directly express an exploitative attitude toward nature; actions taken to satisfy such interests are intrinsically incompatible with respect for nature. Second, there are interests that do not exemplify in themselves an exploitative attitude toward nature, but in many practical circumstances the means taken to satisfy those interests bring about effects on the natural world which, in the eyes of those who have respect for nature, are to be avoided whenever possible. Among this second class of interests are those which are not important enough to (not so highly valued by) a person to make the gains of their pursuit outweigh the undesirable consequences for wildlife. Others are such that their value does outweigh the undesirable consequences, even when such weight is assigned by one who has full respect for nature.

This classification bears on the two priority principles we are now about to consider: the principle of proportionality and that of minimum wrong. Each of the two kinds of nonbasic human interests mentioned above determines the range of application of one of these principles. The principle of proportionality applies to situations of conflict between the basic interests of wild animals and plants and those nonbasic human interests that are intrinsically incompatible with respect for nature. The principle of minimum wrong, on the other hand, applies to conflicts between the basic interests of wild animals and plants and those non-basic human interests that are so highly valued that even a person who has respect for nature would not be willing to abstain from pursuing them, knowing that the pursuit of such interests will bring about conditions detrimental to the natural world.

The accompanying figure schematically represents the relations among the five priority principles and their ranges of application.

Putting aside consideration of the principle of minimum wrong until later, I shall now discuss that of proportionality. The central idea of the principle of proportionality is that, in a conflict between human values and the good of (harmless) wild animals and plants, greater weight is to be given to basic than to nonbasic interests, no matter what species, human or other, the competing claims arise from. Within its proper range of application the principle prohibits us from allowing nonbasic interests to override basic ones, even if the nonbasic interests are those of humans and the basic are those of animals and plants.[5]

The conditions of applicability of this principle are that the human interests concerned are nonbasic ones that are intrinsically incompatible with the attitude of respect for nature, that the competing claims arise from the basic inter-

---

[5] My principle of proportionality is similar to Tom Regan's "Worse-off Principle," differing mainly from it in that the "Worse-off Principle" is stated in terms of rights and is restricted to conflicts between humans and only those animals that satisfy what Regan calls "the subject-of-a-life criterion." These are animals that ". . . have beliefs and desires; perception, memory, and a sense of the future, including their own future; an emotional life together with feelings of pleasure and pain; preference- and welfare-interests; the ability to initiate action in pursuit of their desires and goals; a psychophysical identity over time; and an individual welfare in the sense that their experiental life fares well or ill for them, logically independently of their utility for others and logically independently of their being the object of anyone else's interests" (*The Case for Animal Rights*, p. 243). The "Worse-off Principle" is set forth and discussed by Regan on pp. 307-312 of his book.

WILD ANIMALS AND PLANTS	Harmful to Humans	Harmless to Humans (Or: their harmfulness can reasonably be avoided)		
		Basic Interests		*Basic Interests*
. . . in conflict with . . .		. . . in conflict with . . .		. . . in conflict with . . .
		Nonbasic interests		*Basic interests*
HUMANS		Intrinsically incompatible with respect for nature.	Intrinsically compatible with respect for nature, but extrinsically detrimental to wildlife and natural ecosystems.	
PRIORITY PRINCIPLES	(1) *Self-defense*	(2) *Proportionality*	(3) *Minimum wrong*	(4) *Distributive justice*
			. . . when (3) or (4) have been applied . . . (5) *Restitutive justice*	

ests of wild animals and/or plants, and that these animals and plants are harmless to humans (self-defense is not in question). Examples of conflicts of the relevant sort were given earlier. It should be noted that such practices as recreational fishing and hunting and buying luxury furs made from the pelts of wild creatures are actually accepted by millions of people as morally permissible. This fact merely shows the unquestioned, total anthropocentricity of their outlook on nature and their attitude toward wild creatures. It is clear, however, that from the standpoint of the life-centered system of environmental ethics defended in this book, such practices are to be condemned as being fundamentally exploitative of beings who have as much inherent worth as those who exploit them.

c. The Principle of Minimum Wrong

The principle of minimum wrong applies to situations in which (i) the basic interests of animals and plants are unavoidably in competition with nonbasic interests of humans; (ii) the human interests in question are *not* intrinsically incompatible with respect for nature; (iii) actions needed to satisfy those interests, however, are detrimental to the basic interests of animals and plants; and (iv) the human interests involved are so important that rational and factually informed people who have genuine respect for nature are not willing to relinquish the pursuit of those interests even when they take into account the undesirable consequences for wildlife.

Examples of such situations were given earlier: building a library or art museum where natural habitat must be destroyed; constructing an airport, railroad, harbor, or highway involving serious disturbance of a natural ecosystem; damming a river for a hydroelectric power project; replacing a wilderness forest with a timber plantation; landscaping a natural woodland to make a public park. The problem of priority in these situations is this: How can we tell when it is morally permissible for humans to pursue their nonbasic interests when doing so adversely affects the basic interests of wild animals and plants?

It is true here as it was in the case of the principle of proportionality that human ethics *alone* permits actions (such as destroying wildlife habitat in order to build an art museum) that further nonbasic human interests at the expense of the basic interests of other living things. This is because humans have a freedom-right to pursue their legitimate interests, where an interest is legitimate when its pursuit does not involve wrongdoing *to other humans*. But as soon as the principles of environmental ethics are brought in, what people have a right to do with regard to other persons is no longer the decisive question. The well-being of other living things must be taken into consideration.

Now, fulfilling the nonbasic interests of humans in our present case is held to be so important that, even for those who have the attitude of respect for nature, such fulfillment is deemed to be worth the cost of harming wildlife. What is the basis for this special importance? The answer lies, first, in the role such interests play in the overall view of civilized life that rational and informed people tend to adopt autonomously as part of their total world outlook. Secondly, the special value given to these interests stems from the central place they occupy in people's rational conception of their own true good. The first point concerns the cultural or social aspect of the valued interests—more specifically, the importance of their contribution to human civilization seen from a broad historical perspective. The second concerns the relation of the valued interests to an individual's view of the kind of life which, given one's circumstances and capacities, is most worth living.

With regard to the first point, the interests in question are considered by the people as essential to a whole society's maintaining a high level of culture, when judged from the shared standards of its common way of life as it has developed throughout its history. The judgment of contribution to a high level of culture, I assume here, is being made by persons who are fully rational and enlightened. Not only the endeavor to create meritorious works and make worthwhile discoveries in the intellectual and aesthetic dimensions of human culture will be included among these valued interests, but also the legal, political, and economic systems needed for the community's steady advancement toward a high level of civilized life. Thus the goals and practices that form the core of a rational and informed conception of a community's highest values will be interests that carry great weight when they compete with the (basic) interests of the Earth's nonhuman inhabitants, even in the minds of people who regard those inhabitants as possessing an inherent worth equal to that of humans themselves. Using the concepts of intrinsic value and inherent value introduced earlier in this book, we might say that the system of *intrinsically valued ends* shared by a whole society as the focus of its way of life, along with those human creations and productions that are judged as *supremely inherently valuable* by rational and enlightened members of the society, determine the set of human interests that are to be weighed against the interests of animals and plants in the situations of conflict to which the principle of minimum wrong is applicable. Within the framework of a given culture's way of life when we see it from the perspective of its history, taking into account the *meaning* its history has for the people of that culture, we can make a rational and informed judgment of the kind of civilization that is, within that framework and from that perspective, most worthy of being preserved. The human values, intrinsic and inherent, whose realization is central to that conception of civilization are the values that must be compared in importance with the undesirability of destroying wildlife habitat and natural ecosystems, when that is an unavoidable consequence of realizing those values.

Similarly, when certain human interests are seen to lie at the center of a rational person's system of autonomously chosen ends, thus functioning as the unifying framework for a total conception of an individual's own true good, the value placed on such interests may be given greater weight by the person than the undesirable effects on the natural world the pursuit of those interests might have, even when the person has adopted the attitude of respect for nature.

We have so far dealt with the kinds of conflict to which the principle of minimum wrong applies. It is now time to make clear the content of the principle. The principle states that, when rational, informed, and autonomous persons *who have adopted the attitude of respect for nature* are nevertheless unwilling to forgo the two sorts of values mentioned above, even though they are aware that the consequences of pursuing those values will involve harm to wild animals and plants, it is permissible for them to pursue those values only so long as doing so involves fewer wrongs (violations of duties) than any alternative way of pursuing those values.

This principle sets certain moral constraints on the pursuit of the two types of human values we are concerned with here. In the case of social institutions and practices basic to a community's realization of a high level of civilization, the principle requires that the particular institutions and practices of a community are such that they result in the least wrong being done to the natural world. Here "least wrong" means the lowest number of violations of the rule of nonmaleficence in the ethical system of respect for nature. This lowest number of wrongdoings assumes that there are no alternative institutions and practices which could be used by the community to accomplish the same social ends but which would involve still fewer instances of wrongdoing to wild living things in natural ecosystems.

Concerning the second type of human value, the principle of minimum wrong lays down the requirement that actions taken by individuals in the pursuit of ends that lie at the core of their rational conceptions of their true good must be such that no alternative ways of achieving those ends produce fewer wrongs to wild living things. As before, the key test for moral permissibility is that certain nonbasic interests of humans may be furthered only under the condition of minimizing wrongs done to nonhumans in natural ecosystems.

Is this principle consistent with the idea that wild animals and plants have inherent worth? To answer this we must take into account the difference between a utilitarian calculation of consequences and a deontological or nonconsequential view of minimizing wrongdoings.[6] According to a

[6] The distinction between a utilitarian calculation of least bad consequences and a nonconsequential principle of minimizing violations of duty has been propounded and carefully examined by Tom Regan in *The Case for Animal Rights*, section 8.9, "Should the Numbers Count?" and section 8.10, "The Miniride and Worse-Off Principles" (pp. 297-312). Regan's work in this area, to which I am indebted, makes an original and signifi-

utilitarian ethical system there is always a duty, when harm must be done to some in bringing benefits to others, to do that action (or follow that rule) which produces the least amount of harm when weighed against the benefits. One simply calculates the best consequences, as measuered by quantities of intrinsic value and disvalue. The principle of minimum wrong, on the other hand, does not consider the beings that are benefited or harmed as so many "containers" of intrinsic value or disvalue. They are beings to which are owed prima facie duties. We owe the duty of nonmaleficence, for example, to both humans and nonhumans alike. Each being has inherent worth as an individual and must accordingly be treated with respect, regardless of what species it belongs to. An action that brings harm to any one such being constitutes a prima facie wrong from which moral agents have a duty to refrain. To harm several such beings is not merely to bring about a certain amount of intrinsic disvalue in the world, to be balanced against whatever value might also be produced. It is to commit a number of violations of duty, corresponding to the number of creatures harmed.

Suppose, then, that one alternative way for humans to pursue their interests in situations of the sort we are here concerned with brings harm to a certain number of living things, while another way to pursue the same interests involves harm done to a smaller number of living things. If we were to choose the first alternative we would be knowingly performing more wrong actions than if we chose the second. It is not the aggregate amount of disvalue or harm that is relevant here, but the number of cases in which one fails to carry out one's duty to another being. Each entity that is harmed is thereby treated unjustly and so is wronged. Because the duty of nonmaleficence is owed to each individual organism, it would be morally unjustified to harm a larger number of organisms than a smaller num-

---

cant contribution to human ethics as well as to our understanding of the moral relations between humans and animals.

ber. If a particular act of a certain kind is wrong because it is of that kind, then more wrongs are committed when more particular acts of that kind are done. This is the central consideration that underlies the principle of minimum wrong.

In the light of this consideration we can now see why in general it is worse to harm a species-population than an individual organism, and still worse to harm a biotic community as a whole. We cannot do harm to a species-population without doing harm to a great many of the organisms that make up the population; harming one species-population is not simply doing wrong to one moral subject. Many such subjects, each having the same inherent worth, will also be wronged, namely all the members of the population that are killed or injured. Similarly, by damaging or destroying the ecological balance and integrity on which the well-being of an entire biotic community depends, harm is done to many of the species-populations that constitute the community. A great number of instances of violations of duty are thus involved.

This way of looking at the principle of minimum wrong does not entail a holistic or organicist view of environmental ethics, such as Aldo Leopold's "Land Ethic" or Holmes Rolston's "Ecological Ethic."[7]

The holistic view was critically discussed in Chapter Three in connection with the second component of the biocentric outlook (the natural world as a system of interdependence). What is relevant in the present context is the role that humans should play in relation to the natural world. According to the holistic view, the basic criterion for right action is the tendency of the action to preserve ecological integrity in the natural environment in which the action takes place. From this perspective one begins with the premises that human life is but one component of the

---

[7] Aldo Leopold, "The Land Ethic," in *A Sand County Almanac* (New York: Oxford University Press, 1949), pp. 201–26; Holmes Rolston III, "Is There an Ecological Ethic?" *Ethics* 85/2 (January 1975): 93-109. See also Chapter Three, note 5.

Earth's total ecosystem and that ecological integrity has value in itself. One then argues that the proper moral role of humans on Earth is to function in a biologically sound way in relation to the planet's biosphere. Humans are seen to occupy a certain ecological niche and accordingly should govern their conduct so as to maintain a healthy relationship with the worldwide ecosystem of which they are a part. Such a holistic view includes no conception of moral agents having duties that are owed to individual organisms, each of which is regarded as possessing inherent worth.

In contrast with this, the principle of minimum wrong presupposes that each living thing deserves moral consideration. Since each has inherent worth, a prima facie wrong is done when any one of them is harmed. It is true that a greater wrong is done when a whole species-population or biotic community is harmed. This is not because the group *as such* has a greater claim-to-be-respected than the individual, but because harming the group necessarily involves harming many individuals. Therefore, whenever we are in circumstances to which the principle of minimum wrong applies we are knowingly committing acts that are prima facie wrong. Only if we perform the fewest such acts available to us are we justified in what we do to living things. Our primary obligation in such situations is to choose the alternative which involves the least number of harm-causing acts.

There is, however, a further obligation that is binding upon us in these situations. This obligation must be fulfilled if we are to act consistently with the attitude of respect for nature. It is the duty entailed by the principle of species-impartiality between humans and nonhumans. Since we are aiming at a fair resolution of conflicting claims, whenever we cause harm to animals and plants in the pursuit of our human values, some recognition must be given to the fact that our treatment of them is prima facie wrong. This recognition is expressed in practical terms by our accepting the moral requirement to make restitution for the injustices we have committed. Even though we may have acted in accordance with the principle of minimum wrong, at least some creatures possessing inherent worth equal to our own have been unjustly treated. As a way of restoring the balance of justice between ourselves and them, some form of compensation must be provided for wild animals and plants. Only when that has been done can the actions we have performed in accordance with the principle of minimum wrong also satisfy the criterion of species-impartiality and so be morally justified, all things considered. (I shall discuss this further in connection with the principle of restitutive justice.)

The moral constraints imposed by the principle of minimum wrong are fully acceptable to the very beings whose actions are so constrained. For they are the agents who have adopted the attitude of respect for nature and who view their relation to the natural world from the perspective of the biocentric outlook. Thus they are disposed to *want* to minimize wrongs done to wild creatures while they pursue ends whose value is so great to them that they are unwilling to give them up. Their respect for nature is not diminished or weakened by their valuing of those ends. So they will readily acknowledge their obligation to adopt the principle of minimum wrong as setting valid moral restrictions upon their own decision and conduct. The principle, in other words, will be one to which they voluntarily subscribe and which they follow as their own normative guide.

What is the practical import of the idea of minimizing harm in the kinds of situations covered by the principle of minimum wrong? I shall consider this question by discussing the three chief ways in which such harm is done: (i) by habitat destruction, (ii) by environmental pollution, and (iii) by direct killing.

(i) *Habitat destruction*. In order for humans to pursue valued ends that are fundamental to their cultural ideals of a high-level civilization and to their individual conceptions of their own true good, it is necessary that some of the Earth's natural environment used by wild creatures as habitat be taken over for human purposes. Although this is unavoidable, it is still possible for persons, as free and responsible agents, to choose ways of life that minimize habitat destruction. They can make special efforts to avoid ruining complete ecosystems and to desist from annihilating whole communities of life. They can locate and construct their buildings, highways, airports, and harbors with the good of other species in mind. If they have a sufficient concern for the natural world, they can control their own population growth, change their habits of consumption, and regulate their technology so as to save at least part of the Earth's surface as habitat for wild animals and plants.

One way to minimize habitat destruction is to make use of areas that have already been used for human purposes but are now in a deteriorating state or have been abandoned. Rather than encroaching upon land that is still in a natural condition, it might well be possible simply to reoccupy locations that are no longer part of the natural environment. In this way the used areas of the Earth can be "recycled" and wilderness areas can be preserved as habitat for other species. So even if it is the case that some habitat destruction is unavoidable, there is still a duty to choose the least harmful alternative. This is what the principle of minimum wrong requires of us.

(ii) *Environmental pollution.* To pollute the natural environment is to degrade its quality, where the test of degradation is the capacity to be harmful to living things, human or nonhuman. Pollution is necessarily something undesirable from the standpoint of individual organisms. By its very nature it adversely affects the conditions of life on which the well-being of living things depends. Such adverse consequences need not involve harm to humans.

Although it is true that polluting the environment is not an absolutely necessary accompaniment of human culture in the way that habitat destruction is, nevertheless if people are to carry on a high-level civilization based on the steady

288

advancement of scientific and humanistic knowledge, if they are to enjoy an aesthetically rich culture, and if the values pursued by individuals are to be the result of their autonomous choice, at least some deterioration of the quality of the natural environment will occur.

It is clear how the principle of minimum wrong applies to these conflicts. To abide by that principle we must do all we can to minimize harm to all concerned, regardless of species membership. This means that we should follow certain general policies to ensure that only the least dangerous forms of pollution will be permitted and to clean up presently polluted environments that are harmful to nonhumans as well as to humans. Of course, the complete avoidance of pollution of any kind would be the ideal condition to seek as our ultimate goal. But there are a number of realistic measures we can take as we pursue that goal. We can recycle waste products or render them biologically harmless before depositing them on land or in water. We can use antipollution devices on automobile exhausts and factory smokestacks to eliminate air pollution. We can prevent the dumping of toxic chemicals and radioactive materials and learn how to detoxify present and past dumping sites. If it turns out that there is no safe way to dispose of certain radioactive and chemical wastes, we must simply cease to produce them.

The moral need for such measures is recognized by all who have concern for the natural environment. What is of special interest here is that these policies and practices are followed not only for the good of humans but also for the good of wild creatures themselves. They give concrete expression to our respect for nature as well as to our respect for persons.

One particularly important aspect of this willingness to make changes for the sake of the good of wild creatures by eliminating environment pollution is the attempt to develop what have been called "appropriate technologies."[8]

[8] The idea of appropriate technologies was originated by the economist E. F. Schumacher in his well-known book *Small Is Beautiful* (New York:

These are carefully controlled, small-scale, simplified industrial operations for producing goods and services in ways that are energy-efficient and environmentally clean. By learning to live without the vast scale of mechanization and complex technology typical of modern industrialized societies, we come to enjoy a greater harmony with the natural world. By designing human modes of work and productivity that fit into the natural environment, we do the least possible damage to nature through pollution. In this manner we adhere to the principle of minimum wrong, and the competing claims of both respect for persons and respect for nature are given fair consideration.

(iii) *Direct killing.* A third type of situation of competing claims to which the principle of minimum wrong applies is that in which humans cause the death of wild plants and animals by acts of intentionally killing them. (Such acts are here distinguished from the practices of indirectly bringing about their death through habitat destruction or environmental pollution.) Examples are taking plants and animals from their natural habitats and using them for artistic or educational purposes; collecting specimens of animal and plant life for scientific study; and spraying herbicides and insecticides in wildlife habitats (along highways and power lines, for example). In all such practices humans are going into natural areas and killing animals and plants for certain human purposes. These purposes must be connected with nonbasic interests which are central to a society's way of life or an individual's system of values, if the principle of minimum wrong is to apply.

How does the principle of minimum wrong determine a fair resolution of competing claims in situations of that kind? The following considerations are the relevant ones to be taken into account. First we must ask ourselves whether the human values being furthered are really worth the ex-

---

Harper and Row, 1973). The theme is further explored in his *Good Work* (New York: Harper and Row, 1979). Many examples of appropriate technologies now in use in countries all over the world are described in George McRobie, *Small Is Possible* (New York: Harper and Row, 1981).

treme cost being imposed on wild creatures. In this connection we should reflect on our own value system and on the way of life of our community to see whether a modification in values or a shift in perspective could not be made, consistent with the most fundamental aspects of that system or way of life, which would obviate at least some of the direct killing of nonhumans. Secondly, we should examine carefully all alternative possibilities open to us with regard to the manner of pursuing our values and way of life. The principle of minimum wrong demands that we choose the alternative that either eliminates direct killing entirely or that involves the least numbers killed. Finally, our respect for nature makes us respond with abhorrence to whatever killing is done, and gives rise to the recognition of our duty to make reparation or some form of compensation for the harm we have done to living things in the natural world. Our thoroughness, care, and conscientiousness in carrying out these three steps are then signs of the exercise of a sense of fairness in applying the principle of minimum wrong to cases of this sort.

This completes my account of the third priority principle. In the conflict situations classified above as habitat destruction, environmental pollution, and direct killing, we have seen that the general requirement to do least harm, which is laid down by the principle of minimum wrong, is not left entirely vague and unclear. It does yield some guidelines for resolving practical problems. We have also noted the limiting conditions under which the principle is to be applied. Although no simple "Do this," "Don't do that" prescriptions can be derived from the principle, it does serve to focus our attention on the kinds of consideration that are morally relevant.

d. The Principle of Distributive Justice

This fourth priority principle applies to competing claims between humans and nonhumans under two conditions.

First, the nonhuman organisms are not harming us, so the principle of self-defense does not apply. Secondly, the interests that give rise to the competing claims are on the same level of comparative importance, all being *basic* interests, so the principles of proportionality and of minimum wrong do not apply. The range of application of the fourth principle covers cases that do not fall under the first three.

This principle is called the principle of distributive justice because it provides the criteria for a just distribution of interest-fulfillment among all parties to a conflict when the interests are all basic and hence of equal importance to those involved. Being of equal importance, they are counted as having the same moral weight. This equality of weight must be preserved in the conflict-resolving decision if it is to be fair to all. The principle of distributive justice requires that when the interests of the parties are all basic ones and there exists a natural source of good that can be used for the benefit of any of the parties, each party must be allotted an equal share. A fair share in those circumstances is an equal share.

When we try to put this principle of distributive justice into practice, however, we find that even the fairest methods of distribution cannot guarantee perfect equality of treatment to each individual organism. Consequently we are under the moral requirement to supplement all decisions grounded on distributive justice with a further duty imposed by the fifth priority principle, that of restitutive justice. Since we are not carrying out perfect fairness, we owe some measures of reparation or compensation to wild creatures as their due. As was true in the case of the principle of minimum wrong, recognition of wrongs being done to entities possessing inherent worth calls forth the additional obligation to do what we can to make up for these wrongs. In this way the idea of fairness will be preserved throughout the entire system of priority principles.

In working out the various methods by which the principle of distributive justice can be put into practice, we must keep in mind the fact that the wild animals and plants we are concerned with are not themselves harmful to us. Consequently we are not under any necessity to kill them in self-defense. Since they are not "attacking" us, we can try to avoid or eliminate situations where we are forced to choose between their survival and ours. Thus the principle of distributive justice requires us to devise ways of transforming situations of confrontation into situations of mutual accommodation whenever it is possible to do so. In this way we can share the beneficial resources of the Earth equally with other members of the Community of Life. Our aim is to make it possible for wild animals and plants to carry on their natural existence side by side with human cultures.

Sometimes, however, the clash between basic human interests and the equally basic interests of nonhumans cannot be avoided. Perhaps the most obvious case arises from the necessity of humans to consume nonhumans as food. Although it may be possible for most people to eat plants rather than animals, I shall point out in a moment that this is not true of all people. And why should eating plants be ethically more desirable than eating animals?

Let us first look at situations where, due to severe environmental conditions, humans must use wild animals as a source of food. In other words, they are situations where subsistence hunting and fishing are necessary for human survival. Consider, for example, the hunting of whales and seals in the Arctic, or the killing and eating of wild goats and sheep by those living at high altitudes in mountainous regions. In these cases it is impossible to raise enough domesticated animals to supply food for a culture's populace, and geographical conditions preclude dependence on plant life as a source of nutrition. The principle of distributive justice applies to circumstances of that kind. In such circumstances the principle entails that it is morally *permissible* for humans to kill wild animals for food. This follows from the equality of worth holding between humans and animals.

For if humans refrained from eating animals in those circumstances they would in effect be sacrificing their lives for the sake of animals, and no requirement to do that is imposed by respect for nature. Animals are not of *greater* worth, so there is no obligation to further their interests at the cost of the basic interests of humans.

However, since it is always a prima facie duty of environmental ethics not to destroy whole ecosystems (the duties of nonmaleficence and noninterference), it follows that wherever possible the choice of animal food source and the methods used in hunting should be guided by the principle of minimum wrong. The impact on natural ecosystems of the practice of killing wild animals for food must not involve a greater number of wrongs than any available alternative.

The same considerations apply to the practice of culling wild animals for food (as is done with the Wildebeest and the Water Buffalo in Africa) where environmental conditions make it impossible to use domesticated animals or to grow edible plants for human survival. Here the morally right decision is determined, first by the permissibility of consuming wild animals under the principle of distributive justice, and second, by the obligation to choose the species of animal to be taken and the manner of taking them that entail least harm to all the wild living things in the area. Thus severe damage to natural ecosystems and whole biotic communities must be avoided wherever possible.

I turn now to the issue of meat-eating versus vegetarianism, at least as far as the principles of environmental ethics apply to it. There are two main points to be considered. The first is that, when we raise and slaughter animals for food, the wrong we do to them does not consist simply in our causing them pain. Even if it became possible for us to devise methods of killing them, as well as ways of treating them while alive, that involved little or no pain, we would still violate a prima facie duty in consuming them. They would still be treated as mere means to our ends and so would be wronged. Now, we saw above that it is permissible to kill animals when this is necessary for our survival. But will not the very same be true of our killing plants, in the light of the fact that plants, just like animals, are our equals in inherent worth? Although no pain or conscious suffering to living things is involved here, we are nevertheless using plants wholly for our own purposes. They are therefore being wronged when we kill them to eat them. Yet it is permissible to do this, since we have no duty to sacrifice ourselves to them. Whether we are dealing with animals or with plants, then, the principle of distributive justice applies (and along with it, as we shall see later, the principle of restitutive justice).

Still, the factor of animal suffering does raise important considerations in practice even if no greater wrong is committed in eating animals than in eating plants. Granted that susceptibility to pain does not give animals a higher inherent worth; nevertheless any form of conscious suffering is an intrinsically bad occurrence in the life of a sentient creature. From the standpoint of the animals involved, a life without such experiences is better than a life that includes them. Such a being's good is not fully realized when it is caused to suffer in ways that are not contributory to its overall well-being. We know that this is so in our own case, and must therefore infer that it is so in their case.

Now, insofar as respect is due to sentient animals, moral consideration and concern for their well-being will accordingly include attempts to minimize intrinsic evils in their lives. So when there is a choice between killing plants or killing sentient animals, it will be less wrong to kill plants if animals are made to suffer when they are taken for food.

I consider now the main point regarding the relevance of the principles of environmental ethics to the issue of vegetarianism versus meat eating. It will become clear that, in the light of this second point, anyone who has respect for nature will be on the side of vegetarianism, even though plants and animals are regarded as having the same inherent worth. The point that is crucial here is the amount of arable land needed for raising grain and other plants as food for those animals that are in turn to be eaten by humans when compared with the amount of land needed for raising grain and other plants for direct human consumption.

Consider, for example, the fact that in order to produce one pound of protein for human consumption, a steer must be fed 21 pounds of protein, all from plant sources. For pork the ratio is 8.3 pounds to one and for poultry, 5.5 pounds.[9] When spelled out in terms of the acreage of land required, one acre of cereal grains to be used as human food can produce five times more protein than one acre used for meat production; one acre of legumes (peas, lentils, and beans) can produce ten times more; and one acre of leafy vegetables fifteen times more.[10] So the case for vegetarianism based on the attitude of respect for nature comes down to the following: We can drastically reduce the amount of cultivated land needed for human food production by changing from a meat-eating culture to a vegetarian culture. The land thus saved could be set aside as sanctuaries for wildlife, in accordance with the idea of permanent habitat allocation to be discussed below. Ultimately, far less destruction of natural ecosystems than is now taking place would result. Vegetarians, in short, use much less of the surface of the Earth to sustain themselves than do meat-eaters. And the less humans use for themselves the more there is for other species.

We have been considering situations where conflicts between the basic interests of humans and nonhumans are unavoidable, and what implications the principle of distributive justice has for such situations. I now turn to circumstances where it is possible for humans to make certain ad-

[9] The World Food Problem, a Report of the President's Science Advisory Committee, vol. II, May 1967, p. 249. Full discussion of the problem may be found in Frances Moore Lappé, *Diet for A Small Planet* (New York: Friends of the Earth/Ballantine Books, 1971), part I.

[10] Lappé, *Diet for A Small Planet*, pp. 7-8. See also Singer, *Animal Liberation*, pp. 178-184.

justments in their relations to wild animals and plants, even when their basic interests are in conflict. In these circumstances some approaches to equality of treatment between humans and nonhumans can be realized. Such approaches consist in our transforming situations of rivalry and competition into patterns of mutual accommodation and tolerance.

I shall discuss four methods for accomplishing this task. These methods are: (i) permanent habitat allocation, (ii) common conservation, (iii) environmental integration, and (iv) rotation.

(i) *Permanent habitat allocation.* This method involves setting aside certain land and water areas of the Earth's surface to be "forever wild." It is the familiar policy of wilderness preservation. The justification for such a policy lies in the fact that only by means of it can at least some of the world's wild communities of life continue their existence in a more or less natural state and so receive their share of the benefits of the Earth's physical environment. By allocating a portion of the surface of the planet to them on a permanent basis, we give concrete expression to our respect for them as entities whose good is as worthy of consideration as our own. We accordingly judge it only fair that wild communities of life be given their place in the sun, along with the works of human civilization. Although we cannot avoid taking some of the natural environment and its resources for our own use, we can still make sure that at least some wild animal and plant communities are able to continue their existence in a natural state, living out their evolutionary destinies free from human interference.[11]

[11] There are also, of course, many human-centered reasons for wildlife preservation. See H. J. McCloskey, *Ecological Ethics and Politics*, chapters 5 and 9; Donald H. Regan, "Duties of Preservation"; Terry L. Leitzell, "Extinction, Evolution, and Environment Management"; and Bryan G. Norton, "On the Inherent Danger of Undervaluing Species." The last three papers are available from The Center for Philosophy and Public Policy,

(ii) *Common conservation*. The method of common conservation is the sharing of resources while they are being used by both humans and nonhumans. If people have built a town in a desert or other area where there is a very limited supply of water, the policy of common conservation would mean that humans share the water supply with other species-populations that need it for their survival. The plants of the desert as well as the birds, reptiles, insects, and mammals that live there are all recognized as legitimate users of the water supply along with people. The basic idea is that we do not take it all for ourselves but leave some of it for others, who need it as much as we do.

Conservation is a human practice, but it need not be carried on for the benefit of humans alone. There is nothing in the meaning of conservation that excludes its being done to help other creatures further their well-being. As moral agents we have the freedom to choose to make available to others a portion of a natural resource that we also must use for our own good. Conserving a resource, whether it is renewable or nonrenewable, means using it carefully and wisely, saving some for the future when it will be needed as much as at present. None of it is wasted or rendered unfit for use by pollution. *Common* conservation refers to a human practice of sharing the use of a resource with others, conserving it for the mutual benefit of all.

Common conservation dictates that, if we are to distribute the benefits of nature to all who deserve them, we must make available to nonhuman species as well as to other members of our own species the things they and we need

University of Maryland, and appear in Bryan G. Norton and Henry Shue, eds., *The Preservation of Species* (Princeton, N.J.: Princeton University Press, 1986). Norton discusses some differences between human-centered and life-centered reasons for wildlife preservation in "America's Public Lands: To Use or Not to Use," *Report from the Center for Philosophy and Public Policy* 3/3 (Summer 1983): 9-12. See also "Why Farewell to Plants and Animals?" chapter I of Albert J. Frisch and Science Action Coalition, *Environmental Ethics: Choices for Concerned Citizens* (New York: Doubleday Anchor Books, 1980), and William Godfrey-Smith, "The Value of Wilderness," *Environmental Ethics* 1/4 (Winter 1979): 309-319.

to fulfill basic interests. When there is competition for a limited resource, we must not appropriate all of it for ourselves alone. To do that would be to take something that rightfully belongs to all. The least that we humans can do in recognition of the equal inherent worth of all creatures on Earth is to assign some portion of what we all need to those who cannot demand or obtain it for themselves. Whatever source of good is common to a number of species must accordingly be shared if the due claims of all are to be justly dealt with.

(iii) *Environmental integration*. This is the deliberate attempt to fit human construction and "developments" into natural surroundings in a way that preserves the ecological integrity of a region as a whole. Office buildings and stores, factories and warehouses, hotels and motels, houses and apartment complexes, airports and highways, schools and libraries, bridges and tunnels, and other large-scale human artifacts are designed and located with a view to avoiding serious ecological disturbance and environmental degradation. Natural areas in the region that are essential for ecological stability are left unmodified. Thus certain habitats used by wild species-populations are not destroyed, and some wildlife is given a chance to survive alongside the works of human culture.

When artificial ecosystems are laid out in natural surroundings, the boundary areas can be planned so that various animals can pass across them and some wild trees, shrubs, and other plants can propagate themselves on both sides of the boundary. Certain species-populations may then create their own habitats in the physical environments that have been set out by humans for their own purposes. Thus birds come to nest in neighborhood trees, turtles and frogs inhabit ornamental ponds, insects pollinate the cultivated flowers of gardens, native species of trees grow along the edges of lawns, and microorganisms by the millions live in the soil. Many forms of wildlife can in this way pursue their natural cycles of life in unnatural environments. Such human developments as golf courses, recreational lakes, parks and picnic grounds, suburban housing, seashore and mountain resorts may all be planned with this in mind.

The following list gives a brief indication of a few among the many specific measures that human communities can adopt to preserve and bring about environmental integration in their localities. (Most of these measures are considered by communities under the rubric of "land use planning.")

(1) Natural drainage systems are kept intact and underground aquifers are protected from contamination. Streams are left free-flowing. The original vegetation is allowed to grow on hillsides. No construction is permitted in flood plains.

(2) Special consideration is given to the various types of soil in the area to avoid flooding, sewage problems, and other environmentally damaging effects of human disruption of the natural land.

(3) Construction is controlled and in certain areas prohibited to provide "open space." Stretches of woodland, marsh, sand dunes, rocky slopes and escarpments, and the like are zoned to be left as they are.

(4) In agricultural regions the use of artificial fertilizers and chemical pesticides is restricted. Organic farming is encouraged.

(5) Small-scale technology is preferred to large-scale.

(6) Antipollution devices are required to eliminate air pollution. Dumping of toxic wastes is forbidden. Nontoxic waste is kept to a minimum and whenever possible a system of recycling waste is set up. Past pollution of the land or water in the locality is cleaned up.

(7) Nonrenewable resources are consumed sparingly and new techniques for the most efficient use of renewable resources are adopted.

These are all examples of ways in which the environmental soundness of a developed region can be implemented and preserved. Such measures benefit wild animals and plants and can be adopted as a means to that end, as well as being intended for human benefit. Thus environmental integration is a method that can be used in working toward the ideal of a fair distribution of beneficial resources to be shared by humans and nonhumans alike. Although full equality of treatment is not thereby achieved, serious consideration is given to the well-being of wild living things and practical steps are taken to ensure that at least some of their basic interests are provided for. At the same time that the basic interests of humans are being furthered, those of nonhumans are also being protected.

(iv) *Rotation*. The fourth method of distributing benefits fairly is the method of rotation or "taking turns." The rule is that whenever possible (that is, whenever it can be done consistently with all other valid ethical principles applicable to the situation) we should give the species-populations of a wild biotic community their chance at receiving benefits from inhabiting a particular sector of the Earth's natural environment if we humans have also benefited, for a period of time, by fulfilling our interests in that place. It is only fair that humans and nonhumans take turns at having access to favorable environments and habitats. We might think of this as *time allocation* for a given place, to contrast it with the method of permanent wilderness preservation, which is a form of *space allocation*.

The general scheme of a rotation system works as follows. Suppose there is an area of the natural environment that can be used for satisfying the basic interests *of a certain number of humans for a limited time* without destroying the biological soundness of the ecology of that area. The environment and its living inhabitants are treated in such a way that it is possible at a later time for a wild community of life to satisfy *its* basic interests in the area. By occupying the area at different time periods, both humans and nonhumans can meet basic needs. Under these circumstances a rotation system requires that the nonhuman life community be granted exclusive access to the area for suitable, ecologically functional periods of time, to be alternated with other periods when humans are given access to the area. In this way there is a fair distribution of benefits to both humans and nonhumans in a given part of the environment over time. The following situations illustrate how a rotation system might apply to various types of environments.

(1) Suppose certain minerals are needed for the manufacture of machines and instruments used in the treatment of human diseases. If mining is carried out in a particular mountainous region for a limited time (say, fifty years), these needed minerals can be obtained. Let us further suppose that the mining operation is so controlled that restoration of the original conditions and contours of the land can be approximated after the mineral resource has been exhausted. The rotation principle would then require such restoration, after which the area would be left as a sanctuary for wildlife.

(2) Scuba diving for purposes of scientific observation and collecting specimens of marine life for research might be allowed along a coral reef in tropical waters (assuming that the scientific knowledge gained would be used to meet basic human needs). Then at a later time the undersea area could be set aside as a natural marine preserve, not to be interfered with by humans.

(3) There may be places where some temporary housing or other structures can be located without permanent ecological damage to the natural environment. At a later time, when already-used land in urban or suburban areas becomes available for permanent housing or other construction, the temporary buildings can be removed and the environment allowed to return to its natural condition.

(4) During periods of a severe drought an unspoiled lake could be used by humans for a supplementary water supply. Then as a normal rainfall resumes, the lake could be left alone to refill and again become the habitat of a viable life community.

(5) A saltwater marsh might be designated for a certain period as a place to obtain clams, oysters, and other marine

organisms for human consumption, and then set aside for the same length of time as a wildlife preserve. Afterwards, it might again be open to human use, and then again closed off, and so on indefinitely.

It should be clear from these examples that all the human activities mentioned would require strict monitoring and control for the various rotation schemes to work. However, if the people who engaged in those activities had adopted the attitude of respect for nature (which is being assumed here), they would be willing to be monitored and have their activities controlled. Indeed, they would autonomously discipline themselves and exercise self-restraint in order to make sure that they were not abusing the area to the extent of making it unfit for other creatures at a later time. Out of their respect for nature they would adhere to the priority principle of distributive justice, considering it only fair that other living things have their chance to receive the benefits of nature in the given location. Since the human agents involved would then voluntarily place self-imposed limits on their actions out of consideration for the good of wild living things, the various rotation systems could be said to embody both the attitude of respect for persons and that of respect for nature.

The policies and practices of permanent habitat allocation, common conservation, environmental integration, and rotation show how it is possible to transform what would otherwise be situations of confrontation between humans and nonhumans on the level of basic interests into various means of mutual accommodation. These conditions provide an answer to what at first glance may have appeared to be absurd—that wild animals and plants have an inherent worth equal to that of humans. How could such a position ever make sense, when it is obvious that in order to maintain life humans must consume at least some nonhuman organisms? I hope to have shown that, through conscientious effort enlightened by scientific knowledge of ecology and other related fields (now sometimes called the "environmental sciences"), humans who have respect for nature can devise ways to bring about at least an approximation to a fair distribution of benefits between wild living things and humans themselves. By means of the four methods discussed above a relationship of "live and let live" can replace a life-and-death struggle. The competition between the realization of human values and the ability of wild biotic communities to sustain their natural existence can at least sometimes be overcome.

The ideal of justice in all this is to distribute benefits and burdens equally among the parties. Fair shares are equal shares. We have seen that this ideal is never wholly realizable. Even when the conflict situations are amenable to the four methods, the actions of moral agents always fall short of treating each organism, human or nonhuman, with perfect equality of consideration. The principle of distributive justice, therefore, must be supplemented by another priority principle, that of restitutive justice.

e. The Principle of Restitutive Justice

The idea of restitutive justice (restoring the balance of justice after a moral subject has been wronged) was considered twice before in this book. In Chapter Four it was included as the fourth basic duty of the ethical system of respect for nature. In Chapter Five it was mentioned in connection with human rights, where I argued that when one person's rights are in conflict with another's and it is not possible to accord to both what each has a right to, the one whose rights are infringed is owed a special duty of compensation. As a priority principle in our present context, the principle of restitutive justice is applicable whenever the principles of minimum wrong and distributive justice have been followed. In both cases harm is done to animals and plants that are harmless, so some form of reparation or compensation is called for if our actions are to be fully consistent with the attitude of respect for nature. (In applying the minimum wrong and distributive justice principles, no harm is done to harmless *humans*, so there occurs an inequality of treatment between humans and nonhumans in these situations.) In its role as a priority principle for determining a fair way to resolve conflicts between humans and nonhumans, the principle of restitutive justice must therefore supplement those of minimum wrong and distributive justice.

What kinds of reparation or compensation are suitable? Two factors can guide us in this area. The first is the idea that the greater the harm done, the greater the compensation required. Any practice of promoting or protecting the good of animals and plants which is to serve to restore the balance of justice between humans and nonhumans must bring about an amount of good that is comparable (as far as can be reasonably estimated) to the amount of evil to be compensated for.

The second factor is to focus our concern on the soundness and health of whole ecosystems and their biotic communities, rather than on the good of particular individuals. As a practical measure this is the most effective means for furthering the good of the greatest number of organisms. Moreover, by setting aside certain natural habitats and by maintaining certain types of physical environments in their natural condition, compensation to wild creatures can be "paid" in an appropriate way.

The general practice of wilderness preservation can now be understood as a matter of fairness to wild animals and plants in two different respects. On the one hand it is a practice falling under the principle of distributive justice, and on the other it is a way of fulfilling the requirements of restitutive justice. In its first aspect the preservation of wilderness is simply a sharing of the bounties of nature with other creatures. We allocate certain portions of a source of good so that all receive some benefit. What portions are fair cannot be determined in a piecemeal fashion. It is necessary to envision a whole Earth exemplifying a condition of fundamental harmony between nature and human civilization.

The overall order determines what areas of wilderness, what ecosystems and biotic communities, are to be preserved. (Shortly, I shall discuss in greater detail this vision of an ethically ideal world.)

In a second respect the fairness of wilderness preservation derives from its suitability as a way of compensating for the injustices perpetrated on wildlife by humans. To set aside habitat areas and protect environmental conditions in those areas so that wild communities of animals and plants can realize their good is the most appropriate way to restore the balance of justice with them, for it gives full expression to our respect for nature even when we have done harm to living things in order to benefit ourselves. We can, as it were, return the favor they do us by doing something for their sake. Thus we need not bear a burden of eternal guilt because we have used them—and will continue to use them—for our own ends. There is a way to make amends.

This concludes my examination of the five priority principles for the resolution of competing claims arising from conflicts between humans and nonhumans. The most significant implication of the foregoing investigation is that it gives a reasoned reply to the charge that biotic egalitarianism must break down when it comes to conflicts between humans and other species. I have tried to show that there are various methods for resolving such conflicts in ways that extend fairness to all by giving due recognition to the equal inherent worth of every living thing. In the light of this discussion, we may at least accept the possibility of a life-centered theory of environmental ethics that gives impartial consideration to every species. Such a view, I submit, does not reduce to absurdity in the face of ineluctable biological competition. The five priority principles provide a systematic foundation for the concept of interspecific justice in those situations where the interests of organisms belonging to different species cannot all be fulfilled. In this way the "struggle for survival" is replaced by the constraints of a moral order defined by rational principles of justice.

4. The Ethical Ideal of Harmony between Human Civilization and Nature

I pointed out earlier that the foregoing priority principles do not make up a logically complete system which can tell us what we ought to do in every situation of conflict between duties of human ethics and those of environmental ethics. There will always be some cases of conflict in which the right thing to do is undecidable. In those cases we simply do not know what would be a fair way to resolve a situation of competing claims, since the principles give no clear indication of what priorities to assign. The immediate question then arises: Must we make an arbitrary decision in those cases, letting the resolution we adopt be randomly chosen?

We can avoid arbitrariness and randomness in these situations, I suggest, by referring to our total picture or vision of what kind of world order would be ideal according to the structure of normative principles we have accepted. In the light of this unified and comprehensive vision we have guidance in our search for a resolution to such conflicts. For we are in search of a resolution that fits coherently into the total world order pictured as ideal. This "coherent fit" means not only that our decision is not incompatible with the general nature of that world order, that is, with its pervading, deep, and salient characteristics; it also means that the decision tends to clarify and reinforce those characteristics. The characteristics in question are those that make that world order the kind of condition of life and environment at which we would all aim as an ideal that is truly worthy of being pursued if we were committed to the total set of rules and standards contained in the systems of human ethics and environmental ethics propounded earlier in this book and to the priority principles discussed in the preceding sections.

The ideal gives us an imaginative picture of what it would mean for all moral agents to exemplify in their character and conduct the two attitudes of respect for persons and respect for nature. The most apt phrase for describing this "best possible world" in its simplest terms is: *a world order on our planet where human civilization is brought into harmony with nature*. By understainding what "harmony" means as used in this phrase we can better grasp the central features of the content of the ideal. But first we must consider what is covered by the term "human civilization."

Human civilization is to be taken here as equivalent to the total set of cultures on Earth at any given time. In an ethically ideal world where all cultures are in harmony with nature, it is understood that each carries on its way of life *within the constraints of the human ethics of respect for persons*. Thus in each community, individuals and organizations pursue their varying interests without violating each other's moral rights. At the same time they are bound by the laws and directives of legal and political systems that make their rights secure. However varied may be their beliefs about reality, whatever might be their understanding of the meaning of their history and traditions, whatever religious beliefs they might accept, and however they might conceive of the kinds of life most worth living, their beliefs and values do not conflict with the fundamental moral attitude of respect for persons.

Similarly, when we turn to the cultures' ways of regarding nonhuman living things and their views concerning the proper place of human life in the natural world, we may again have great variation in what constitutes human civilization in the ethical ideal. But this variation must always be consistent with the attitude of respect for nature. Whether a culture accepts a mystical view of the identity of the human soul with the world-soul or looks at the relation between human and other forms of life in some nonmystical way (romantic primitivism, religious transcendental- ism, animism, Earth-stewardship, existential alienation, or what not), the belief-system in question must allow the at- titude of respect for nature to be adopted and put into prac- tice. Although some or all of the elements of the biocentric outlook may not be accepted as part of a culture's own world view, the outlook on nature it does have must not lend support to an exploitative attitude toward wild living things or any other attitude incompatible with that of re- spect. Thus it is perfectly possible in the ethically ideal world that there be religious communities, having either monotheistic or polytheistic beliefs, according to which God or the gods command that humans love and care for all the Earth's wild creatures. A mysticism in which the high- est state of human consciousness is understood as a matter of having one's self become one with the natural world is also quite compatible with the moral attitude of respect for nature. The biocentric outlook is a rational and scientifically enlightened way of conceiving of the place of humans in the natural world, but it need not be the only world view accepted by cultures when the ethical ideal of harmony be- tween human civilization and nature is achieved.

In order further to clarify the content of the ideal, the no- tion of harmony must be explained. As it is used here "har- mony" means the preserving of a balance between human values and the well-being of animals and plants in natural ecosystems. It is a condition on Earth in which people are able to pursue their individual interests and the cultural ways of life they have adopted while at the same time al- lowing many biotic communities in a great variety of natu- ral ecosystems to carry on their existence without interfer- ence. Whatever harm comes to the individual members of those communities results from the ongoing processes of evolution, adaptation, and natural changes in environmen- tal circumstances, not from human actions.

In this ethical ideal our role as moral agents is to direct and control our conduct so that, with regard to animals and plants living in the wild, we comply with the four basic rules of environmental ethics (as set forth in Chapter Four). Although we cannot avoid some disruption of the natural world when we pursue our cultural and individual values, we nevertheless constantly place constraints on ourselves so as to cause the least possible interference in natural eco-systems and their biota. The realm of nature is not considered as something to be consumed, exploited, or controlled only for humans ends, but is shared with other creatures. Although one part of human civilization, the bioculture, does consist in making use of other living things for the benefit of people, no such relationship of dominance and subordination is found in the human treatment of the creatures of the wild.

Not only are different areas of the Earth's surface apportioned to humans and to wild communities of life, but an allocation of time periods is worked out with regard to certain favorable habitats so that humans and nonhumans can take turns in benefiting from the use of those habitats. Balance is further shown in the policy of "common conservation," where certain resources of nature are shared by humans and nonhumans alike. In these and other ways the ethically ideal world is seen to be a place where the good of nonhumans can be realized along with the (partly controlled) fulfillment of human values.

5. The Normative Function of the Ethical Ideal

I shall conclude with a brief account of the way in which the ethical ideal described above functions normatively in the practical decision making of those who accept it. The main function of the ideal is to provide a focus for practical goals. It does this by specifying a kind of world order whose gradual realization is the permanent long-range moral purpose behind the exercise of instrumental rationality by moral agents. In getting a clear grasp of the content of the ideal, agents know the overall direction they wish to take in setting practical goals. The immediate tasks they set for themselves are aimed at changes in the actual world that they believe will make it more closely approximate the ideal world as they conceive of it. It is because they envision the final outcome of their endeavors in terms of the ethical ideal that they use their factual knowledge the way they do in choosing practical ends and the best means to those ends. (The goal of increasing their factual knowledge when needed in these endeavors is, of course, one of their most important practical ends.)

The ethical ideal not only clarifies the ultimate end for instrumental rationality, but also, as it were, lends value to it. The goals that moral agents set for themselves in pursuing the gradual realization of the ideal are judged to be *worthy* of their best efforts because the ethical ideal itself represents a *summum bonum* (the greatest good). Achieving the immediate, practical goals has only instrumental value. The ends and means are sought not for their own sake but for the sake of the ideal, that is, for the sake of making the world a better place by bringing it one step closer to what it should be. The world so changed is judged to be better than what it would have been without the change precisely because the ethically ideal world contains as much good (both moral and nonmoral) as is empirically possible for our world to contain.

The normative function of the ethical ideal as a focus for instrumental rationality in the lives of moral agents must not be thought of as *replacing* the system of reasons-for-action already in place in their lives in virtue of their having adopted the attitudes of respect for persons and respect for nature. Whatever ways moral agents devise to change the actual world in the direction of greater harmony between civilization and nature, the means they take to do this must never violate those basic moral constraints imposed by respect for persons and for nature. Persons and other living things must not be looked at merely in terms of their actual or potential usefulness in bringing about a future world closer to the ideal. Their duties as moral agents cannot be overriden by their instrumental rationality. The process of bringing about ever closer approximations to the ideal is itself a moral process. To accomplish a good end, evil means must not be used, when the evilness of the means consists in the performance of actions that are wrong, all things considered. It is only within the boundaries set by the rules of duty of human ethics and environmental ethics that acts performed as "best means" toward ends in the realization of the ethical ideal are permissible

I hope the entire investigation of the Ethics of Respect for Nature presented in this book has made it clear that people *can* put this ethics into practice. A world of harmony between human civilization and nature, when structured in the way indicated by the foregoing analysis, is a distinct empirical possibility. Although I have not proposed any political, legal, or economic changes in the world's present cultures as specific measures that must be taken to make a start in the direction toward the ethical ideal, it should be evident from my discussion of the biocentric outlook and the attitude of respect for nature that an *inner* change in our moral beliefs and commitments is the first, indispensable step. And this inner change is itself a psychological possibility. Some people have actually made such a change, exercising their autonomy in the decision to adopt new moral principles regarding their treatment of the natural environment and its living inhabitants. They have accepted at least the rudiments of a life-centered outlook in the domain of environmental ethics. Thus the moral shift from anthropocentricity to biocentricity is not psychologically impossible for human moral agents to accomplish.

In this connection we must not confuse the difficulty of a task with its impracticability. There should be no illusions about how hard it will be for many people to change their values, their beliefs, their whole way of living if they are sincerely to adopt the attitude of respect for nature and act accordingly. Psychologically, this may require a profound moral reorientation. Most of us in the contemporary world have been brought up in a thoroughly anthropocentric culture in which the inherent superiority of humans over other species has been taken for granted. Great efforts will be needed to emancipate ourselves from this established way of looking at nonhuman animals and plants. But it is not beyond the realm of practical possibility. Nothing prevents us from exercising our powers of autonomy and rationality in bringing the world as it is gradually closer to the world as it ought to be.

BIBLIOGRAPHY

Attfield, Robin. *The Ethics of Environmental Concern*. New York: Columbia University Press, 1983.

Auxter, Thomas. "The Right Not to Be Eaten." *Inquiry* 22 (Summer 1979): 221–230.

Baier, Annette. "For the Sake of Future Generations." In T. Regan, ed., *Earthbound: New Introductory Essays in Environmental Ethics*. New York: Random House, 1984.

Baier, Kurt. *The Moral Point of View: A Rational Basis of Ethics*. Ithaca, N.Y.: Cornell University Press, 1958.

Barbour, Ian G. *Technology, Environment, and Human Values*. New York: Praeger, 1980.

Blackstone, William T., ed. *Philosophy and Environmental Crisis*. Athens, Ga.: University of Georgia Press, 1974.

———. "Ethics and Ecology." In W. T. Blackstone, ed. *Philosophy and Environmental Crisis*. Athens, Ga.: University of Georgia Press, 1974.

———. "The Search for an Environmental Ethic." In T. Regan, ed., *Matters of Life and Death: New Introductory Essays in Moral Philosophy*. New York: Random House, 1980.

Callicott, J. Baird. "Non-Anthropocentric Value Theory and Environmental Ethics." *American Philosophical Quarterly* 21 (October 1984):299-309.

Clark, Stephen R. L. *The Moral Status of Animals*. Oxford: Oxford University Press, 1977.

———. "The Rights of Wild Things." *Inquiry* 22 (Summer 1979):171-187.

———. "Gaia and the Forms of Life." In R. Elliot and A. Gare, eds., *Environmental Philosophy: A Collection of Readings*. University Park, Pa.: Pennsylvania State University Press, 1983.

Daly, Herman E. *Steady-State Economics: The Economics of Biophysical Equilibrium and Moral Growth*. San Francisco: W. H. Freeman, 1977.

Darwall, Stephen. *Impartial Reason*. Ithaca, N.Y.: Cornell University Press, 1983.

———. "Two Kinds of Respect." *Ethics* 88 (October 1977):36-49.

Devall, Bill, and George Sessions. *Deep Ecology: Living As If Nature Mattered*. Layton, Utah: Gibbs M. Smith, Inc., 1985.

Disch, Robert, ed. *The Ecological Conscience: Values for Survival*. Englewood Cliffs, N.J.: Prentice-Hall, 1970.

Donagan, Alan. *The Theory of Morality*. Chicago: University of Chicago Press, 1977.

Ehrenfeld, David W. *Conserving Life on Earth*. New York: Oxford University Press, 1972.

———. *The Arrogance of Humanism*. New York: Oxford University Press, 1978.

Elliot, Robert, and Arran Gare, eds. *Environmental Philosophy: A Collection of Readings*. University Park, Pa.: Pennsylvania State University Press, 1983.

Feinberg, Joel. *Social Philosophy*. Englewood Cliffs, N.J.: Prentice-Hall, 1973.

———. *Rights, Justice, and the Bounds of Liberty: Essays in Social Philosophy*. Princeton, N.J.: Princeton University Press, 1980.

Foot, Philippa. *Virtues and Vices and Other Essays in Moral Philosophy*. Oxford: Basil Blackwell, 1978.

Forstner, Lorne J., and John H. Todd, eds. *The Everlasting Universe: Readings on the Ecological Revolution*. Lexington, Mass.: D. C. Heath, 1971.

Frankena, William K. "The Concept of Morality." *Journal of Philosophy* 63 (1966):688-696.

———. "On Defining Moral Judgements, Principles, and Codes." *Etyka*, 2 (1973):45-56.

———. "Ethics and the Environment." In K. E. Goodpaster and K. M. Sayre, eds., *Ethics and Problems of the 21st*

Century. Notre Dame, Ind.: University of Notre Dame Press, 1979.

Fried, Charles. *Right and Wrong*. Cambridge, Mass.: Harvard University Press, 1978.

Frisch, Alfred J., and Science Action Coalition. *Environmental Ethics: Choices for Concerned Citizens*. Garden City, N.Y.: Anchor Press/Doubleday, 1980.

Godfrey-Smith, William. "The Value of Wilderness." *Environmental Ethics* 1 (Winter 1979):309-319.

Goodpaster, Kenneth E., ed. *Perspectives on Morality: Essays by William K. Frankena*. Notre Dame, Ind.: University of Notre Dame Press, 1976.

————. "On Being Morally Considerable." *Journal of Philosophy* 75 (June 1978):308-325.

————. "From Egoism to Environmentalism." In K. E. Goodpaster and K. M. Sayre, eds., *Ethics and Problems of the 21st Century*. Notre Dame, Ind.: University of Notre Dame Press, 1979.

Goodpaster, Kenneth E., and K. M. Sayre, eds. *Ethics and Problems of the 21st Century*. Notre Dame, Ind.: University of Notre Dame Press, 1979.

Gunn, Alastair S. "Preserving Rare Species." In T. Regan, ed., *Earthbound: New Introductory Essays in Environmental Ethics*. New York: Random House, 1984.

Hardin, Garrett. *Exploring New Ethics for Survival: The Voyage of the Spaceship* Beagle. New York: Viking Press, 1972.

————. "The Tragedy of the Commons." *Science* 162 (December 1968): 1243-1248. (Reprinted in G. Hardin, *Exploring New Ethics for Survival*.)

Hill, Thomas E., Jr. "Servility and Self-Respect." *The Monist* 57 (January 1973):87-104.

Johnson, Edward. "Treating the Dirt: Environmental Ethics and Moral Theory." In T. Regan, ed. *Earthbound: New Introductory Essays in Environmental Ethics*. New York: Random House, 1984.

Johnson, Lawrence E. "Humanity, Holism, and Environmental Ethics." *Environmental Ethics* 5 (Winter 1983):345-354.

Kant, Immanuel. *Foundations of the Metaphysics of Morals* (1785). Translated by Lewis White Beck. Indianapolis: Bobbs-Merrill, 1959.

————. *The Doctrine of Virtue: Part II of The Metaphysics of Morals* (1797). Translated by Mary J. Gregor. Philadelphia: University of Pennsylvania Press, 1964.

Kassiola, Joel. "The Limits to Economic Growth: Politicizing Advanced Industrial Society." *Philosophy and Social Criticism* 8 (Spring 1981): 87-113.

Lappé, Frances Moore. *Diet for a Small Planet.* New York: Friends of the Earth/Ballantine Books, 1971.

Leitzell, Terry L. "Extinction, Evolution, and Environment Management." In Bryan G. Norton and Henry Shue, eds., *The Preservation of Species.* Princeton, N.J.: Princeton University Press, 1986.

Leopold, Aldo. *A Sand County Almanac and Sketches Here and There.* New York: Oxford University Press, 1949.

Lewis, Clarence Irving. *An Analysis of Knowledge and Valuation.* LaSalle, Ill.: Open Court, 1946.

Lockwood, Michael. "Singer on Killing and the Preference for Life." *Inquiry* 22 (Summer 1979):157-170.

Lombardi, Louis G. "Inherent Worth, Respect, and Rights." *Environmental Ethics* 5 (Fall 1983):257-270.

Lovejoy, Arthur O. *The Great Chain of Being: A Study of the History of an Idea.* Cambridge, Mass.: Harvard University Press, 1936.

MacCallum, Gerald C., Jr. "Negative and Positive Freedom." *Philosophical Review* 76 (July 1967): 312-334.

McCloskey, H. J. *Ecological Ethics and Politics.* Totowa, N.J.: Rowman and Littlefield, 1983.

————. "Moral Rights and Animals." *Inquiry* 22 (Summer 1979):23-54.

McGinn, Colin. "Evolution, Animals, and the Basis of Morality." *Inquiry* 22 (Summer 1979): 81-99.

McRobie, George. *Small Is Possible.* New York: Harper and Row, 1981.

Naess, Arne. "The Shallow and the Deep, Long-Range Ecology Movements: A Summary." *Inquiry* 16 (1973):95-100.

———. "Self-Realization in Mixed Communities of Humans, Bears, Sheep, and Wolves." *Inquiry* 22 (Summer 1979):231-241.

Nash, Roderick. *Wilderness and the American Mind*. New Haven, Conn.: Yale University Press, 1967. (Second edition, 1973; third edition, 1982.)

Nell, Onora. *Acting On Principle: An Essay On Kantian Ethics*. New York: Columbia University Press, 1975.

Norton, Bryan G. "On the Inherent Danger of Undervaluing Species." In Bryan G. Norton and Henry Shue, eds., *The Preservation of Species*. Princeton, N.J.: Princeton University Press, 1986.

Norton, Bryan G., and Henry Shue, eds. *The Preservation of Species*. Princeton, N.J.: Princeton University Press, 1986.

Ophuls, William. *Economics and the Politics of Scarcity: A Prologue to a Political Theory of the Steady State*. San Francisco: William H. Freeman, 1977.

Partridge, Ernest, ed. *Responsibilities to Future Generations: Environmental Ethics*. Buffalo, N.Y.: Prometheus Books, 1981.

Passmore, John. *Man's Responsibility for Nature: Ecological Problems and Western Traditions*. New York: Charles Scribner's Sons, 1974.

———. "Attitudes to Nature." In R. S. Peters, ed., *Nature and Conduct*. New York: St. Martin's Press, 1975.

Paton, H. J. *The Categorical Imperative: A Study in Kant's Moral Philosophy*. London: Hutchinson and Co., 1947.

Pluhar, Evelyn B. "The Justification of an Environmental Ethic." *Environmental Ethics* 5 (Spring 1983):47-61.

Rawls, John. *A Theory of Justice*. Cambridge, Mass.: Harvard University Press, 1971.

Regan, Donald H. "Duties of Preservation." in Bryan G. Norton and Henry Shue, eds., *The Preservation of Species*. Princeton, N.J.: Princeton University Press, 1986.

Regan, Tom. *All That Dwell Therein: Animal Rights and Environmental Ethics*. Berkeley and Los Angeles: University of California Press, 1982.

————. *The Case for Animal Rights*. Berkeley and Los Angeles: University of California Press, 1983.

————, ed. *Earthbound: New Introductory Essays in Environmental Ethics*. New York: Random House, 1984.

————. "The Nature and Possibility of an Environmental Ethic." *Environmental Ethics* 3 (Spring 1981):19-34. (Reprinted in T. Regan, *All That Dwell Therein*.)

————. "On the Right Not to be Made to Suffer Gratuitously." *Canadian Journal of Philosophy* 10 (September 1980):473-478.

Regan, Tom, and Peter Singer, eds. *Animal Rights and Human Obligations*. Englewood Cliffs, N.J.: Prentice-Hall, 1976.

Rodman, John. "The Liberation of Nature?" *Inquiry* 20 (Spring 1977):83-145.

————. "Animal Justice: The Counter-Revolution in Natural Right and Law." *Inquiry* 22 (Summer 1979):3-22.

Roelofs, R. T., J. N. Crowley, and D. L. Hardesty, eds. *Environment and Society: A Book of Readings on Environmental Policy, Attitudes, and Values*. Englewood Cliffs, N.J.: Prentice-Hall, 1974.

Rolston, Holmes III. "Is There an Ecological Ethic? *Ethics* 85 (1975):93-109.

————. "Just Environmental Business."In T. Regan, ed., *Just Business: New Introductory Essays in Business Ethics*. New York: Random House, 1984.

————. "Valuing Wildlands." *Environmental Ethics* 7 (Spring 1985):23-48.

Routley, R. and V. "Against the Inevitability of Human Chauvinism." In K. E. Goodpaster and K. M. Sayre, eds., *Ethics and Problems of the 21st Century*. Notre Dame, Ind.: University of Notre Dame Press, 1979.

Ruse, Michael. *The Philosophy of Biology*. London: J. M. Dent, 1973.

————. *Sociobiology: Sense or Nonsense?* Dordrecht, Holland: D. Reidel, 1979.

Schumacher, E. F. *Small Is Beautiful*. New York: Harper and Row, 1973.

————. *Good Work*. New York: Harper and Row, 1979.

Shepard, Paul, and Daniel McKinley eds. *The Subversive Science: Essays toward an Ecology of Man*. Boston: Houghton Mifflin, 1969.

Shrader-Frechette, K. S., ed., *Environmental Ethics*. Pacific Grove, Calif.: The Boxwood Press, 1981.

Shue, Henry. *Basic Rights: Subsistence, Affluence, and U. S. Foreign Policy*. Princeton, N. J.: Princeton University Press, 1980.

Simmons, John A. "Inalienable Rights and Locke's *Treatises*." *Philosophy and Public Affairs* 12 (Summer 1983):175-204.

Simpson, George Gaylord. *The Meaning of Evolution: A Study of the History of Life and Its Significance for Man*. New Haven, Conn.: Yale University Press, 1949.

Singer, Peter. *Animal Liberation: A New Ethics for Our Treatment of Animals*. New York: The New York Review, 1975.

————. "All Animals Are Equal." In Tom Regan and Peter Singer, eds., *Animal Rights and Human Obligations*. Englewood Cliffs, N.J.: Prentice-Hall, 1976.

————. "Killing Humans and Killing Animals." *Inquiry* 22 (Summer 1979):145-156.

————. "Not for Humans Only: The Place of Nonhumans in Environmental Issues." In K. E. Goodpaster and K. M. Sayre, eds., *Ethics and Problems of the 21st Century*. Notre Dame, Ind.: University of Notre Dame Press, 1979.

Sprigge, T.L.S. "Metaphysics, Physicalism, and Animal Rights." *Inquiry* 22 (Summer 1979): 101-143.

Stone, Christopher. *Should Trees Have Standing? Toward Legal Rights for Natural Objects*. Los Altos, Calif.: William Kaufmann, Inc., 1974.

Taylor, Paul W. "The Ethics of Respect for Nature." *Environmental Ethics* 3 (Fall 1981):197-218.

———. "Frankena on Environmental Ethics." *The Monist* 64 (July 1981):313-324.

———. "In Defense of Biocentrism." *Environmental Ethics* 5 (Fall 1983):237-243.

———. "Are Humans Superior to Animals and Plants?" *Environmental Ethics* 6 (Summer 1984):149-160.

Tribe, Laurence H., Corinne S. Schelling, and John Voss, eds. *When Values Conflict: Essays on Environmental Analysis, Discourse, and Decision*. Cambridge, Mass.: Ballinger Publishing Co., 1976.

VanDeVeer, Donald. "Interspecific Justice." *Inquiry* 22 (Summer 1979):55-79.

Vlastos, Gregory. "Justice and Equality." In R. B. Brandt, ed. *Social Justice*. Englewood Cliffs, N.J.: Prentice-Hall, 1962.

Von Wright, Georg Henrik. *The Varieties of Goodness*. New York: Humanities Press, 1963.

Wallace, James D. *Virtues and Vices*. Ithaca, N. Y.: Cornell University Press, 1978.

Watson, Richard A. "A Critique of Anti-Anthropocentric Biocentrism." *Environmental Ethics* 5 (Fall 1983):245-256.

Williams, George C. *Adaptation and Natural Selection: A Critique of Some Current Evolutionary Thought*. Princeton, N.J.: Princeton University Press, 1966.

Wilson, Edward O. *Sociobiology: The New Synthesis*. Cambridge, Mass.: Harvard University Press, 1975.

Woodfield, Andrew. *Teleology*. New York: Cambridge University Press, 1976.

Wright, Larry. *Teleological Explanation*. Berkeley and Los Angeles: University of California Press, 1976.

Young, Robert. "Autonomy and the 'Inner Self'." *American Philosophical Quarterly* 17 (January 1980):35-43.

———. "Autonomy and Socialization." *Mind* 89 (October 1980):565-576.

Zimmerman, David. "The Force of Hypothetical Commitment."*Ethics* 93 (April 1983):467-483.

INDEX

agent, 14-16, 47-53, 57, 131-33, 150-51, 232-34, 246-47

anthropocentrism, 11-12, 11n, 20, 143, 146, 177, 226, 312, 313

appraisal respect, 60n, 183

appropriate technologies, 289-90, 289n

Aristotle, 61n, 198n

Attfield, R., 270n

attitude of respect, 41-43, 46, 71-72, 80-90, 100; as an ultimate attitude, 41-42, 90-98. *See also* recognition respect; respect for nature; respect for persons

autonomy rights, 239-40, 250

Baier, A., 12n

Baier, K., 25n, 28n

balance of nature, 8-9

belief-system, 41-45, 98, 99-100, 119, 158-68, 309

biocentric outlook on nature, 44-46, 99-158; argument for, 158-68; relation among components of, 153-55; and respect for nature, 44-47, 99-100, 134, 155-56, 167-68, 226, 252, 309

biocentrism, 11-14, 20-21, 306, 312

bioculture, 53-55, 310; ethics of, 53-58

biology, its relation to ethics, 47-53, 102-104

Blackstone, W., 68n, 236n

Brandt, R., 76n

character. *See* standards of character; virtue

competing claims, 20-21, 244-45, 258-60, 262-64, 268. *See also* priority principles

conflict between humans and non-humans. *See* competing claims

conservation, common, 298-99, 303

considerateness, 207-208, 213

Daly, H., 258n

Darwall, S., 25n, 60n, 65n

Descartes, R., 143-46

direct killing, 290-91

distributive justice, 270, 291-304, 305

Donagan, A., 43n

ecology, 50-52; evolutionary, 6-7, 8n

ecosystem, 3-9, 7n, 101, 103, 116-17, 182, 189-90, 194

Ehrenfeld, D., 104n

Elliot, R., 118n

endangered species, protection of, 11, 194, 196, 198, 223

environmental ethics, 9-10, 59, 75n, 168, 219; compared with human ethics, 40-47, 89, 150-52, 226, 255, 256-60, 275-76, 307-309; distinguished from the ethics of the bioculture, 53-54. *See also* biocentrism; respect for nature

environmental integration, 299-301, 303

equity, 211-12, 213

ethical ideal, 264, 306, 307-13. *See also* harmony between civilization and nature

ethics of the bioculture. *See* bioculture, ethics of

evolution, 49-50, 111-13, 113n, 177. *See also* ecology, evolutionary

exploitative attitude, 51-52, 95-96, 133, 226, 273-75, 277, 309

327

Library of Congress Cataloging-in-Publication Data

Taylor, Paul W.
Respect for nature.

(Studies in moral, political, and legal philosophy)
Bibliography: p.   Includes index.
1. Human ecology—Moral and ethical aspects.   2. Environmental
protection—Moral and ethical aspects.   I. Title.   II. Series.
GF80.T39 1986   170   85-43318
ISBN 0-691-07709-6 (alk. paper)
ISBN 0-691-02250-X (pbk.)